Salamaat! سلامات
Learning Arabic
with Ease

HEZI BROSH, Ph.D.

TUTTLE Publishing

Tokyo | Rutland, Vermont | Singapore

ABOUT TUTTLE
"Books to Span the East and West"

Our core mission at Tuttle Publishing is to create books which bring people together one P .at a time. Tuttle was founded in 1832 in the small New England town of Rutland, Vermont (USA). Our fundamental values remain as strong today as they were then—to publish best-in-class books informing the English-speaking world about the countries and peoples of Asia. The world has become a smaller place today and Asia's economic, cultural and political influence has expanded, yet the need for meaningful dialogue and information about this diverse region has never been greater. Since 1948, Tuttle has been a leader in publishing books on the cultures, arts, cuisines, languages and literatures of Asia. Our authors and photographers have won numerous awards and Tuttle has published thousands of books on subjects ranging from martial arts to paper crafts. We welcome you to explore the wealth of information available on Asia at **www.tuttlepublishing.com**.

Published by Tuttle Publishing, an imprint of Periplus Editions (HK) Ltd.

Copyright © 2018 by Hezi Brosh
Cover image © aldomurillo l istockphoto.com

Library of Congress Cataloging-in-Publication Data is in progress

ISBN 978-0-8048-5015-5

First edition
22 21 20 19 18   5 4 3 2 1   1805RR

Printed in China

Distributed by:

North America, Latin America & Europe
Tuttle Publishing,
364 Innovation Drive,
North Clarendon, VT 05759-9436 U.S.A
Tel: 1 (802) 773 8930
Fax: 1 (802) 773 6993
info@tuttlepublishing.com
www.tuttlepublishing.com

Japan
Tuttle Publishing
Yaekari Building, 3rd Floor
5-4-12 Osaki
Shinagawa-ku
Tokyo 141 0032
Tel: (81) 3 5437-0171
Fax: (81) 3 5437-0755
sales@tuttle.co.jp
www.tuttle.co.jp

Asia-Pacific
Berkeley Books Pte Ltd,
61 Tai Seng Avenue #02-12,
Singapore 534167
Tel: (65) 6280-1330
Fax: (65) 6280-6290
inquiries@periplus.com.sg
www.periplus.com

DEDICATION

I dedicate this book to:

My wife Sarit,

My daughter Shani and her husband Nadav,

My son Rahn and his wife Teresa,

My grandchildren Shira, Rotem and Raphael and Nina,

and to the lovers of Arabic wherever they are.

TABLE OF CONTENTS

CULTURE الثقافة

42–82 UNIT 2 وَحْدَة ٢

CONVERSATIONS أَلْمُحَادثَات

v

LETTERS & PRONUNCIATION أَلْحُرُوفُ ٱلْعَرَبِيَّة وَٱلنُّطْق

GRAMMAR أَلْقَوَاعِد

CULTURE أَلثَّقَافَة

CONVERSATIONS   أَلْمُحَادثَات

LETTERS & PRONUNCIATION   أَلْحُرُوفُ ٱلْعَرَبِيَّة وَٱلنُّطْق

GRAMMAR   أَلْقَوَاعِد

GRAMMAR
ألْقَوَاعِد

CULTURE
ألثَّقَافَة

165-206 UNIT 5
وَحْدَة ٥

CONVERSATIONS
ألْمُحَادَثَات

248–291   UNIT 7   وَحْدَة ٧

CULTURE　　　　　　　　　　　　　　أَلثَّقَافَة

*　　*　　*

Appendices

INTRODUCTION

The *Salamaat!* series has adopted the communicative approach in the teaching of Modern Standard Arabic (MSA). In spite of the common perceptions that learning the standard variety (MSA) simply doesn't comply with communication needs, *Salamaat!* demonstrates—as do the many native English speakers who have learned Arabic using *Salamaat!*—that this is not the case. The learners start to develop their communicative skills from the first phases of learning.

    Salamaat! is extremely effective in developing students' communicative skills using flexible teaching methods that make sense to learners. It offers a combination of a wide range of dialogues, which are close to the spoken language, useful vocabulary items and phrases, simple grammatical explanations and regional and cultural knowledge in context. This, in turn, enables learners to constantly develop their communicative capability bit by bit.

    Salamaat! introduces Arabic grammatical structures and patterns in a spiral and functional way, that is, centered around learners' needs in developing their language proficiency. Language structures are explained clearly and simply and introduced in a logical sequence: easy then hard, passive then active, simple then complex. It also introduces the Arab-Islamic and Christian cultures of the Arabic-speaking areas of the globe, embedded in the language learning process. Thus, cultural knowledge becomes more accessible and easily comprehended.

    Salamaat! targets learners both in academia and in professional arenas such as governmental agencies and business who are beginning to study MSA. It can also be used in other educational settings such as high schools, adult language classes and community centers. Individuals who want to study Arabic on their own will find it useful as well. No previous knowledge is assumed.

    No matter where learners may eventually find themselves in the Arabic-speaking world, the language skills they develop with *Salamaat!* will remain with them and serve them well.

Highlights:
1. *Salamaat!* focuses on fluency and accuracy starting with the first lesson in the book. Throughout, the student is at the core of the teaching–learning cycle in this series, and the teacher is a facilitator.
2. By presenting standard Arabic in a modern way that balances linguistic correctness and conversational fluency, *Salamaat!* aims to take the student from the novice-low

level to the low-intermediate level of proficiency: the learner will be capable of using studied/memorized phrases and vocabulary in various topics, and put them to use in basic daily communicative situations.

3. Furthermore, *Salamaat!* provides Arabic learners with a semantic and linguistic knowledge through familiar and expected topics related to daily life which enables students to communicate using Arabic for greetings, introducing oneself and others, apologizing, simple descriptions, requesting info, expressing what he/she likes and dislikes, hobbies, housing, the hospital and visiting a doctor, family, work, daily routines, traveling, food, clothing, and so on.

4. *Salamaat!* is not more of the same. Its new approach is manifested in the systematic, clear and simple teaching of the letters and grammatical structures and in finding the right balance between accuracy and fluency. While the book focuses on accuracy in grammar and pronunciation, it is also enhancing fluency by using dialogues in simplified Modern Standard Arabic (MSA) that are structured as close as possible to the spoken language. Unlike other books, this book presents the words with vowels and gradually eliminates them once the learners feel confident to function without them.

5. *Salamaat!* is an important contribution in the field of teaching Arabic for non-speakers, and I believe that this book will leave a mark on the teaching of Arabic among all non-speakers—particularly English speakers—all around the world.

Khaled H. Abu Amsha, Ph.D., *is Educative Director of CASA in Amman, the Academic Director at the Qasid Institute of Classical and Modern Standard Arabic, and AMIDEAST's Arabic Studies Consultant in the Middle East. He has taught and lectured at the University of Jordan, the International Islamic University in Malaysia, and Brigham Young University in Provo, Utah, where he served as visiting professor in the Department of Asian and Near Eastern Languages. He holds a Ph.D. in curriculum development and methods of teaching Arabic as a second language. Dr. Abu Amsha has written widely and has participated in several international conferences on Arabic teaching and linguistics.*

TO THE INSTRUCTOR

Dear Instructor,

Salamaat! was developed to answer the need for a systematic textbook in Modern Standard Arabic (MSA) as a language of both written and oral communication. It is designed to make teaching and learning easier for you and your students. While it offers a fast and effective technique for learning the letters and the sounds they represent, it also aims to establish solid linguistic foundations to build upon. *Salamaat!* further aims to develop a new kind of learning environment intended to tap into students' own sources of motivation. This textbook contains many stimuli related to language, culture and locale. The incorporation of such information into language instruction promotes the development of intercultural competence and therefore of effective communication with native Arabic speakers.

    Salamaat! takes a learner-centered approach, as it acknowledges the varying needs and learning styles of each student. Through a wide range of oral and written activities, students are provided with various learning strategies and assisted in identifying their individual style of comprehension. They develop criteria for self-evaluation parallel to the learning process, acknowledging their capacity to learn independently. From the first phase of learning, students are simultaneously exposed to the four basic linguistic skills: listening, reading, speaking and writing.

    Salamaat! targets learners both in academia and in professional arenas such as governmental agencies and business, who are beginning to study MSA. This book can also be used in other educational settings such as high schools and adult language classes, and can serve as a self-teaching tool for individuals who are interested in learning Arabic on their own. No previous knowledge is assumed.

    As you know, your teaching is not equal to your students' learning. The intake of your students does not match your input. Students differ in their interests and learning styles, and they move forward in different ways. Each will take something unique from your teaching. Your philosophy of teaching might differ from that of other teachers, just as you have different priorities, approaches and methods. However, we all share the same goal: to make our students independent of us, to teach them how to think for themselves and how to work on their own. We all do our best to realign our teaching to the students' learning in order to maximize that learning. To that end, this book is a tool in your hand. You can add texts, drills and cultural information to suit the needs of your students and your teaching style, methods and philosophy.

Ten suggestions for you:

1. Make sure your students write the letters correctly and develop the ability to identify and produce the Arabic sounds accurately from the first stages of learning. This is an ongoing process beyond the learning of letters and sounds.

2. Understanding a grammatical structure does not mean that students can successfully apply it. They will need many repetitions from different angles and a lot of practice inside and outside the classroom.

3. Emphasize the difference between MSA and the spoken variety when the opportunity presents itself.

4. Plan a weekly quiz (reading aloud, dictation, vocabulary, conjugation of verbs, prepositions, nouns, and so on.)

5. Develop additional activities to practice listening comprehension in groups and individually.

6. Language is culture. Point out how culture has shaped language use.

7. Encourage students to elaborate on the cultural components presented in each unit, or other pertinent cultural themes not included in the textbook, with writing assignments in English and with oral presentations.

8. Expose students to authentic Arabs through movies and lectures, planning excursions to Arab places (mosques, shops, neighborhoods, restaurants), and coordinating Arabic events, such as parties and dinners.

9. Encourage students to make use of the Internet and other available resources to further enhance their language skills and cultural knowledge.

10. Plan an intensive Arabic summer course in an Arabic speaking country.

Hezi Brosh
March, 2018

TO THE LEARNER

Dear learner!

Arabic is an easy language to study!

   In all phases of the development of *Salamaat!* I was thinking of you, the learner: about your needs, learning strategies, and interests. Above all, I am seeking to introduce you to a new language in a very easy, simple and systematic way to help you to get a lot for your time and effort.

   You are about to embark on a fascinating journey into the Arab world, its rich culture, religion and history through learning its language. Throughout the Middle East and beyond its boundaries, decorative Arabic letters can be seen on every corner, down every street, and in the wallets of every citizen. Even non-Arabs, such as Pakistanis and Persians, have adopted the Arabic alphabet to represent their respective native languages. During the Golden Age of Arab culture, a rich body of literature was created and preserved in the Arabic alphabet, reinforcing its eminence among other languages. And today Arabic retains its importance as modern Arab writers continue to use the Arabic script. Arab authors and poets are widely studied and honored, from the 13th century (but still bestselling) poet Rumi to the modern Egyptian novelist and Nobel laureate Nagib Mahfuz. Arabic, the gateway to Jerusalem, Cairo, Casablanca, and Tunis, the gateway to the pyramids and the Qur'an, is also a language of conflict and of the endeavor towards reconciliation.

   This is the language that you are about to learn. I am sure you know that nothing worthwhile comes cheaply and if you don't do the work it won't be done. I wish you an enjoyable journey, and as the Arabic proverb says:

بَدْرْب وَصَلَلَّمن سُارَع ى أَ

(*man sara 'ala-ddarbi waṣala.*)
He who starts walking will arrive.

Hezi Brosh
March, 2018

* * *

UNIT 1

Listen to the conversation.

إِسْتَمِعُوا إِلَى ٱلْمُحَادَثَة.

ma-smuka?   مَا ٱسْمُكَ؟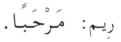

What is your name?

رِيم: مَرْحَبًا.

سَامِي: مَرْحَبًا.

رِيم: مَا ٱسْمُكَ؟

سَامِي: إِسْمِي سَامِي، وَمَا ٱسْمُكِ أَنْتِ؟

رِيم: إِسْمِي رِيم.

سَامِي: تَشَرَّفْنَا.

رِيم: تَشَرَّفْنَا.

تَمْرِين ١. إِسْتَمِعُوا إِلَى ٱلْمُحَادَثَة مَرَّة ثَانِيَة وَخَمِّنُوا مَعْنَى كَلِمَة "تَشَرَّفْنَا."

Exercise 1. Listen to the conversation again and guess the meaning of "tasharrafna."

تَمْرِين ٢. تَعَرَّفُوا عَلَى زُمَلائِكُمْ. سَلِّمُوا عَلَيْهِمْ وَٱسْأَلُوهُمْ عَنْ أَسْمَائِهِمْ.

Exercise 2. Meet your classmates. Greet them and ask them their names.

Gender   *'aljins*   أَلْجِنْس

The Arabic language differentiates grammatically between masculine (*mudhakkar*) and feminine (*mu'annath*). Nouns that relate to human beings (and animals) have two forms, masculine and feminine. Nouns for inanimate objects such as *table* or *window* are also either masculine or feminine. Unlike English, in Arabic there is no gender neutral "it."

What (before nouns)   *ma*   مَا

The question word مَا (*ma*) means **what**. It comes before nouns.

ma–smuka? What is your (*m. s.*) name?   مَا ٱسْمُكَ؟

ma–smuki? What is your (*f. s.*) name?   مَا ٱسْمُكِ؟

It is a pleasure   *tasharrafna*   تَشَرَّفْنَا

When someone is introduced to you (or introduces himself or herself), you say *tasharrafna* (تَشَرَّفْنَا). The answer could be the same or:

tasharrafna bika (تَشَرَّفْنَا بِكَ). It is a pleasure to meet you (*m. s.*).

tasharrafna biki (تَشَرَّفْنَا بِكِ). It is a pleasure to meet you (*f. s.*).

ألحروف العربية

THE ARABIC ALPHABET

أ ب ت ث

ج ح خ د ذ ر ز

س ش ص ض ط ظ

ع غ ف ق ك ل

م ن هـ و ي

تَمْرِين ٣ . أُنْظُرُوا إِلَى ٱلْخَطِّ ٱلْعَرَبِيّ . مَاذَا تُلاحِظُونَ؟

Exercise 3. Look at the Arabic writing (print and script). What do you notice?

Script	Print
	أَلـسَّلامُ عَلَيْكُمْ .
	وَعَلَيْكُمُ ٱلسَّلام .
	كَيْفَ حَالُكَ؟
	أَلْحَمْدُ لله بِخَيْرٍ .

1. Arabic is written from right to left.

2. _____

3. _____

4. _____

5. _____

Writing Arabic

You are about to learn how to write Arabic letters and how to differentiate between print and script. Usually **you read print and write script.** To write the letters correctly, keep in mind an imaginary set of six lines, similar to a staff of written music. The lines are numbered 1 through 6 from top to bottom. Lines 1 and 6 are heavy, while lines 2 through 5 are light. The printed Arabic text is above the staff and the script (handwriting) is written on the staff. For letters which are written below line 6, the staff is doubled (1-11).

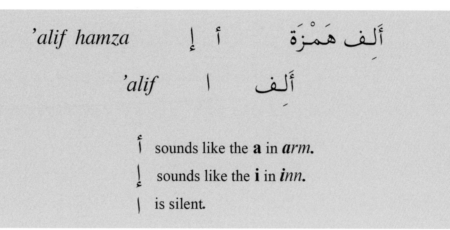

'alif hamza   أ   إ   أَلِف هَمْزَة

'alif   ا   أَلِف

أ sounds like the **a** in *arm*.

إ sounds like the **i** in *inn*.

ا is silent.

تَمْرِين ٤ . إِسْتَمِعُوا وَأَعِيدُوا ثُمَّ حَدِّدُوا حَرْفَ اَلْأَلِف مَعَ اَلْهَمْزَة وَبِدُونِ اَلْهَمْزَة .

Exercise 4. Listen and repeat, then identify *'alif and 'alif hamza*.

٤ . إسمي   ٣ . أبي   ٢ . إيراني   ١ . أنا

Exercise 5. Write.   تَمْرِين ٥ . أُكْتُبُوا .

ا   أ إ

First write the *'alif* and then write the *hamza* above or underneath it.

أ إ

Remember: The examples above the staff of lines are print, and those within the staff of lines are script. **Imitate the script only.** Continue writing until the end of the staff. When you practice writing a letter or a combination of letters, say the letters to yourself while writing them.

1. The position of the ء, above or underneath the ا, depends on the vowel the *'alif* represents. When the vowel is /a/ or /u/, the ء is written above the *'alif* (أ ﺍ). When the vowel is /i/ the ء is written underneath the *'alif* (إِ).

2. *'alif* without *hamza* (ا) is silent. It can appear only at the middle or end of a word.

3. **Words in Arabic do not start with silent letters.**

أ إ ا **is one of six non-connector letters.**

When you complete the writing of the *'alif,* break the writing continuum; that is, lift your pen from the page:

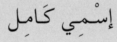

إسْمِي كَامِل

تَمْرِين ٦ . إِسْتَمِعُوا وَأَضِيفُوا ٱلْهَمْزَة لِحَرْفِ ٱلْأَلِفِ ٱلَّذِي تَسْمَعُونَهُ.

Exercise 6. Listen and add *hamza* to the *'alif* that you hear.

٤. ابي   ٣. اسمها   ٢. امي   ١. اسمي

٨. بنات   ٧. اختـ   ٦. ا.   ٥. انا

باء   بـ   ب   *baa*

ب sounds like **b**.

تَمْرِين ٧ . إِسْتَمِعُوا وَأَعِيدُوا ثُمَّ حَدِّدُوا حَرْفَ ٱلْبَاءِ.

Exercise 7. Listen and repeat, then identify the letter *baa*.

٤. بنت   ٣. كلب   ٢. بيت   ١. كبير

Exercise 8. Write.   تَمْرِين ٨ . أُكْتُبُوا.

Final *baa* ب   بـ

بابا

ببا

أَب father

باب door

تَمْرِين ٩. حَدِّدُوا ٱلْأَلِف وَٱلْبَاء فِي ٱلْجُمْلَة ٱلتَّالِيَة.

Exercise 9. Identify the 'alif and the baa in the following sentence.

زا رامي البيت الأبيض

THE WHITE HOUSE
WASHINGTON

nuun　　ن　ـن　نون

ن sounds like **n**.

تَمْرِين ١٠. إِسْتَمِعُوا وَأَعِيدُوا ثُمَّ حَدِّدُوا حَرْفَ ٱلنُّون.

Exercise 10. Listen and repeat, then identify the letter *nuun*.

١. لبنان　　٢. إبن　　٣. أنا　　٤. نبيل

Exercise 11. Write.　　تَمْرِين ١١. أُكْتُبُوا.

final *nuun*　ن　　　　　ـن

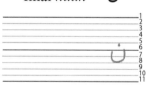

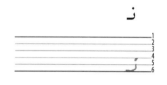

أنا　ا

son　إبن

تَمْرِين ١٢ . حَدِّدُوا ٱلْأَلِف وَٱلْبَاء وَٱلنُّون فِي ٱلْجُمْلَة ٱلتَّالِيَة .

Exercise 12. Identify the *'alif*, the *baa* and the *nuun* in the following sentence.

تَسْكُنُ بِنْتِي فِي كَالِيفُورنِيا فِي مَدِينَة لُوس أَنجِليس .

تَمْرِين ١٣ . صِلُوا ٱلْحُرُوف وَٱكْتُبُوا كَلِمَات .

Exercise 13. Connect the letters and write words.

_____ ←	١ . أ + ب
_____ ←	٢ . إ + ب + ن
_____ ←	٣ . ب + ا
_____ ←	٤ . أ + ن + ا

taa   ت   ﺗ   تاء

ت sounds like **t**.

تَمْرِين ١٤. إِسْتَمِعُوا وَأَعِيدُوا ثُمَّ حَدِّدُوا حَرْفَ ٱلتَّاء.

Exercise 14. Listen and repeat, then identify the letter *taa*.

٤. تركيا   ٣. بيتي   ٢. تونس   ١. أنت

Exercise 15. Write.   تَمْرِين ١٥. أُكْتُبُوا.

final *taa* ت   ﺗ

> The *taa* has two dots centered above the initial downward stroke.
> On the final *taa* the two dots are in the middle. In script, the two
> dots are written as a short horizontal line.

you   أنت

girl, daughter   بنت

girls, daughters   بنات

بَنَاتِ

Important notes about writing Arabic

1. Connecting letters in Arabic cursive is basically simple. Letters that have an **initial**, **medial** and **final** form can be joined to one another continuously to form a word. **After writing the first letter, continue to the spot where the second letter starts and write it, then continue to the spot where the following letter starts and write it, and so on until you finish writing the word.**

2. Any letter that follows a **non-connector** takes its initial form.

3. A letter written on its own is in its **isolated** form. Example: ب ن.

4. In general, there are three sizes of letters in Arabic: small (ب), medium (ن), and large (tall) (أ). The medium letters are as twice as tall as the small ones, and the large letters are as twice as tall as the medium letters. Some letters are written on line 6 and others - below line 6. Keep these proportions and your handwriting will be neat.

Listen to the conversation.

إِسْتَمِعُوا إِلَى ٱلْمُحَادَثَة.

min 'ayna 'anti?   مِنْ أَيْنَ أَنْتِ؟

Where are you (*f. s.*) from?

سَامِي: صَبَاحُ ٱلْخَيْرِ يَا رِيم.

رِيم: صَبَاحُ ٱلنُّورِ يَا سَامِي.

سَامِي: مِنْ أَيْنَ أَنْتِ يَا رِيم؟

رِيم: أَنَا مِنْ لُبْنَان وَمِنْ أَيْنَ أَنْتَ يَا سَامِي؟

سَامِي: أَنَا مِنَ مِصْر.

Exercise 16. Answer.   تَمْرِين ١٦. أَجِيبُوا.

1. Where are Rim and Sami from?   (مِنْ أَيْنَ رِيم وَمِنْ أَيْنَ سَامِي؟)

2. Guess the meaning of the word "*min.*"   (خَمِّنُوا مَعْنَى كَلِمَة "مِنْ".)

تَمْرِين ١٧. سَلِّمُوا عَلَى زُمَلائِكُمْ وَٱسْأَلُوهُمْ مِنْ أَيْنَ هُمْ.

Exercise 17. Greet your classmates and ask them where they are from.

Vocative Particle   *ya*   يَا

The vocative particle يَا (*ya*) is used when addressing someone.

It appears before names and titles. Usually it is not translated into English: *

ya Rim!	يَا رِيم!
ya 'ustadh Hani (Professor Hani)!	يَا أُسْتَاذ هَانِي!
ya duktuur!	يَا دُكْتُورا!
ya rabb (O Lord)!	يَا رَبّ!

*   Of course there are some English expressions that use the vocative "O,"
as in, "O Lord!" The vocative in English was common in earlier times.

Where?   *'ayna?*   أَيْنَ؟

'ayna Rim?	Where is Rim?	أَيْنَ رِيم؟
'ayna Sami?	Where is Sami?	أَيْنَ سَامِي؟

Where ... from?   *min 'ayna?*   مِنْ أَيْنَ؟

min 'ayna 'anta?	Where are you (*m. s.*) from?	مِنْ أَيْنَ أَنْتَ؟
min 'ayna Nawal?	Where is Nawal from?	مِنْ أَيْنَ نَوَال؟

Exercise 18. Translate out loud.   تَمْرِين ١٨ . تَرْجِمُوا شَفَهِيًّا .

1. - Where are you (*f. s.*) from?

    - I am from America (*'amrika*).

2. - Where is Rami from?

    - Rami is from Lebanon.

3. - What is your (*m. s.*) name?

    - My name is ... .

4. - It is a pleasure.

    - It is a pleasure (to meet you).

Where are you **from**? (*min 'ayna 'anti?*) ؟ مِنْ أَيْنَ أَنْتِ –

I am **from** Lebanon. (*'ana min lubnan.*) . أَنَا مِنْ لُبْنَان –

In this example, the preposition *"min"* is added to the question word *'ayna*.

If a preposition is added to a question word it should be used in the answer.

yaa　　ي　يـ　　ياء

ي sounds like **y**.

تَمْرِين ١٩ . إِسْتَمِعُوا وَأَعِيدُوا ثُمَّ حَدِّدُوا حَرْفَ ٱلْيَاءِ .

Exercise 19. Listen and repeat, then identify the letter *yaa*.

٤ . مريم　　٣ . يوم　　٢ . بيت　　١ . أين

تَمْرِين ٢٠ . إِسْتَمِعُوا إِلَى هٰذِهِ ٱلْكَلِمَاتِ ٱلَّتِي فِيهَا يَاء وَأَعِيدُوا .

Exercise 20. Listen to these words that include *yaa* and repeat.

٥ . نبيل　　٤ . كبير　　٣ . دين　　٢ . تين　　١ . بنتي

هَلْ تَسْمَعُونَ ٱلْيَاءَ؟ مَاذَا تُلاحِظُونَ بِٱلنِّسْبَةِ لِحَرْفِ ٱلْيَاءِ؟

Do you hear the *yaa*? What do you notice about the *yaa*?

Exercise 21. Write.　　تَمْرِين ٢١ . أُكْتُبُوا .

final *yaa*　ي　　　　يـ

yaa is the only letter in Arabic that has two dots **beneath** it.

Vocative particle preceding names and titles يا

يا

house بيت

بيت

where أين

أين

my father أبي

أبي

my house بيتي

بيتي

my daughters بناتي

بناتي

وا و *waaw*

و sounds like **w**.

تَمْرِين ٢٢. إِسْتَمِعُوا وَأَعِيدُوا ثُمَّ حَدِّدُوا حَرْفَ ٱلْوَاو.

Exercise 22. Listen and repeat, then identify the letter *waaw*.

٤. أولاد   ٣. يوم   ٢. مروان   ١. ولد

تَمْرِين ٢٣. إِسْتَمِعُوا إِلَى هٰذِهِ ٱلْكَلِمَاتِ ٱلَّتِي فِيهَا وَاو وَأَعِيدُوا.

Exercise 23. Listen to these words that include *waaw* and repeat.

١. كمبيوتر ٢. تلفزيـون ٣. مسلمون ٤. تونس ٥. بيروت

هَلْ تَسْمَعُونَ ٱلْوَاو؟ مَاذَا تُلاحِظُونَ بِٱلنِّسْبَة لِحَرْفِ ٱلْوَاو؟

Do you hear the *waaw*? What do you notice about the *waaw*?

Exercise 24. Write   تَمْرِين ٢٤. أُكْتُبُوا.

و **is one of six non-connector letters.**

When you complete the writing of the *waaw,* break the writing

continuum; that is, lift your pen from the page: بيوت

a son and a father   إبن وأب

إبن وأب

houses   بيوت

بيوت

thaa   ثاء ث ث

ث sounds like the **_th_** in **th**anks.

تَمْرِين ٢٥. إِسْتَمِعُوا وَأَعِيدُوا ثُمَّ حَدِّدُوا حَرْفَ ٱلثَّاء.

Exercise 25. Listen and repeat, then identify the letter *thaa.*

١. ثَلاث   ٢. ثَوْر   ٣. مَثَل   ٤. ثَعْلَب

Exercise 26. Write.   تَمْرِين ٢٦. أُكْتُبُوا.

Final *thaa*   ث   ثَ

ث has three dots centered above the initial downward stroke.

In script, the three dots are written like ∧ from left to right.

solid, firm   ثابت

dress, clothes   ثوب

تَمْرِين ٢٧. صِلُوا ٱلْحُرُوف وَٱكْتُبُوا ٱلْكَلِمَات.

Exercise 27. Connect the letters to write the words.

١.   أ + ب + و + ا + ب ⟵ _____

٢.   ب + ن + ا + ت ⟵ _____

٣.   ب + ي + ت + ي ⟵ _____

٤.   ت + ي + ن ⟵ _____

٥.   أ + ي + ن ⟵ _____

‏٦. ب + ن + ت + ي ← _____

‏٧. ث + و + ب ← _____

‏٨. ث + ا + ب + ت ← _____

‏تَمْرِين ٢٨ . حَدِّدُوا:

‏– ثَلاثَة حُرُوف لَهَا مِيزَة مُشْتَرَكَة . مَا هِيَ ٱلْمِيزَة؟

‏– حَرْفَانِ لَهَمَا مِيزَة مُشْتَرَكَة . مَا هِيَ ٱلْمِيزَة؟

Exercise 28. Identify:

- Three letters that share a distinguishing feature. What is that feature?

- Two letters that share a distinguishing feature. What is that feature?

ث	ي	و	ن	ت	ب	أ

‏تَمْرِين ٢٩ . أَحِيطُوا ٱلْحَرْفَ ٱلَّذِي تَسْمَعُونَهُ.

Exercise 29. Circle the letter you hear.

‏١.	أ	ب	و	ن	ي	ث	ت
‏٢.	ت	ت	ث	ي	ن	و	ب	إ
‏٣.	أ	ن	و	ب	ت	ث	ي

The vowels   *'alḥarakaat*   أَلْحَرَكَات

Arabic has three short vowels: and three silent letters which lengthen the vowels preceding them (long vowels).

The short vowels

ḍamma /u/   ُ — ضَمَّة

A small و above the letter.

Pronounced like /u/ as in "blue": أُ , تُ , نُ.

fatḥa /a/   َ — فَتْحَة

Short downward sloping line drawn from right to left above the letter.

Pronounced like /a/ as in "fat": أَ , نَ , تَ.

kasra /i/ as   ِ — كَسْرَة

Short downward sloping line drawn from right to left under and to the left of the letter.

Pronounced like /i/ as in "Alli": إِ , وِ , بِ.

تَمْرِين ٣٠. شَكِّلُوا ٱلْحُرُوف ثُمَّ ٱلْفِظُوهَا.

Exercise 30. Add the vowels above or below the letters, then pronounce
the resultant syllable.

ḍamma   ت   ي   ب   ن   ث   و   أ

fatḥa   أ   ن   ث   و   ب   ي   ت

kasra   ن   و   ت   ب   إ   ث   ي

> The *hamza* is written under the *'alif* only when
>
> the *hamza* has *kasra* – إِ

Exercise 31. Read the letters.   تَمْرِين ٣١. إِقْرَؤُوا ٱلْحُرُوف.

ب   بْ   تَ   وِ   إِ   نُ   يِ   أُ   نَ   ثِ   وَ

وُ   نِ   نَ   أَ   بُ   إِ   يُ   وِ   تَ   بَ   ثُ

تَمْرِين ٣٢. إِسْتَمِعُوا وَضَعُوا ٱلْحَرَكَات.

Exercise 32. Listen and add the corresponding vowels.

١	٢	٣	٤	٥	٦	٧	٨	٩	١٠

ب   أ   ي   ث   ت   ب   أ   إ   ن   و

تَمْرِين ٣٣. أَحيطُوا ٱلْحَرْفَ ٱلَّذي تَسْمَعُونَهُ.

Exercise 33. Circle the letter that you hear.

١. وُ وَ وُ وِ   ٢. تَ تُ تِ تَ   ٣. تُ ثُ وُ

٤. بِ بُ بَ   ٥. يَ يِ يُ   ٦. ثِ يِ إِ

٧. نِ نَ نُ   ٨. أُ أَ إِ   ٩. وَ أَ ثَ

تَمْرِين ٣٤. إِخْتَارُوا خَمْسَة حُرُوف وَٱكْتُبُوهَا وَضَعُوا عَلَيْهَا حَرَكَات ثُمَّ
ٱلْفِظُوهَا.

Exercise 34. Choose five letters, write them, add vowels, and then pronounce them.

بِسْمِ ٱللهِ ٱلرَّحْمَنِ ٱلرَّحِيمِ

ḥurufu-lmadd   حُرُوفُ ٱلْمَدّ

Lengthening letters

1. The letters ا و and ي could be silent in the middle or at the end of a word.

2. In the **middle of a word**, a silent letter **lengthens** the vowel that precedes it:

Silent ا lengthens the *fatḥa* that precedes it [ا —] producing the long vowel

sound in *far*: بَاب ، بَنَات.

Silent و lengthens the *ḍamma* that precedes it [و —ُ] producing the

long vowel sound in *tool*: تُوت ، بُيُوت.

Silent ي lengthens the *kasra* that precedes it [ي —ِ] producing the

long vowel sound in *cheese*: دِين ، تِين (diin).

3. **At the end of a word a silent letter does not lengthen the vowel**

preceding it: أَبِي ، أَبُو ، أَنَا.

Note: Mispronunciation of the lengthening letters can create spelling

mistakes and may affect the meaning of words. For example, the word

بَنَات means *girls*, as opposed to the word بَنَتْ which means *she built*.

Likewise the word مَطَار (*maṭaar*) means *airport*, as opposed to the word

مَطَر (*maṭar*) which means *rain*.

تَمْرِين ٣٥. إِسْتَمِعُوا وَأَعيدُوا. أَحيطُوا ٱلْكَلِمَاتِ ٱلَّتِي تَحْتَوِي عَلَى

حُرُوفِ ٱلْمَدّ.

Exercise 35. Listen and repeat. Circle the words which include lengthening letters.

٤. أَوْلاد   ٣. أُسْتَاذ   ٢. أَسْكُنُ   ١. تَسْكُنِينَ

٨. أَلْقَاهِرَة   ٧. مَرْكَز   ٦. بُيُوت   ٥. لُبْنَان

١٢. أَبُو   ١١. حَالُكَ   ١٠. يَوْم   ٩. تَرْجِم

تَمْرِين ٣٦. إِسْتَمِعُوا إِلَى ٱلْكَلِمَات وَأَحيطُوا حَرْفَ ٱلْمَدّ.

Exercise 36. Listen to the words and circle the lengthening letter.

| ١. | ا | و | ي | | ٢. | ا | و | ي |

| ٣. | ا | و | ي | | ٤. | ا | و | ي |

| ٥. | ا | و | ي | | ٦. | ا | و | ي |

| ٧. | ا | و | ي | | ٨. | ا | و | ي |

| ٩. | ا | و | ي | | ١٠. | ا | و | ي |

تَسْكُنِينَ ، سُورِيّ ، حَالُكَ ، مَحْمُود ، صَبَاح

تَمْرِين ، لُبْنَان ، تُوت ، تِين ، أُسْتَاذ

سُكُون ْ – *sukuun*

A small circle written above the letter indicates the absence of a vowel.

تَمْرِين ٣٧. إِسْتَمِعُوا وَأَعِيدُوا. إِنْتَبِهُوا إِلَى أَلسُّكُون.

Exercise 37. Listen and repeat paying attention to the *sukuun*.

٣. أَدْرُسُ	٢. تَسْكُنُ	١. لُبْنَان
٦. عَلَيْكُمْ	٥. مُمْتَاز	٤. بَيْرُوت

تَمْرِين ٣٨. إِسْتَمِعُوا وَأَعِيدُوا. أَحِيطُوا كَلِمَات تَحْتَوِي عَلَى سُكُون.

Exercise 38. Listen and repeat. Circle the words which include *sukuun*.

٣. أَنت	٢. مدينة	١. أولاد
٦. جديد	٥. تدرسين	٤. ولاية

تَمْرِين ٣٩. إِسْتَمِعُوا إِلَى أَلْكَلِمَات وَضَعُوا أَلسُّكُون عَلَى أَلْحَرْفِ أَلْمُلَائِم.

Exercise 39. Listen to the words and add the *sukuun* to the appropriate letter.

٤. إبني	٣. بنتي	٢. أنت	١. بيتي

shadda — شَدَّة

The _shadda_ looks like a small "w" above a consonant. It indicates that the consonant has been doubled. To pronounce a consonant with _shadda_, extend the length of the consonant's normal pronunciation. For example, the word _kassara_ (to brake) is pronounced: _kas + sara_ – hold the /s/ sound for twice as long.

تَمْرِين ٤٠ . إِسْتَمِعُوا وَأَعِيدُوا. إِنْتَبِهُوا إِلَى ٱلشَّدَّة.

Exercise 40. Listen and repeat paying attention to the _shadda_.

٣. طَبَّاخ	٢. أَلسَّلام	١. مُحَمَّد
٦. مُعَلِّم	٥. يَتَكَلَّمُ	٤. تَشَرَّفْنَا

تَمْرِين ٤١ . إِسْتَمِعُوا وَأَعِيدُوا. أَحِيطُوا كَلِمَات تَحْتَوِي عَلَى ٱلشَّدَّة.

Exercise 41. Listen and repeat. Circle the words that include _shadda_.

٣. يهود	٢. تلميذ	١. محمد
٦. معلم	٥. ألسلام	٤. تشرفنا

1. A _sukuun_ cannot be used with the _shadda_.

2. In **both print and script,** the _fatḥa_ and _ḍamma_ are written over

   the _shadda_: —   —   أَلْعَرَبِيَّة ، لُبْنَانِيُّونَ

3. In modern print the _kasra_ is written under the _shadda_: أُمِّي.

   When you write script, write the _kasra_ under the letter.

تَمْرِين ٤٢. حَدِّدُوا ٱلْحُرُوف وَٱلْحَرَكَات ثُمَّ ٱقْرَؤُوا.

Exercise 42. Identify the letters and the vowels, then read.

٣. أَنْتَ وَأَنْتِ	٢. بَيْت بِنْتِي	١. إِبْن وَبِنْت
٦. ثَوْب بِنْتِي	٥. أَنَا وَأَنْتَ	٤. إِبْنِي وَبِنْتِي
٩. إِبْنِي وَبَنَاتِي	٨. أَيْنَ أَبِي؟	٧. أَنَا وَأَبِي
١٢. بَاب بَيْتِي	١١. أَيْنَ أَنْتِ؟	١٠. يَا بِنْتِي.

If the final letter of a word does not have a vowel, read it as if it has a *sukuun*:

أَب ، بَيْت ، بِنْت

وَاوُ ٱلْعَطْف   وَ   The conjunction "and"

1. The word "and" in Arabic is وَ.

2. It is used to join words, clauses, and sentences.

3. **It is always added to the word that follows it:**

My son and my daughter   إِبْنِي وَبِنْتِي

4. When three or more words, phrases, or clauses appear in a series, they are connected by وَ and are not separated by commas, as they are in English.

A son, a daughter, and a father   إِبْن وَبِنْت وَأَب

I and you　أَنَا وَأَنْتَ

Unlike English, which places the first person pronoun last, Arabic follows a "first, second, third" person word order. I precedes you, which in turn precedes he/she. Examples: I and you, you and he, I and he.

تَعَلَّمُوا هٰذِهِ ٱلْمُفْرَدَات

my father	أَبِي	father	أَب	I	أَنَا
doors	أَبْوَاب	door	بَاب	you (m. s.)	أَنْتَ
houses	بُيُوت	house	بَيْت	you (f. s.)	أَنْتِ
girls, daughters	بَنَات	girl, daughter	بِنْت	son	إِبْن
strawberry	تُوت	figs	تِين	my son	إِبْنِي
dress, clothes	ثَوْب	solid, firm	ثَابِت	where?	أَيْنَ

إِسْتَمِعُوا إِلَى ٱلْمُحَادَثَة.

Listen to the conversation.

'ana min wilaayat new york   أَنَا مِنْ وِلَايَة نِيو يُورك

I am from New York State.

نَبِيل: مَسَاءُ ٱلْخَيْر يَا نَادِيَا.

نَادِيَا: مَسَاءُ ٱلنُّور يَا نَبِيل.

نَبِيل: مِنْ أَيْنَ أَنْتِ؟

ناديا: أَنَا مِنْ وِلَايَة كَالِيفُورنِيَا مِنْ مَدِينَة

لُوس أَنْجِلِيس وَمِنْ أَيْنَ أَنْتَ؟

نَبِيل: أَنَا مِنْ وِلَايَة نِيو يُورك مِنْ مَدِينَة نِيو يُورك.

Exercise 43. Answer out loud.   تَمْرِين ٤٣. أَجِيبُوا شَفَهِيًّا.

١. مِنْ أَيْنَ نَبِيل؟   ⟸   نَبِيل مِنْ مَدِينَة نِيو يُورك.

٢. مِنْ أَيْنَ نَادِيَا؟

٣. مِنْ أَيْنَ أَنْتَ؟ / مِنْ أَيْنَ أَنْتِ؟

٤. مَا مَعْنَى "وِلَايَة كَالِيفُورنِيَا"؟   (What is the meaning of ...?)

Listen to the conversation.   إِسْتَمِعُوا إِلَى ٱلْمُحَادَثَة.

kayfa ḥaluka?   كَيْفَ حَالُكَ؟

How are you (*m. s.*)?

رِيم: أَلسَّلامُ عَلَيْكُمْ، يَا نَبِيل.

نَبِيل: وَعَلَيْكُمُ ٱلسَّلام، يَا رِيم.

رِيم: كَيْفَ حَالُكَ؟

نَبِيل: أَلْحَمْدُ لله أَنَا بِخَيْر، وَكَيْفَ حَالُكِ أَنْتِ يَا رِيم؟

رِيم: أَلْحَمْدُ لله بِخَيْر.

'alḥamdu lillaah   أَلْحَمْدُ لله

Praise be to God

'alḥamdu lillah rabbi-l'alamin أَلْحَمْدُ لله رَبِّ ٱلْعَلَمِين (*Praise be to God the lord of the worlds*) is the second verse of the opening *suura* (سُورَة *chapter*) in the Qur'an. Its short version, *'alḥamdu lillaah* أَلْحَمْدُ لله is frequently used in daily life in Arabic–speaking countries to thank God for blessings and favors. When learning about a positive outcome, such as being successful on a test, or solving a problem, a person says *'alḥamdu lillaah*. This expression is also used after finishing a meal, or to politely refuse additional food that is offered. The phrase *'alḥamdu lillaah* is also used after sneezing. In the Arab culture the sneeze is associated with the superstitious belief that it stops the heart or releases the soul. By saying *'alḥamdu lillaah* one thanks God for not letting these things happen to him or her. If a person hears a sneeze, he or she should courteously respond saying *yarḥamukumu-LLaah* يَرْحَمُكُمْ ٱلله which means "May the mercy of God be upon you," or simply, "God bless you," and the person who sneezes then responds *'alḥamdu lillaah*. In Arab culture, the attitude is that one should praise God in either good or bad situations because things could always be worse, and one should be thankful for what God has given. The phrase *'alḥamdu lillaah* is commonly used as a reply to *kayfa ḥaluka?* كَيْفَ حَالُكَ which means, "How are you (*m. s.*)?" (Literally: "*How is your* [*m. s.*] *condition?*")

تَمْرِين ٤٤ . إِسْتَمِعُوا وَأَعِيدُوا ثُمَّ تَرْجِمُوا إِلَى ٱلْإِنْجِلِيزِيَّة .

Exercise 44. Listen and repeat, then translate into English.

١. – كَيْفَ حَالُكَ؟   ٢. – اَلسَّلَامُ عَلَيْكُمْ.

– اَلْحَمْدُ للهِ بِخَيْرٍ.   – وَعَلَيْكُمُ ٱلسَّلَام.

٣. – مَرْحَبًا يَا أُسْتَاذ.   ٤. – صَبَاحُ ٱلْخَيْرِ . (Good morning)

– مَرْحَبًا يَا نَبِيل.   – صَبَاحُ ٱلنُّور.

٥. – مَسَاءُ ٱلْخَيْرِ . (Good evening)   ٦. – مِنْ أَيْنَ أَنْتِ؟

– مَسَاءُ ٱلنُّور.   – أَنَا مِنْ أَنَابُولِيس.

Exercise 45. Translate into Arabic .   تَمْرِين ٤٥ . تَرْجِمُوا إِلَى ٱلْعَرَبِيَّة .

1. - Hello, Professor.

   - Hello, Nabil.

2. - Where are you (*m. s.*) from?

   - I am from Iran.

3. - Good morning, Nawal (*f.*).

   - Good morning, Rim (*f.*).

4. - How are you, Linda?

   - Thank God, I am fine.

تَمْرِين ٤٦ . إِسْتَمِعُوا وَقُولُوا أَسْمَاءَكُمْ وَمِنْ أَيْنَ أَنْتُمْ حَسَبَ ٱلْمِثَال .

Exercise 46. Listen, then say your name and where you are from, following

the example.

أَلسَّلامُ عَلَيْكُمْ . إِسْمِي ... (ران) وَأَنَا مِنْ مَدِينَة ...

(لُوس أَنْجِلِيس) مِنْ وِلايَة ... (كَاليفُورنِيَا) .

تَمْرِين ٤٧ . سَلِّمُوا عَلَى زُمَلائِكُمْ وَٱسْأَلُوهُمْ عَنْ أَسْمَائِهِمْ، وَمِنْ أَيْنَ هُمْ وَكَيْفَ

أَحْوَالُهُمْ .

Exercise 47. Greet your classmates and ask them their names, where

they are from, and how they are doing.

The Arab Name

The Arab name is composed of three parts:

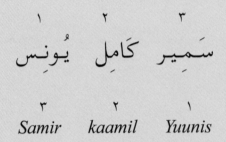

Samir　　kaamil　　Yuunis

The first name is the given name. The second name is the father's given name. The last name is the family name. In some cases, the paternal grandfather's name is used after the father's given name:

سَمِير كَامِل نَبِيل يُونِس

Samir　　kaamil　　Nabil　　Yuunis

The full name is usually used in formal documents and settings. In casual daily conversations only the given name is used.

تَمْرِين ٤٨. إِخْتَارُوا أَسْمَاء لِأَنْفُسِكُمْ وَلِثَلَاثَة مِنْ زُمَلَائِكُمْ مِنْ قَائِمَة ٱلْأَسْمَاء فِي ٱلصَّفْحَة ٱلْإِلِكْتُرُونِيَّة لِسَلَامَات.

Exercise 48. Pick an Arabic name for three of your classmates from the name list on the *Salamaat!* website.

Exercise 49. Circle the correct answer.   تَمْرِين ٤٩ . أَحِيطُوا ٱلْجَوَابَ ٱلصَّحِيح .

1. The first letter in the word ثَوْب is:

    a. *baa*   b. *taa*   c. <u>*thaa*</u>   d. *nuun*

2. The last letter in the word إِبْن is:

    a. *yaa*   b. *nuun*   c. *taa*   d. *baa*

3. The *'alif* in the word بَنَات is silent.

    a. True   b. False

4. The *hamza* is written either on top of the *'alif* or underneath it.

    a. True   b. False

5. The letter *waaw* is a non-connector.

    a. True   b. False

6. The letter *yaa* is always a consonant.

    a. True   b. False

7. In the word بَيْتِي there are five letters.

    a. True   b. False

8. How many times does the letter *yaa* appears in the phrase بَيْت بِنْتِي ؟

    a. One tine   b. Two times   c. Three times   d. Four times

9. The letters أ و ي at the beginning of a word could be silent.

    a. True   b. False

Arabic numerals أَلأَعْدَادُ ٱلْعَرَبِيَّة

Two sets of numerals were developed in India by the Hindus as early as 500 B.C., and are used today throughout the world. One set, popularly known as "Arabic numerals" (0, 1, 2, 3, 4, ...), was transmitted by the Arabs to the West, replacing the cumbersome Roman numerals. The other set, used in most of the Arab world, can also be called Arabic numerals. These new symbols, including the symbol which represents zero, make it easier to cope with big numbers.

		٠	0
٦	6	١	1
٧	7	٢ (٢)	2
٨	8	٣ (٣)	3
٩	9	٤	4
١٠	10	٥	5

The numerals are identical in print and script except for ٢ and ٣.

تَمْرِين ٥٠. إِسْتَمِعُوا إِلَى ٱلأَعْدَاد مِنْ صِفْر إِلَى عَشَرَة وَأَعِيدُوا.

Exercise 50. Listen to the numbers from zero to ten and repeat.

ṣifr ٠ صِفْر

sitta	سِتَّة	٦	*waḥid*	وَاحِد	١
sab‘a	سَبْعَة	٧	*’ithnan*	إِثْنَان	٢
thamaniya	ثَمَانِية	٨	*thalatha*	ثَلاثَة	٣
tis‘a	تِسْعَة	٩	*’arba‘a*	أَرْبَعَة	٤
‘ashara	عَشَرَة	١٠	*khamsa*	خَمْسَة	٥

khamsa خَمْسَة

In the Arab culture the number five, *khamsa** خَمْسَة is superstitiously perceived as having power and strength. It can thus provide protection from the evil eye. "*khamsa*" is also the name of a palm-shaped talisman, that sometimes includes an eye symbol. It is also called "the hand of Faṭima" after Prophet Muḥammd's daughter. People tend to hang "*khamsa*" on the wall as a decoration, mainly at the entrance to the house, or wear it as a necklace for protection. The "*khamsa*" image also appears as decorative element in jewelry, paintings and sculptures.

* *kh* is pronounced like **ch** in German.
(Johann Sebastian Bach)

Exercise 51. Write the numbers.　　　تَمْرِين ٥١ . أُكْتُبُوا أَلْأَعْدَاد.

١٠　٩　٨　٧　٦　٥　٤　٣　٢　١

١٠　٩　٨　٧　٦　٥　٤　٣　٢　١

Compound numbers, unlike text, are written from left to right , as in English:

2020 ⟹ ٢٠٢٠

Exercise 52. Write the following numbers.　　　تَمْرِين ٥٢ . أُكْتُبُوا أَلْأَرْقَام أَلتَّالِيَة.

1. 4831 _____

2. 7326 _____

3. 5462 _____

4. 6900 _____

5. 1895 _____

6. 2013 _____

تَمْرِين ٥٣. إِسْتَمِعُوا وَأَحِيطُوا ٱلْعَدَدَ ٱلَّذِي تَسْمَعُونَهُ.

Exercise 53. Listen and circle the number you hear.

١.   ١   ٢   ٣   ٤   ٥   ٦   ٧   ٨   ٩   ١٠

٢.   ١   ٢   ٣   ٤   ٥   ٦   ٧   ٨   ٩   ١٠

٣.   ١   ٢   ٣   ٤   ٥   ٦   ٧   ٨   ٩   ١٠

٤.   ١   ٢   ٣   ٤   ٥   ٦   ٧   ٨   ٩   ١٠

٥.   ١   ٢   ٣   ٤   ٥   ٦   ٧   ٨   ٩   ١٠

٦.   ١   ٢   ٣   ٤   ٥   ٦   ٧   ٨   ٩   ١٠

مَنْ سَارَ عَلَى ٱلدَّرْبِ وَصَلَ.

man sara 'ala-ddarbi waṣala.

He who starts walking will arrive.

UNIT 2

Listen to the conversation.

إِسْتَمِعُوا إِلَى ٱلْمُحَادَثَة .

'ayna taskunu?   أَيْنَ تَسْكُنُ؟

Where do you (*m. s.*) live?

نَبِيل: أَلسَّلامُ عَلَيْكُمْ .

نَوَال: وَعَلَيْكُمُ ٱلسَّلام .

نَبِيل: مَا ٱسْمُك؟

نَوَال: إِسْمِي نَوَال، وَما ٱسْمُكَ أَنْتَ؟

نَبِيل: إِسْمِي نَبِيل، أَهْلاً .

نَوَال: أَهْلاً بِكَ يا نَبِيل، هَلْ أَنْتَ طالِب جَدِيد؟

نَبِيل: نَعَمْ .

نَوَال: أَيْنَ تَسْكُنُ؟

نَبِيل: أَسْكُنُ فِي وِلايَة نيو يُورك فِي مَدِينَة أَلْبَنِي،
وَأَيْنَ تَسْكُنِينَ أَنْتِ يا نَوَال؟

نَوَال: أَنَا أَيْضًا أَسْكُنُ فِي وِلايَة نيو يورك وَلٰكِنْ فِي مَدِينَة
نيو يُورك .

نَبِيل: عَظِيم! عَمِّي (my paternal uncle) داوُد يَسْكُنُ أَيْضًا فِي مَدِينَة
نيو يُورك .

Exercise 1. Answer out loud.

تَمْرِين ١. أَجِيبُوا شَفَهِيًّا.

١. أَيْنَ تَسْكُنُ نَوَال؟   ٢. أَيْنَ يَسْكُنُ نَبِيل؟   ٣. أَيْنَ يَسْكُنُ داوُد؟

٤. أَيْنَ تَسْكُنُ أَنْتَ / أَيْنَ تَسْكُنِينَ أَنْتِ؟

Exercise 2. Answer with yes or no.

تَمْرِين ٢. أَجِيبُوا، نَعَمْ أَمْ لا.

١. هَلْ تَسْكُنُ نَوَال فِي وِلايَة نيو يُورك؟   نَعَمْ / لا

٢. هَلْ يَسْكُنُ نَبِيل فِي مَدِينَة أَلْبَنِي؟   نَعَمْ / لا

٣. هَلْ تَسْكُنُ نَوَال فِي مَدِينَة لُوس أَنْجِلِس؟   نَعَمْ / لا

٤. هَلْ يَسْكُنُ داوُد فِي وِلايَة كَالِيفورنِيَا؟   نَعَمْ / لا

Exercise 3. Ask your classmates:

تَمْرِين ٣. إِسْأَلُوا زُمَلاءَكُمْ:

1. - What is your name (m. s.)?
   - My name is John.

2. - Where do you (f. s.) live, Nadia?
   - I live in the city of Beirut.

3. - Where are you (m. s.) from?
   - I am from the state of New York.

4. - How are you (f. s.), Laṭifa?
   - Praise be to Allaah, I'm fine.

5. - Are you (m. s.) from Lebanon?
   - No. I am from Egypt.

6. - Hello (Peace be upon you.)
   - Hello

تَمْرين ٤ . أَنْتُمُ ٱلْآنَ فِي حَفْلَة. تَعَرَّفُوا عَلَى زُمَلائِكُمْ وَسَلِّمُوا عَلَيْهِمْ وَٱسْأَلُوهُمْ

عَنْ أَسْمَائِهِمْ وَأَحْوَالِهِمْ وَمِنْ أَيْنَ هُمْ وَأَيْنَ يَسْكُنُونَ.

Exercise 4. You are now at a party. Meet your peers, greet them, ask them their

names, how they are, where they are from, and where they live.

دال   د   *daal*

د sounds like **d**.

تَمْرِين ٥ . إِسْتَمِعُوا وَأَعِيدُوا ثُمَّ حَدِّدُوا حَرْفَ ٱلدَّال .

Exercise 5. Listen and repeat, then identify the letter *daal*.

١. أَدْرُسُ   ٢. بَدَوِيّ   ٣. أَلْأُرْدُنّ   ٤. أَلْحَمْدُ لله .

Exercise 6. Write.   تَمْرِين ٦ . أُكْتُبُوا .

د

د is a non-connector. When you complete it, break the writing continuum.
That is, lift your pen from the paper.

writer, author, well mannered   أَدِيب

bear   *   دُبّ

* If the <u>shadda</u> at the end of a word has no vowel ignore it in pronunciation.

Pay special attention to the way the ﺩ is written when connected to a letter preceding it. For example: ﻳﺪ (hand).

hand يَـد

يـد

nomad, bedouin بَـدَوِيّ

بـدوِيّ

Writing a word with vowels - an important note

Write the consonants of the word (بـدوي). Then return to the beginning, say the word in your mind, and give each letter, first, the diacritical marks (dots) and then the necessary orthographic marks such as *fatḥa, ḍamma, kasra, sukuun* and *shadda*: بَـدَوِيّ

The vowels are introduced to help you read the words correctly. After you have learned how to pronounce the words properly, you will gradually be "liberated" from the need to use vowels.

dhaal   ذ   ذال

ذ sounds like the **th** in _that_.

تَمْرِين ٧ . إِسْتَمِعُوا وَأَعِيدُوا ثُمَّ حَدِّدُوا حَرْفَ ٱلذَّال .

Exercise 7. Listen and repeat, then identify the letter _dhaal_.

١. أُسْتَاذ   ٢. مَاذَا   ٣. ذَنَب   ٤. هٰذَا

Exercise 8. Write.   تَمْرِين ٨ . أُكْتُبُوا .

ذ

ذ

ذ is a non-connector. When you complete it, break the writing continuum. That is, lift your pen from the paper.

tail   ذَنَب

ذَنَب

ear   أُذْن

أُذْن

تَمْرِين ٩ . أُكْتُبُوا ٱلْحَرْفَ ٱلْأَوَّل لِكُلّ كَلِمَة تَسْمَعُونَهَا .

Exercise 9. Write the first letter of each word you hear.

_____ . ٤   _____ . ٣   _____ . ٢   _____ . ١

_____ . ٨   _____ . ٧   _____ . ٦   _____ . ٥

ثَلاثَة ، دُرْزِيّ ، نَهْر ، وَلَد ، إِنْسَان ، دِمَشْق

ذَهَب ، يَسْكُنُ

تَمْرِين ١٠. صِلُوا ٱلْحُروف وَٱكْتُبُوا ٱلْكَلِمَات .

Exercise 10. Connect the letters to write the words.

_____ ← ١. دِ + ي + نَ + ا

_____ ← ٢. دَ + ا + وُ + د

_____ ← ٣. ذَ + نَ + ب

_____ ← ٤. يَ + دِ + ي

_____ ← ٥. أَ + دَ + ب

_____ ← ٦. أَ + دِ + ي + ب

raa   ر   را

ر sounds similar to the Spanish or Russian **r**.

There is no precise English equivalent.

تَمْرِين ١١. إِسْتَمِعُوا وَأَعِيدُوا ثُمَّ حَدِّدُوا حَرْفَ ٱلرَّاء.

Exercise 11. Listen and repeat, then identify the letter *raa*.

١. أَدْرُسُ   ٢. يَا رَبّ!   ٣. أَمْرِيكَا   ٤. أَلْعَرَبِيَّة

Exercise 12. Write.   تَمْرِين ١٢. أُكْتُبُوا.

ر

ر is a non–connector. When you complete it, break the writing continuum.

That is, lift your pen from the paper.

God   رَبّ

house   دَار

path, road دَرْب

بَيْرُوت Beirut

post, mail بَرِيد

Dinar (The name of the currency used in Iraq, Jordan, Kuwait, Tunisia, and Bahrain) * دِينَار

إِيرَان * Iran

* When there are two lengthening letters in the middle of a word, you lengthen
only the vowel preceding the second one: إِيرَان دِينَار

زاي ز *zaai*

ز sounds like **z**.

تَمْرِين ١٣. إِسْتَمِعُوا وَأَعِيدُوا ثُمَّ حَدِّدُوا حَرْفَ ٱلزَّاي.

Exercise 13. Listen and repeat, then identify the letter *zaai*.

١. زَيْت   ٢. زَيْتُون   ٣. زَارَ   ٤. دُرْزِيّ

Exercise 14. Write.   تَمْرِين ١٤. أُكْتُبُوا.

ز

ز is a non-connector. When you complete it, break the writing continuum.

That is, lift your pen from the paper.

to visit   زَارَ

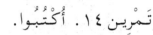

olives   زَيْتُون

minister (goverment)   وَزِير

وَزِير

The six non-connectors are:

أ   د   ذ   ر   ز   و

تَمْرِين ١٥. صِلُوا ٱلْحُروف وَٱكْتُبُوا ٱلْكَلِمَات.

Exercise 15. Connect the letters to write the words.

١.	⟵	دُ + رْ + زِ + يّ
٢.	⟵	إ + ي + رَ + ا + ن
٣.	⟵	بَ + يْ + رُ + و + ت
٤.	⟵	بَ + ر + ي + د
٥.	⟵	زَ + يْ + ت

تَمْرِين ١٦. أَحِيطُوا ٱلْحَرْفَ ٱلَّذِي تَسْمَعُونَهُ.

Exercise 16. Circle the letter that you hear.

١. زُ ذُ وُ   ٢. ذُ رِ زَ   ٣. وِ ذُ زُ

٤. ذِ دِ رِ   ٥. دَ دُ ذِ   ٦. تَ ذَ زَ

تَعَلَّمُوا هٰذِهِ ٱلْمُفْرَدَات

Iran	إِيرَان	hand	يَد
son	إِبْن	house	دَار (ج)* دُور
daughter, girl	بِنْت (ج) بَنَات	bedouin	بَدَوِيّ
ear	أُذْن	he visited	زَارَ
Beirut	بَيْرُوت	Dinar (currency)	دِينَار
olives	زَيْتُون	oil	زَيْت

* The letter ج (*jiim*) stands for the word جَمْع (*jam‘*) meaning *plural*.

Exercise 17. Read, then copy.   تَمْرِين ١٧ . إِقْرَؤُوا ثُمَّ ٱنْسَخُوا.

١. دَاوُد بَدَوِيّ.

_____

٢. يَد بِيَد

_____

٣. إِبْن وَبِنْت

_____

٤. إِبْن وَبِنْت وَأَب

_____

٥. دِينَا وَنَادِيَا وَدَاوُد _____

٦. دَانِي إِيرَانِيّ. _____

٧. زَيْت زَيْتُون _____

٨. بَنَات دِينَا _____

تَمْرِين ١٨ . يَسْتَمِعُ مَرْوَان إِلَى رِسَالَة صَوْتِيَّة مِنْ نَبِيل.

Exercise 18. Marwan is listening to a voice mail from Nabil.

أَنَا فِي ٱلْبَيْت. أَيْنَ أَنْتَ؟ هَلْ أَنْتَ فِي ٱلْجَامِعَة؟

Answer out loud. Where is Nabil?   أَجِيبُوا شَفَهِيًّا. أَيْنَ نَبِيل؟

تَمْرِين ١٩ . يَسْتَمِع نَبِيل إِلَى رِسَالَة صَوْتِيَّة مِنْ مَرْوَان.

Exercise 19. Nabil is listening to a voice mail from Marwan.

نَعَمْ. أَنَا فِي ٱلْمَكْتَبَة. أَدْرُس ٱلْعَرَبِيَّة. دِينَا هُنَا أَيْضًا.

Where are Dina and Marwan?   أَيْنَ دِينَا وَأَيْنَ مَرْوَان؟

Exercise 20. Describe the picture.   تَمْرِين ٢٠. صِفُوا ٱلصُّورَة.

laam   ل   ل   ل   لا.

ل sounds like the **l** as in **Linda**.

تَمْرِين ٢١. إِسْتَمِعُوا وَأَعِيدُوا ثُمَّ حَدِّدُوا حَرْفَ ٱللام.

Exercise 21. Listen and repeat, then identify the letter *laam*.

٤. لِسَان   ٣. نَبِيل   ٢. طَالِب   ١. لُبْنَانِيّ

Exercise 22. Write.   تَمْرِين ٢٢. أُكْتُبُوا.

ل

I have   لِي

city   بَلَد

boy   وَلَد

laam'alif   لا   أَلِف   لا

Write the *laam* and then the *'alif*   أُكْتُبُوا ٱللام وَبَعْدَ ذٰلِكَ ٱلأَلِف

2   1   لا

no   لا

After completing لا, lift your pen from the page because ا أ إ

is a non-connector.

cities, country   بِلاد

بِلاد

boys   أَوْلاد

أَوْلاد

Final *laam*   لام فِي آخِرِ ٱلْكَلِمَة

---

connected   بل   not connected   ل

بل   ل

to come down, stay   نَزَلَ

نَزَلَ

night   لَيْل

لَيْل

A connected ل at the end of a word shifts downward.

تَمْرِين ٢٣ . صِلُوا ٱلْحُرُوف وَٱكْتُبُوا ٱلْكَلِمَات .

Exercise 23. Connect the letters to write the words.

١. وَ + ا + لِ + دِ + ي ←————

٢. دُ + و + ل + ا + ر ←————

٣. دِ + ي + نَ + ا + ر ←————

٤. أَ + وْ + ل + ا + د ←————

٥. لَ + يْ + ل ←————

٦. بِ + لَ + ا + دِ + ي ←————

٧. لُ + بْ + نَ + ا + ن ←————

٨. لَ + ا ←————

٩. نَ + بِ + ي + ل ←————

١٠. لَ + نْ + دَ + ن ←————

تَعَلَّمُوا هٰذِهِ ٱلْمُفْرَدَات

father of...	أَبُو ...	Lebanon	لُبْنَان
father of Nabil	أَبُو نَبِيل	Lebanese	لُبْنَانيّ
(f. name)	نَوَال	Libya	لِيبِيَا
London	لَنْدَن	Libyan	لِيبِيّ
night	لَيْل	Japan	أَلْيَابَان
father	وَالِد	Japanese	يَابَانيّ
boy, child	وَلَد (ج) أَوْلاد	Greece	أَلْيُونَان
city	بَلَد (ج) بِلاد	Greek	يُونَانيّ
I have	لِي	Jordan	أَلأُرْدُنّ
no, not	لا	Jordanian	أُرْدُنّي
well mannered (also m. name)	أَدِيب	light (also f. name)	نُور

تَمْرِين ٢٤ . إِقْرَؤُوا ثُمَّ ٱنْسَخُوا فِي دَفَاتِرِكُمْ.

Exercise 24. Read, then copy in your notebooks.

٢. أَوْلاد وَبَنَات		١. لَنْدَن وَبَيْرُوت
٤. أَلْيَابَان وَإِيرَان		٣. بِنْتِي بِلَنْدَن.
٦. زُرْتُ (I visited) نُور وَنَوَال.		٥. أَلأُرْدُنّ وَلِيبِيَا
٨. وَالِد أَدِيب أُرْدُنِّيّ.		٧. أُرْدُنِيّ وَلِيبِي *
١٠. أَنْتَ يُونَانِيّ؟ لا، أَنَا يَابَانِي.		٩. لُبْنَانِيّ وَيَابَانِيّ *

* Remember, the _shadda_ is ignored in pronunciation at the end of a word when it does not have a vowel.

بِ in

بِ is attached to the word that follows it:

My son is in London.   إِبْنِي بِلَنْدَن.

Dina's house is in Beirut.   دَار دِينَا بِبَيْرُوت.

siin   سـ   ـسـ   سِـين

س sounds like **s**.

تَمْرِين ٢٥. إِسْتَمِعُوا وَأَعِيدُوا ثُمَّ حَدِّدُوا حَرْفَ ٱلسِّين.

Exercise 25. Listen and repeat. Then identify the letter *siin*.

١. سَلام   ٢. إِسْلام   ٣. سُورِيَا   ٤. إِنْسَان

تَمْرِين ٢٦. أُكْتُبُوا.

Exercise 26. Write.

final *siin*   س   ـسـ

Syria   سُورِيَا

man, human being   إِنْسَان

I study   أَدْرُسُ

teeth   أَسْنَان

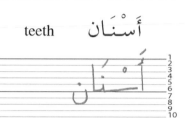

tongue, language   لِسَان

Teacher, professor   أُسْتَاذ

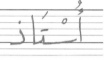

shiin   ش   شـ   شـيـن

ش sounds like <u>sh</u> in *<u>sh</u>adow*.

تَمْرِين ٢٧ . إِسْتَمِعُوا وَأَعِيدُوا ثُمَّ حَدِّدُوا حَرْفَ ٱلشِّين .

Exercise 27. Listen and repeat, then identify the letter *shiin*.

١. شَهْر   ٢. شَرِبَ   ٣. شَبَاب   ٤. تَشَرَّفْنَا

Exercise 28. Write.   تَمْرِين ٢٨ . أُكْتُبُوا .

final *shiin* ش   شـ

On the ش there are three dots (like those in the letter ث) centered above the letter.

young man   شَابّ

(m. name)   بَشِير

he drank　شَرِب

he drinks / he will drink　يَشْرَبُ

تَمْرِين ٢٩. صِلُوا ٱلْحُرُوف وَٱكْتُبُوا ٱلْكَلِمَات .

Exercise 29. Connect the letters to write the words.

١. س َ + و ْ + س َ + ن ← _____

٢. س ُ + و + ر ِ + ي َ + ا ← _____

٣. إ + ن ْ + س َ + ا + ن ← _____

٤. ب َ + ش ِ + ي + ر ← _____

٥. ش َ + ب َ + ا + ب ← _____

٦. أ ُ + س ْ + ت َ + ا + ذ ← _____

٧. ي َ + ش ْ + ر َ + ب ُ ← _____

Listen to the conversation.

hiya 'arabiyya masiḥiyya   هِيَ عَرَبِيَّة مَسِيحِيَّة

She is a Christian Arab.

نَوال: يَا نَبِيل، تِلْكَ أُسْتَاذَةُ ٱلْعَرَبِيَّة.

نَبِيل: مَا ٱسْمُهَا؟

نَوال: ٱلْأُسْتَاذَة مَارِي. هِيَ أُسْتَاذَة مُمْتَازَة.

نَبِيل: مِنْ أَيْنَ هِيَ؟

نَوال: مِن لُبْنَان. هِيَ عَرَبِيَّة مَسِيحِيَّة.

نَبِيل: هَلْ تَسْكُنُ (live) فِي ٱلْجَامِعَة؟

نَوال: لا. تَسْكُنُ فِي بَيْت قَرِيب مِنَ ٱلْجَامِعَة.

Exercise 30. Answer out loud.   تَمْرِين ٣٠. أَجِيبُوا شَفَهِيًّا.

٢. أَيْنَ تَسْكُنُ ٱلْأُسْتَاذَة مَارِي؟   ١. مَنْ هِيَ مَارِي؟

٤. مِنْ أَيْنَ هُوَ؟ / مِنْ أَيْنَ هِيَ؟   ٣. مَا ٱسْمُ أُسْتَاذِكَ؟ / مَا ٱسْمُ أُسْتَاذِكِ؟

٦. أَيْنَ تَسْكُنُ أُسْتَاذُكَ / أُسْتَاذُكِ؟   ٥. أَيْنَ يَسْكُنُ أُسْتَاذُكَ / أُسْتَاذُكِ؟

أُسْتَاذ

The word أُسْتَاذ (pl. *'asatidha* أَسَاتِذَة) means master, high school teacher, or university professor. As a title, أُسْتَاذ is a form of address for intellectuals such as lawyers, engineers, officials, journalists, writers, and poets.

عَرَبِيّ مُسْلِم وَعَرَبِيّ مَسِيحِيّ

Muslim and Christian Arabs

An Arab is a member of the Arabic-speaking semitic people of the Arabian Peninsula. Not all Arabs are Muslims and not all Muslims are Arabs. There are in fact many Christian Arabs. Muslims who do not speak Arabic, in countries such as Iran, Turkey and Indonesia, are not Arabs.

تَمْرِين ٣١. يَتَكَلَّمُ سَامِي فِي skype. إِسْتَمِعُوا.

Exercise 31. Sami is speaking on Skype. Listen.

أَلسَّلامُ عَلَيْكُمْ. إِسْمِي سَامِي وَأَسْكُنُ فِي مَدِينَة أَلْبَنِي فِي وِلَايَة نيو يُورك. أَنَا طَالِب فِي جَامِعَة أَلْبَنِي وَأَدْرُسُ ٱلْعَرَبِيَّة وَٱلْعِبْرِيَّة.

تَمْرِين ٣٢ . أَجِيبُوا شَفَهِيًّا. مَاذَا تَعْرِفُونَ عَنْ سَامِي؟

Exercise 32. Answer out loud. What do you know about Sami?

Exercise 33. Introduce yourself (*m. s.*) to Sami.   تَمْرِين ٣٣ . قَدِّمْ نَفْسَكَ لِسَامِي .

Introduce yourself (*f. s.*) to Sami.   قَدِّمِي نَفْسَكِ لِسَامِي .

تَمْرِين ٣٤ . إِقْرَؤُوا ثُمَّ ٱنْسَخُوا فِي دَفَاتِرِكُمْ.

Exercise 34. Read, then copy in your notebooks.

١. – يَا رَشِيد، أَنْتَ إِيرَانِيّ؟   ٢. – أَيْنَ بِنْت يَاسِر؟

– لَا. أَنَا أُرْدُنِّيّ.   – بِنْت يَاسِر بِدَار نَادِيَا.

٣. – أَيْنَ دَار رَشِيد؟   ٤. – أَيْنَ أَسَد وَدَاوُد؟

– دَار رَشِيد بِبَيْرُوت.   – أَسَد وَدَاوُد بِبَيْت رَان.

haa   ه   ـ   ـه   هَاء

هـ sounds like the **h** in *happy*

تَمْرِين ٣٥. إِسْتَمِعُوا وَأَعِيدُوا ثُمَّ حَدِّدُوا حَرْفَ ٱلْهَاء.

Exercise 35. Listen and repeat, then identify the letter *haa*.

٤. يَـهُودِيّ   ٣. هُنَا   ٢. هِيَ   ١. هُوَ

Exercise 36. Write.   تَمْرِين ٣٦. أُكْتُبُوا.

هـ

Unlike the other letters, when you write the letter هـ on its own,
write it in its initial form.

this, this is (.)   هٰذَا

here   هُنَا

he   هُوَ

river   نَهْر

her father   وَالِدُهَا

India   أَلْهِنْد

haa in the middle of a word.   هَاء فِ وَسَطِ ٱلْكَلِمَة

ـهـ

Final *haa*	هَاء في آخِرِ ٱلْكَلِمَة

not connected ه　　　　　connected ــ

God　أَللّٰه

his hand　يَدُهُ

this, this is (*f. s.*)　هٰذه

his house　بَيتُهُ

his father　وَالِدُهُ

'alif mu'allaqa   أَلِف مُعَلَّقَة

Dagger 'alif

1. There are few words in Arabic in which a short vertical stroke appears above one of the letters. It serves as a replacement for a lengthening 'alif. This mark is called 'alif mu'allaqa (أَلِف مُعَلَّقَة – dagger 'alif):

هٰذَا هٰذِهِ أَللّٰه.

2. The Dagger 'alif functions exactly like a lengthening 'alif (ا).

3. This kind of writing represents an old phase in the development of Arabic script, in which the lengthening 'alif (ا) was not used.

4. 'alif mu'allaqa (أَلِف مُعَلَّقَة) is written in texts that have the vowels marked.

هٰذَا أَبُو نَبِيل

This is 'abu Nabil.

هٰذِهِ شَهْرَزَاد

This is Shahrazad.

هٰذَا رَشِيد

This is Rashid.

Father of Nabil   أَبُو نَبِيل

The Arabs of ancient Arabia lived in tribes that were constantly attacking one another. In order to strengthen the tribe and win battles, there was a constant need for fighters. Siring a son was considered a sign of manhood and was therefore a matter of great pride. When an Arab was successful in that important mission, he received the 67 nickname (*kunya* كُنْيَة) *father of* (أَبُو *followed by the name of the first-born son*). If, for example, the name of his first-born son is نَبِيل then he would be addressed as أَبُو نَبِيل. Likewise the mother (*'um* أُمّ) is addressed as *'um* Nabil (أُمّ نَبِيل). This tradition of the *kunya* still exists today, and many Arabs address each other using it. The *kunya* أَبُو الْبَنَات indicates that the person has three daughters or more. Such a *kunya* is undesirable in the Arab culture.

وَهٰذَا أَبُو نَبِيل   هٰذَا نَبِيل

تَمْرِين ٣٧ . أُكْتُبُوا هٰذَا أَوْ هٰذِهِ فِي ٱلْفَرَاغ .

Exercise 37. Write هٰذَا or هٰذِهِ in the blank.

٢ . _____ نَهْر . (m.)   ١ . هٰذِهِ _____ نَادِيَا . (f.)

٤ . _____ أَبُو رَان . (m.)   ٣ . هٰذَا _____ وَلَد . (m.)

٦ . _____ نَوَال . (f.)   ٥ . _____ بِنْتِي . (f.)

٨ . _____ دِينَار . (m.)   ٧ . _____ وَالِدِي . (m.)

تَمْرِين ٣٨ . أَضِيفُوا ٱلضَّمَائِر حَسَبَ ٱلْمِثَال .

Exercise 38. Add the pronouns according to the example.

My professor   أُسْتَاذِي   ⟵   أُسْتَاذ + ي

My hand   _____   ⟵   يَد + ي

His professor   أُسْتَاذُهُ   ⟵   أُسْتَاذ + هُ

His hand   _____   ⟵   يَد + هُ

Her professsor   أُسْتَاذُهَا   ⟵   أُسْتَاذ + هَا

Her hand   _____   ⟵   يَد + هَا

Exercise 39. Read and complete.   تَمْرِين ٣٩ . إِقْرَؤُوا وَأَكْمِلُوا .

هٰذِهِ بِنْتُهُ .   هٰذِهِ بِنْت ران .   ١ .

_____   هٰذا وَالِد نَبِيـل .   ٢ .

هٰذِهِ بِنْتُهَا   هٰذِهِ بِنْت دِينَا .   ٣ .

_____   هٰذا بَيْت نَوَال .   ٤ .

تَمْرِين ٤٠ . صِلُوا ٱلْحُرُوف وَأَكْتُبُوا ٱلْكَلِمَات .

Exercise 40. Connect the letters to write the words.

_____ ◄   أَ + لْ + هـِ + نْ + د   . ١

_____ ◄   سُ + و + رِ + يَ + ا   . ٢

_____ ◄   إِ + نْ + سَ + ا + ن   . ٣

_____ ◄   بَ + شِ + ي + ر   . ٤

_____ ◄   شَ + بَ + ا + ب   . ٥

_____ ◄   أُ + سْ + تَ + ا + ذ   . ٦

كَاف   ك   ك   *kaaf*

كـ sounds like **k**.

تَمْرِين ٤١. إِسْتَمِعُوا وَأَعِيدُوا ثُمَّ حَدِّدُوا حَرْفَ ٱلْكَاف .

Exercise 41. Listen and repeat, then identify the letter *kaaf*.

٤. كَبِير   ٣. دُكْتُور   ٢. كَاتِب   ١. كَيْفَ

Exercise 42. Write.   تَمْرِين ٤٢. أُكْتُبُوا .

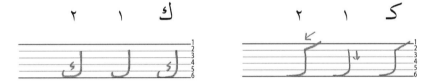

he wrote   كَتَبَ

book   كِتَاب

there, there is / are   هُنَاكَ

your (*m. s.*) house   بَيْتُكَ

big   كَبِير

---

kaaf followed by *'alif* or *laam*   كَاف + أَلِف أَوْ لَا،

كَلْب   كَاتِب

writer, clerk   كَاتِب

dog   كَلْب

every, each   كُلّ

the writer   أَلْكَاتِب

أَلْكَاتِب

تَمْرِين ٤٣. صِلُوا ٱلْحُرُوف وَٱكْتُبُوا ٱلْكَلِمَات.

Exercise 43. Connect the letters to write the words.

‏_____ ← ‏أَ + لْ + كَ + لْ + ب .١

‏_____ ← ‏أَ + لْ + كَ + ا + ت + ب .٢

‏_____ ← ‏نَ + كْ + ت + بُ .٣

‏_____ ← ‏هُ + نَ + ا + كَ .٤

‏_____ ← ‏بَ + يْ + ت + كَ .٥

‏_____ ← ‏أَ + لْ + كُ + وَ + يْ + ت .٦

‏_____ ← ‏كَ + بِ + ي + ر .٧

‏_____ ← ‏سَ + يَّ + ا + رَ + ت + كِ .٨

taa marbuuṭa   ة ـة   تَاء مَرْبُوطَة

The feminine marker ة, comes only at the end of nouns and adjectives.
It is preceded by *fatḥa*. It never appears at the end of verbs.

1. *taa marbuuṭa* looks like ending *haa* (connected or not connected) with
   two dots on top.

2. *taa marbuuṭa* is usually silent.

3. *taa marbuuṭa* can be pronounced as ت in two cases:

   a) When the *taa marbuuṭa* has a vowel: أَلْكَاتِبَةُ

   b) When the *taa marbuuṭa* appears in the first noun of a noun-noun

      phrase (*'iḍaafa*): *madinat new york* مَدِينَة نِيو يُورك.

4. You can make many nouns and adjectives feminine by adding ةَ -

   to the singular masculine form:

   كَبِيرَة ← كَبِير ، كَاتِبَة ← كَاتِب

5. When a suffix is added after ة it becomes ت:

   Your (*m. s.*) car   سَيَّارَة ← سَيَّارَتُكَ

6. There are a few feminine nouns that do not end in ة, such as:

   بِنْت ؛ أُمّ (*mother 'um*) ؛ أُخْت (*'ukht* sister)

Exercise 44. Write   تَمْرِين ٤٤. أُكْتُبُوا.

not connected ة   connected ـة

family   أُسْرَة

writer (f.)   كَاتِبَة

تَمْرِين ٤٥. حَوِّلُوا ٱلاسْم إِلَى ٱلْمُؤَنَّث حَسَبَ ٱلْمِثَال.

Exercise 45. Change the noun to feminine according to the example.

١. هُوَ إِيرَانِيّ.	هِيَ	إِيرَانِيَّة.	She is Iranian.
٢. هُوَ كَاتِب.	هِيَ		
٣. هُوَ أُرْدُنِّيّ.	هِيَ		
٤. نَبِيل لُبْنَانِيّ.	رَشِيدَة		
٥. إِبْرَاهِيم لِيبِيّ.	وَرْدَة		
٦. هَانِي أُسْتَاذ.	هَنَادَة		

Thank you   _shukran_   شُكْرًا

When the vowel at the end of a word is doubled, the sound "_nuun_" is added to the vowel. This is called تَنْوِين (nunation). Additional example: أَهْلاً وَسَهْلاً.

Exercise 46. Listen and repeat, then read.   تَمْرِين ٤٦ . إِسْتَمِعُوا وَأَعِيدُوا ثم أَقْرَؤُوا .

٢.   سَيَّارَة كَبِيرَة   ١.   شُكْرًا لَكَ .

٤.   أُسْرَة لُبْنَانِيَّة   ٣.   أَهْلاً وَسَهْلاً .

٦.   كُلّ لِسَان إِنْسَان .   ٥.   هٰذِهِ وَالِدَة رَشِيدَة .

٨.   أَبُو رَشِيد أُسْتَاذ .   ٧.   كَاتِب كَبِير

١٠.   هَلْ هٰذا كَلْبُهَا؟   ٩.   أُسْتَاذَة سُورِيَّة

١٢.   يَا شَبَاب !   ١١.   كَاتِبَة كُوَيْتِيَّة

١٤.   سَيَّارَة بِنْتِي   ١٣.   هٰذا وَالِد رَشِيــــد *

* Only in print, a long straight line can be inserted between letters for style purposes. This line has no meaning: رَشِيـــد. In handwriting, however, such a long line represents the letter س (_siin_).

Welcome   أَهْلاً وَسَهْلاً

This greeting expresses Arab hospitality. It is a short way of saying, "You came

to our family (أَهْل) and your stay with us will be easy and pleasant (سَهْل)."

The appropriate answer is بكِ / بكَ أَهْلاً وَسَهْلاً. (*Welcome to you.*)

Rashida's mother   وَالِدَة رَشِيدَة

The word وَالِدَة means "mother." When this noun is followed by another noun

(رَشِيدَة) it creates a noun-noun phrase. In this structure the ة is pronounced

as ت: *waalidat Rashida* (وَالِدَة رَشِيدَة). Examples: وِلَايَة نِيُو يُورْك

(the State of New York); سَيَّارَة بِنْتِي (my daughter's car).

Exercise 47. True or false. تَمْرِين ٤٧ . صَوَاب أَمْ خَطَأ .

1. The letter ي is a non-connector.

2. In the word أُسْتَاذ the second *'alif* is pronounced.

3. In the word كَاتِبَة the letter after the *taa* is *nuun*.

4. In the word دِينَار you should lengthen only the *fatha* before the *'alif*.

5. In the phrase أَبُو نَبِيل the و in أَبُو does not lengthen the *damma* preceding it.

6. The vowel preceding the lengthening letter و is always *damma*.

7. The letter ك does not have a similar sound in English.

8. The vowel before ة is always *fatha*.

9. A connected ل at the end of a word shifts downward.

10. In the phrase وَالِدَة نَادِيَا the ة is silent.

11. When the vowel at the end of a word is doubled, the sound "*nuun*" is added to the vowel.

12. When a suffix is added after ة it becomes ت .

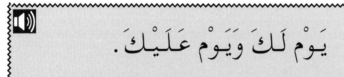

يَوْمٌ لَكَ وَيَوْمٌ عَلَيْكَ .

Literally: **A day for you and a day against you.**

Meaning: A good day and a bad day (It is said on a "bad day.")

(One of those days)

UNIT 3

Listen to the conversation.

إِسْتَمِعُوا إِلَى ٱلْمُحَادَثَة.

أَدْرُسُ ٱلدِّينَ ٱلْإِسْلامِيّ

I study the Islamic religion.

دِينَا: أَلسَّلامُ عَلَيْكُمْ يَا نَبِيل.

نَبِيل: وَعَلَيْكُمُ ٱلسَّلام يَا دِينَا.

دِينَا: مَاذَا تَدْرُسُ فِي ٱلْجَامِعَة؟

نَبِيل: أَدْرُسُ لُغَات. أَللُّغَة ٱلْعَرَبِيَّة وَٱللُّغَة ٱلْإِسْبَانِيَّة وَٱللُّغَة ٱلْفَرَنْسِيَّة.

دِينَا: مُمْتَاز! مَا شَاءَ ٱلله!

نَبِيل: وَمَاذَا تَدْرُسِينَ أَنْتِ يَا دِينَا؟

دِينَا: أَدْرُسُ ٱلدِّينَ ٱلْإِسْلامِيّ وَٱلْأَدَب ٱلْعَرَبِيّ.

نَبِيل: عَظِيم! مَنْ أُسْتَاذُ ٱلدِّين؟

دِينَا: أَلأُسْتَاذ كَرِيم، هُوَ أُسْتَاذ مُمْتَاز.

Exercise 1. Answer out loud.   تَمْرِين ١. أَجِيبُوا شَفَهِيًّا.

١. مَنْ هُوَ نَبِيل؟   ٢. مَاذَا يَدْرُسُ نَبِيل؟   ٣. مَنْ أُسْتَاذُ لدين؟

٤. مَاذَا تَدْرُسُ دِينَا؟   ٥. مَاذَا تَدْرُسُ أَنْتَ؟ / مَاذَا تَدْرُسِينَ أَنْتِ؟

Exercise 2. Translate out loud.   تَمْرِين ٢. تَرْجِمُوا شَفَهِيًّا.

1. -   Where is the professor?   2. -   What does Nabil study?

   -    In the library.   -   He studies languages.

3. -   What do you study?   4. -   Hello (Peace be upon you).

   -    I study Arabic and Spanish.   -   Hello.

تَمْرِين ٣. إِسْأَلُوا زُمَلاءَكُمْ مَاذَا يَدْرُسُونَ.

Exercise 3. Ask your classmates what they study.

مَاذَا تَدْرُسُ يَا جُون؟   أَدْرُسُ ٱلـ...

مَاذَا تَدْرُسِينَ يَا لِيلِي؟   أَدْرُسُ ٱلـ...

تَمْرِين ٤. هٰذا نَبِيل وَهٰذِهِ دِينَا. تَكَلَّمُوا عَنْهُمَا.

Exercise 4. This is Nabil and this is Dina. Talk about them.

ma–shaa'a–LLaah   مَا شَاءَ ٱلله

What God has given [amazing!]

"*ma–shaa'a–LLaah*" (مَا شَاءَ ٱلله) literally means "What God has given!"
[meaning: Amazing! How nice! How beautiful!]. In *Ammiyya* (the spoken
variety) these three words are combined together and are pronounced as
one word: *mashaLLa*. This expression includes the name of God to protect
one from evil spirits and from the evil eye that might unintentionally
destroy goodness. People hang signs with this expression on it in houses
and businesses, and stick them on car windows for protection. *ma–
shaa'a–LLaah* also expresses happiness, thanks and appreciation to God
for the blessings and the good things that He gives. If, for example, you
see a friend's child and learn about his or her success in school, you
should say *ma–shaa'a–LLaah*. Or if you want to tell your friend that his
new car is beautiful, you should say, *ma–shaa'a–LLaah*.

The religion professor   أُسْتَاذُ ٱلدِّين

أُسْتَاذُ ٱلدِّين is a phrase in which two nouns come one after the other (a
noun-noun phrase – *'iḍaafa* - إِضَافَة). In the *'iḍaafa* construction the
second noun modifies the first one (professor of religion). This
phenomenon of a noun which modifies another noun exists also in
English: fire truck, school bus, cheesecake, university professor, cat
food, and so on.

miim   م   ـ   ـمـ   مـيـم

م sounds like **m**.

تَمْرِين ٥ . إِسْتَمِعُوا وَأَعِيدُوا ثُمَّ حَدِّدُوا حَرْفَ ٱلْمِيم.

Exercise 5. Listen and repeat, then identify the letter *miim*.

١ . رَامِي   ٢ . سَلام   ٣ . أَلْيَمَن   ٤ . مِنْ

Exercise 6. Write.   تَمْرِين ٦ . أُكْتُبُوا.

مـ

did not (preceded by a verb in the past tense);   **what** (preceded by a noun)   مَا

king   مَلِك

office   مَكْتَب

miim in the middle of a word　　　أَلْمِيم فِي وَسَطِ ٱلْكَلِمَة

Every letter preceding the *miim* ends on line 5 and the *miim* is written on line 6.

When م follows a ل that is not connected to the previous letter the م can

connect with the ل in two ways: لِمَاذَا لِمَاذَا

لِمَاذَا　　　　　　why　لِمَاذَا

لِمَّا　　　　when (not a question)　لَمَّا

أَلْمَلِك　　　　the king　أَلْمَلِك

أَلْمُهَنْدِس　　the engineer　أَلْمُهَنْدِس

أَلْمِيم فِي آخِرِ ٱلْكَلِمَة   Final *miim*

not connected   م   connected   ـم

they (*m. pl*)   هُمْ

how many, how much   كَمْ

day   يَوْمْ

in front of   أَمَامَ

The letters ي ن ث ت ب preceding م

When م follows ب or ت or ث or ن or ي the connecting line of these

letters comes from the top so that the م could be written on line 6.

سَليمَة

(f. name) سَليمَة

exercise تَمْرين   تمرين

Yemen أَلْيَمَن

تَمْرِين ٧. صِلُوا ٱلْحُرُوف وَٱكْتُبُوا ٱلْكَلِمَات.

Exercise 7. Connect the letters to write the words.

١. مَ + لِ + ك ⟸ _____

٢. كَ + ا + مِ + ل ⟸ _____

٣. كَ + رِ + ي + مَ + ة ⟸ _____

٤. أ + لْ + يَ + مَ + ن ⟸ _____

٥. إِ + سْ + مُ + كَ ⟸ _____

تَعَلَّمُوا هٰذِهِ ٱلْمُفْرَدَات

I study	أَدْرُسُ	name	إِسْم (ج) أَسْمَاء
you (m. s.) study	تَدْرُسُ	from	مِنْ
you (f. s.) study	تَدْرُسِينَ	from where?	مِنْ أَيْنَ؟
Muslim	مُسْلِم (ج) مُسْلِمُونَ	Yemen	أَلْيَمَن
Islam	أَلْإِسْلَام	what (before nouns)	مَا
office	مَكْتَب (ج) مَكَاتِب	what (before verbs)	مَاذَا
post, mail	بَرِيد	Jew, Jewish	يَهُودِيّ
in front of	أَمَامَ	(question word)	هَلْ؟

Exercise 8. Which word does not fit (in each group)?　　تَمْرِين ٨. جِدُوا ٱلشَّاذّ.

٢. تَدْرُسُ ، مَاذَا ، مَا　　　　١. يَهُودِيّ ، هَلْ ، مَكْتَب

Exercise 9. Translate.　　　　　　تَمْرِين ٩. تَرْجِمُوا

1. What is your (f. s.) name?

2. Where are you (f. s.) from?

3. I am from Syria.

4. What do you study?

5. Nabil is Muslim.

6. Are you (m. s.) Jewish?

7. Are you (f. s.) from Lebanon?

8. Are you (m. s.) from Syria?

'alif waṣla　　أُ　　أَلِف وَصْلَة

The symbol above the 'alif is called **waṣla** (أُ). **'alif waṣla is silent.**

It indicates that the two consonants, preceding and following it, should be

connected in pronunciation: وَٱبْنِي (wabni [and my son]). If these two

consonants belong to two different words then you have to pronounce the two

words as if they are one, for example, مَا ٱسْمُكَ؟ (ma-smuka? "What is your

(m. s.) name?"). 'alif waṣla (أُ) should always be preceded by a vowel to

facilitate pronunciation.

Exercise 10. Write.   تَمْرِين ١٠. أُكْتُبُوا.

أ

I and my son   أَنَا وَٱبْنِي

What is your (f. s.) name?   مَا ٱسْمُكِ؟

Where is your (f. s.) son?   أَيْنَ ٱبْنُكِ؟

لامُ ٱلتَّعْرِيف   أَلْ / أَلْ   *lamu–tta'riif*

The definite article

The definite article in Arabic is أَلْ / أَلْ (equivalent to "the"). Unlike in English, **to make a noun or an adjective definite in Arabic**, add the definite article to the beginning of the word, for example:

أَلْوَلَد   ←   وَلَد

أَلْبَنَات   ←   بَنَات

If the definite article is preceded by a letter or a word, the *'alif* of the definite article takes *waṣla* (أَلْ), for example:

أَلْوَلَد   ←   وَٱلْوَلَد ، أَيْنَ ٱلْوَلَد؟

أَلْبَنَات   ←   وَٱلْبَنَات ، أَبُو ٱلْبَنَات

The *'alif* of the definite article (أَلْ) is called *hamzatu–lwaṣl* as the *hamza* changes into *waṣla* when preceded by a letter or a word. Actually, the definite article in Arabic is لْ (*lamu–tta'riif* لامُ ٱلتَّعْرِيف) and *'alif hamza* (أَ) is added to prevent سُكُون at the beginning of a word, thus to facilitate pronunciation (أَلْوَلَد).

تَمْرِين ١١. أَضِيفُوا لَامَ ٱلتَّعْرِيف لِلْكَلِمَاتِ ٱلتَّالِيَة.

Exercise 11. Add the definite article to the following words.

٢. أَوْلَاد ـــــــــــــــــــــ   ١. وَلَد ⟸ أَلْوَلَد

٤. أُرْدُنِّيّ ـــــــــــــــــــــ   ٣. بَلَد ـــــــــــــــــــــ

٦. وَالِدَة ـــــــــــــــــــــ   ٥. أَدَب ـــــــــــــــــــــ

٨. إِيرَانِي ـــــــــــــــــــــ   ٧. مُسْلِم ـــــــــــــــــــــ

١٠. بَنَات ـــــــــــــــــــــ   ٩. أُسْتَاذ ـــــــــــــــــــــ

١٢. أُسْرَة ـــــــــــــــــــــ   ١١. يَابَانِيّ ـــــــــــــــــــــ

١٤. بَرِيد ـــــــــــــــــــــ   ١٣. مَكْتَب ـــــــــــــــــــــ

تَمْرِين ١٢. إِقْرَؤُوا وَٱنْتَبِهُوا إِلَى هَمْزَةِ ٱلْوَصْل.

Exercise 12. Read paying attention to *hamzatu–lwaṣl.*

🔊

١. أَبُو ٱلْبَنَات   ٢. أَنَا وَٱبْنِي   ٣. أَدْرُسُ ٱلْإِسْبَانِيَّة.

٤. أَلْوَلَد وَٱلْبِنْت   ٥. أَيْنَ ٱلْأُسْتَاذ؟   ٦. أَلْوَالِد وَٱلْوَالِدَة

٧. أَيْنَ ٱلْمَكْتَب؟   ٨. هٰذَا ٱبْنِي.   ٩. مَكْتَبُ * ٱلْبَرِيد

١٠. مَا ٱسْمُك؟   ١١. أَلْأَب وَٱلْبِنْت   ١٢. أَلْأُرْدُنّ وَٱلْيَمَن **

---

* In the phrase مَكْتَبُ ٱلْبَرِيد the word مَكْتَبُ has **ḍamma** on its last letter. As previously mentioned, **a vowel must appear before waṣla to facilitate pronunciation**. In Arabic, a noun or an adjective can have a vowel on or underneath its last letter. This vowel is determined by grammatical considerations. For now, if you see such a vowel on or underneath the last letter of a word pronounce it as usual.

** The definite article could be part of names of cities and countries, for example: أَلْأُرْدُنّ (Jordan), أَلْيَابَان (Japan) and ٱلْيُونَان (Greece), compare in English, The Bronx, The Netherlands, and The Philippines. The *'alif* of the definite article takes **waṣla** *(as usual)* when preceded by a letter or a word:

بِ + أَلْأُرْدُنّ ⬅ بِٱلْأُرْدُنّ

تَمْرِين ١٣ . أَضِيفُوا "أَلْ" لِلْكَلِمَات . أُكْتُبُوهَا وَٱقْرَؤُوهَا . إِنْتَبِهُوا إِلَى ٱلْوَصْلَةِ .

Exercise 13. Add the definite article to the words. Write and read them.

      Pay attention to 'alif waṣla.

١ . وَلَد وَبِنْت   أَلْوَلَد وَٱلْبِنْت

٢ . أَب وَبِنْت   _____

٣ . وَالِد وَوَالِدَة   _____

٤ . مُسْلِم وَيَهُودِيّ   _____

٥ . أُرْدُنِّيّ وَإِيرَانِيّ   _____

٦ . أَوْلاد وَبَنَات   _____

An important note about reading aloud

In order to acquire good habits in reading aloud, never pause before ا.

If you must pause, do so only after you have pronounced the first

consonant following the ا. For example, when you read أَبُو ٱلْبَنَات,

say **abu - l** first; then determine how to pronounce the word بَنَات.

Finally, return to the beginning and say the two words together:

أَبُو ٱلْبَنَات.

Exercise 14. Read with your classmates.

تَمْرين ١٤. إِقْرَؤُوا مَعَ زُمَلائِكُمْ.

٢. ‒ مَاذَا تَدْرُسُ؟

‒ أَدْرُسُ ٱلْهَنْدَسَة.

١. ‒ مَا ٱسْمُكَ؟

‒ إِسْمي سَلِيم.

٤. ‒ أَيْنَ بَيْتُكَ؟

‒ أَمَامَ مَكْتَبِ ٱلْبَرِيد.

٣. ‒ مِنْ أَيْنَ أَنْتَ يَا سَلِيم؟

‒ أَنَا مِنَ * ٱلْيَمَن.

٦. ‒ مَاذَا تَدْرُسِينَ؟

‒ أَدْرُسُ ٱلإِسْبَانِيَّة.

٥. ‒ هَلْ أَنْتِ مِنَ ٱلْيَمَن؟

‒ لَا. أَنَا مِنْ لُبْنَان.

٨. ‒ هَلْ أَبُو رَامِي يَهُودِيّ؟

‒ لَا. أَبُو رَامِي مُسْلِم.

٧. ‒ أَيْنَ ٱبْنُكِ؟

‒ إِبْني هُنَا.

* The preposition مِنْ takes *faṭha* on the ن before the definite article to facilitate pronunciation: مِنَ ٱلْيَمَن

هَلْ ، أَ

هَلْ or أَ is an interrogative particle which changes a statement sentence into a yes / no question. While هَلْ is a separate word, أَ is added to the word that follows:

هٰذا بَيْتُهُ.   ←   هَلْ هٰذا بيتُهُ؟ / أَهٰذا بَيْتُهُ؟

Is this his house?   This is his house.

تَمْرين ١٥. حَوِّلُوا ٱلْجُمَلَ إِلَى أَسْئِلَة حَسَبَ ٱلْمِثَال.

Exercise 15. Change the sentences to questions according to the example.

١. هٰذا كِتَابِي.   ←   هَلْ هٰذا كِتَابِي؟   أَهٰذا كِتَابِي؟

٢. هٰذا بَيْتُكَ. _____

٣. هٰذِهِ سَيَّارَتُك. _____

٤. هٰذِهِ أُسْتَاذَتُهَا. _____

٥. هُوَ لُبْنَانِيّ. _____

٦. هِيَ مِنْ إِيرَان. _____

أَلِف مَقْصُورَة   ى   'alif maqṣuura

Short 'alif

1. It is written like ending ي (connected or unconnected) without the two dots

   beneath it: ى

2. It appears at the end of nouns, adjectives, proper nouns, verbs, prepositions,

   and question words: مَبْنَى (building), مَتَى (when?), مُنَى (Muna).

3. It is silent and always preceded by *fatḥa*.

4. When a suffix is added after ى it usually becomes ْي:

   to you (*m. s.*)   إِلَيْكَ   ←   إِلَى + كَ

تَمْرِين ١٦. إِسْتَمِعُوا وَأَعِيدُوا ثُمَّ حَدِّدُوا ٱلْأَلِفَ ٱلْمَقْصُورَة.

Exercise 16. Listen and repeat, then identify the *'alif maqṣuura*.

٤. رَأَى   ٣. مَبْنَى   ٢. مَتَى   ١. مُنَى

Exercise 17. Write.   تَمْرِين ١٧. أُكْتُبُوا.

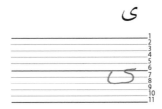
ى

building   مَبْنَى

مَبْنَى

1
2
3
4
5
6
7
8
9
10
11

to   إِلَى

إِلَى

1
2
3
4
5
6
7
8
9
10
11

When?   مَتَى؟

مَتَى

1
2
3
4
5
6
7
8
9
10
11

Muna (f. name)   مُنَى

مُنَى

1
2
3
4
5
6
7
8
9
10
11

Moses   مُوسَى

مُوسَى

1
2
3
4
5
6
7
8
9
10
11

faa   ف   ـ   ـف   فَاء

ف sounds like **f**.

تَمْرِين ١٨. إِسْتَمِعُوا وَأَعيدُوا ثُمَّ حَدِّدُوا حَرْفَ أَلْفَاء.

Exercise 18. Listen and repeat, then identify the letter *faa*.

٤. أَلْف   ٣. فِكْرَة   ٢. كَيْفَ؟   ١. فِي

Exercise 19. Write.   تَمْرِين ١٩. أُكْتُبُوا.

ف   ـف   ف

in, into   فِي

falafel   فَلافِل

idea   فِكْرة

فِكْرَة

singular   مُفْرَد

مُفْرَد

thousand   أَلْف

أَلْف

how   كَيْفَ

كَيْف

useful (also m. name)   مُفِيد

مُفِيد

قَاف   ق   ـقـ   ق   *qaaf*

ق sounds like an emphatic كَ from the back of the throat.

There is no English equivalent.

تَمْرِين ٢٠. إِسْتَمِعُوا وَأَعِيدُوا ثُمَّ حَدِّدُوا حَرْفَ ٱلْقَاف .

Exercise 20. Listen and repeat, then identify the letter *qaaf*.

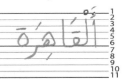

١. قَرِيب   ٢. أَلْقُرْآن   ٣. أَلْقَاهِرَة   ٤. دِمَشْق

Exercise 21. Write.   تَمْرِين ٢١. أُكْتُبُوا.

ق   ـقـ   ق

close to   قَرِيب مِنْ

Cairo   أَلْقَاهِرَة

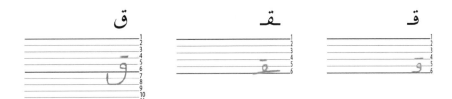

سُوق   market

رَفِيق   companion, friend (also m. name)

دِمَشْق   Damascus

تَمْرِين ٢٢ . إِقْرَؤُوا وَٱنْتَبِهُوا إِلَى ٱلْفَرْقِ بَيْنَ ٱلْكَافِ وَٱلْقَاف .

Exercise 22. Read, paying attention to the difference between كـ and ق.

dog	٢. كَلْب	heart	١. قَلْب
close, relative	٤. قَرِيب	big	٣. كَبِير
friend	٦. رَفِيق	Cairo	٥. أَلْقَاهِرَة
poor	٨. فَقِير	Kuwait	٧. أَلْكُوَيْت
the Qur'an	١٠. أَلْقُرْآن	king	٩. مَلِك

تَمْرِين٢٣. إِقْرَؤُوا ٱلْكَلِمَات فِي ٱلتَّمْرِين ٱلسَّابِق لِزُمَلائِكُمْ وَٱطْلُبُوا مِنْهُمْ أَنْ

يَقُولُوا هَلْ تَحْتَوِي ٱلْكَلِمَة عَلَى حَرْفِ ٱلْكَاف أَمْ عَلَى حَرْفِ

ٱلْقَاف .

Exercise 23. Read the words in the previous exercise to your classmates and ask

them to indicate if the word contains the letter ك or the letter ق.

تَمْرِين ٢٤. أُكْتُبُوا ٱلْحَرْفَ ٱلأَوَّل لِكُلّ كَلِمَة تَسْمَعُونَهَا .

Exercise 24. Write the first letter of each word you hear.

٤. _____	٣. _____	٢. _____	١. _____
٨. _____	٧. _____	٦. _____	٥. _____
١٢. _____	١١. _____	١٠. _____	٩. _____

كَلْب قَلْب كَبِير قَرِيب فِكْرَة مُطْرِب هَدِيَّة

قَرَأَ كَتَبَ قَبْلَ إلى شَفِيق

وَعْدُ ٱلْحُرّ دَيْن عَلَيْهِ .

wa'du-lḥur dayn 'alyhi.

The promise of a free man is a debt on him.

تَعَلَّمُوا هٰذِهِ ٱلْمُفْرَدَات

close to	قَرِيب مِنْ	who?	مَنْ؟
friend	رَفيق (ج) رِفَاق	you (*pl. m.*)	أَنْتُمْ
Cairo	أَلْقَاهِرَة	here	هُنَا
Damascus	دِمَشْق	there, there is/are	هُنَاكَ
in	فِي	library	مَكْتَبَة
thousand	أَلْف	idea	فِكْرَة
school	مَدْرَسَة	before (time)	قَبْلَ

تَمْرِين ٢٥. تَرْجِمُوا إلى ٱلْإنجِليزِيَّة.　　Exercise 25. Translate into English.

٢. رَفِيقِي مِنْ دِمَشْق.　　١. هُنَا وَهُنَاكَ

٤. قَرِيب مِنْ هُنَا　　٣. مِنْ أَيْنَ أَنْتُمْ؟

٦. أَلْف دِينَار　　٥. أَمَامَ ٱلْمَدْرَسَة

٨. بَيْتِي فِي ٱلْقَاهِرَة.　　٧. أَلْمَكْتَبَة قَرِيبَة.

Listen to the conversation, then read it.

إِسْتَمِعُوا إِلَى ٱلْمُحَادَثَة ثُمَّ ٱقْرَؤُوهَا .

مَنْ أَنْتَ؟

فَارُوق : مَنْ أَنْتَ؟

ران : أَنَا رَان، وَمَنْ أَنْتُمْ؟

فَارُوق : أَنَا فَارُوق وَهٰذِهِ مَرْيَم وَهٰذَا رَفِيقِي تَوْفِيق .

ران : مِنْ أَيْنَ أَنْتُمْ، يَا فَارُوق؟

فَارُوق : أَنَا مِنَ ٱلْقَاهِرَة وَمَرْيَم مِنْ بَيْرُوت وَرَفِيقِي تَوْفِيق مِنْ دِمَشْق، وَمِنْ أَيْنَ أَنْتَ، يَا رَان؟

ران : أَنَا مِنْ نِيو يُورك .

فَارُوق : وَأَيْنَ بَيْتُكَ؟

ران : بَيْتِي قَرِيب مِنْ هُنَا . هُنَاكَ، أَمَامَ ٱلْمَدْرَسَة .

تَمْرِين ٢٦ . أَجِيبُوا شَفَهِيًّا ثُمَّ ٱكْتُبُوا ٱلْجَوَاب .

Exercise 26. Answer out loud, then write the answer.

١ . مِنْ أَيْنَ ران؟ _____

٢ . مِنْ أَيْنَ فَارُوق؟ _____

٣ . مِنْ أَيْنَ مَرْيَم؟ _____

٤ . مِنْ أَيْنَ تَوْفِيق؟ _____

٥ . مِنْ أَيْنَ أَنْتُمْ؟ _____

تَمْرِين ٢٧ . صِلُوا ٱلْحُرُوف وَٱكْتُبُوا ٱلْكَلِمَات .

Exercise 27. Connect the letters to write the words.

١ . سُ + و + ق ◀ _____

٢ . دِ + مَ + شْ + ق ◀ _____

٣ . أَ + لْ + قَ + ا + هِـ + رَ + ة ◀ _____

٤ . فَ + ل + ا + فِ + ل ◀ _____

٥ . مُ + سْ + لِ + مُ + و + نَ ◀ _____

٦ . قَ + ر + ي + ب ◀ _____

٧ . قَ + بْ + لَ ◀ _____

Long *'alif*   آ   أَلِف مَمْدُودَة

The mark above the آ is called مَدَّة.

أَلِف مَمْدُودَة with مَدَّة is called أَلِف.

آ is pronounced as a long /a/ ⟹ /aa/

There is no English equivalent.

Exercise 28. Listen and repeat.   تَمْرِين ٢٨. إِسْتَمِعُوا وَأَعِيدُوا.

٤. آلاف   ٣. أَلآنَ   ٢. آسِف   ١. أَلْقُرآن

Exercise 29. Write.   تَمْرِين ٢٩. أُكْتُبُوا.

٢   ١   آ

أَلِف مَمْدُودَة has two parts: أَلِف and مَدَّة.

the Qur'an   أَلْقُرآن

آسِف (m. s.) , آسِفَة (f. s.)   Sorry

I eat, I am eating, I will eat   آكُلُ

أَأَ ⇐ آ
أَنَا لا آكُلُ فِي ٱللَّيْل.

أَأَ ⇐ آ
ألْقُرآنُ ٱلْكَرِيم

The Generous Qur'an   أَلْقُرْآنُ ٱلْكَرِيـم

The Qur'an is the holy book of Muslims. They believe it consists of the word of God (ALLaah) revealed in Arabic to the Prophet Muhammad through the angel Gabriel in a series of revelations over about a 23-year period. The Qur'an consists of 114 chapters (سُوَر), which are each further divided into verses (آيَات). The first chapter (سُورَة) in the Qur'an is called *suratu-lfatiḥa* (سُورَةُ ٱلْفَاتِحَة "The Opening Chapter"). It consists of seven verses and it is recited several times in the daily prayer as well as on important occasions such as a death or birth. After *suratu-lfatiḥa* the chapters are arranged according to their length, from the longest to the shortest. At the beginning of each chapter there is a notation indicating where the chapter was revealed, in Mecca (مَكَّة) or in Medina (أَلْمَدِينَة). The consolidation of the Qur'an into the version that exists today is attributed to the third Caliph (*khalifa* خَلِيفَة) *'uthmaan bnu 'affan* (644-656 AD, عُثْمَان بْنُ عَفَّان). The Qur'an has been translated into many languages and is one of the most read books in the world.

Caliph   *khalifa*   خَلِيفَة

The meaning of the word *khalifa* (خَلِيفَة) is "successor." This title was given to the Islamic rulers after the death of Prophet Muhammad. The first caliph was *Abu Bakr* (أَبُو بَكْر). A caliph is both a religious and a civil leader.

The Opening Chapter

1. In the name of ALLaah, most gracious, most merciful.

2. Praise be to ALLaah, the Lord of the worlds,

3. The most Gracious, the most Merciful,

4. Master of the Day of Judgement.

5. You do we worship, and your aid do we seek.

6. Guide us on the right path,

7. The path of those upon whom you have bestowed your grace, not of those upon whom wrath is brought down, nor of those who go astray.

'ayn   ع ‐ ـ ـ عـ   عَيْن

ع sounds like the هَمْزة articulated with friction in the pharynx,

resembling the <u>Ein</u> in Einstein, a strong guttural sound.

There is no English equivalent.

تَمْرِين ٣٠. إِسْتَمِعوا وأَعيدوا ثُمَّ حَدِّدُوا حَرْفَ ٱلْعَيْن.

Exercise 30. Listen and repeat, then identify the letter *'ayn*.

١. أَلْعَرَبِيَّة   ٢. عِنْدِي   ٣. مَمْنُوع   ٤. عَرَبِيّ

Exercise 31. Write.   تَمْرِين ٣١. أُكْتُبُوا.

عـ

At the place of   عِنْدَ

Arab   عَرَبِيّ

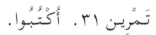

'*ayn* in the middle of a word   أَلْعَيْن فِ وَسَطِ ٱلْكَلِمَة

ـعـ

Iraq   أَلْعِرَاق

teacher   مُعَلِّم

Final '*ayn*   أَلْعَيْن فِ آخِرِ ٱلْكَلِمَة

not connected   ع   connected   ـع

with   مَعَ

four   أَرْبَع

forbidden   مَمْنُوع

to hear   سَمِعَ

Peace be upon you.   أَلسَّلامُ عَلَيْكُمْ.

Muslims usually use أَلسَّلامُ عَلَيْكُمْ (*m. pl.*) to greet any single

person, man or a woman, upon meeting or departing. The usual

answer is وَعَلَيْكُمُ ٱلسَّلام. It is also possible to use the long answer:

وَعَلَيْكُمُ ٱلسَّلام وَرَحْمَةُ (*waraḥmatu*) ٱللهِ وَبَرَكَاتُهُ.

(Peace be upon you and the mercy of ALLaah and his blessings.)

ghayn   غ ـ ـغ ـغـ غَيْن

غ sounds like the French **r** similar to gargling.

There is no English equivalent.

تَمْرِين ٣٢. إِسْتَمِعُوا وَأَعِيدُوا ثُمَّ حَدِّدُوا حَرْفَ ٱلْغَيْن.

Exercise 32. Listen and repeat, then identify the letter *ghayn*.

١. لُغَة   ٢. بَغْدَاد   ٣. أَلْمَغْرِب   ٤. غُرْفَة

Exercise 33. Write.   تَمْرِين ٣٣. أُكْتُبُوا.

غ   ـغ   ـغـ   غـ

west   غَرْب

language   لُغَة

تَمْرِين ٣٤. صِلُوا ٱلْحُرُوف وَٱكْتُبُوا ٱلْكَلِمَات.

Exercise 34. Connect the letters to write the words.

١. لُ + غَ + ة ⟵ _____

٢. دِ + مَ + شْ + ق ⟵ _____

٣. أَ + لْ + مَ + غْ + رِ + ب ⟵ _____

٤. مَ + مْ + نُ + و + ع ⟵ _____

٥. أَ + لْ + عِ + رَ + ا + ق ⟵ _____

٦. أَ + لْ + قُ + رْ + آ + ن ⟵ _____

٧. بَ + غْ + دَ + ا + دِ + يّ ⟵ _____

٨. مَ + تْ + بُ + و + ع ⟵ _____

٩. غُ + رْ + فَ + ة ⟵ _____

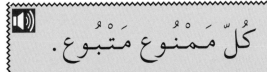

كُلّ مَمْنُوع مَتْبُوع.

Every forbidden thing is desired.

تَمْرِين ٣٥. إِقْرَؤُوا وَٱنْتَبِهُوا إِلَى ٱلْفَرْقِ بَيْنَ ٱلرَّاءِ وَٱلْغَيْن.

Exercise 35. Read, paying attention to the difference between ر and غ.

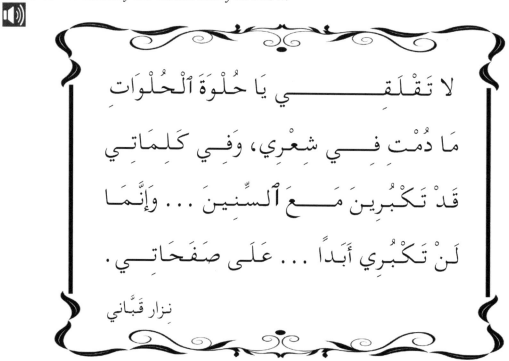

strange, stranger	٢. غَرِيب	room	١. غُرْفَة
Baghdad	٤. بَغْدَاد	to order	٣. أَمَرَ
river	٦. نَهْر	God	٥. رَبّ
Morocco	٨. أَلْمَغْرِب	to gargle	٧. غَرْغَرَ
languages	١٠. لُغَات	language	٩. لُغَة

تَمْرِين ٣٦. مَيِّزُوا ٱلْحُرُوفَ ٱلَّتِي تَعْرِفُونَهَا.

Exercise 36. Identify the letters that you know.

لا تَقْلَقِي يَا حُلْوَةَ ٱلْحُلْوَاتِ

مَا دُمْتِ فِي شِعْرِي، وَفِي كَلِمَاتِي

قَدْ تَكْبُرِينَ مَعَ ٱلسِّنِينَ ... وَإِنَّمَا

لَنْ تَكْبُرِي أَبَدًا ... عَلَى صَفَحَاتِي.

نِزَار قَبَّانِي

تَعَلَّمُوا هٰذِهِ ٱلْمُفْرَدَات

to speak	تَكَلَّمَ (م) يَتَكَلَّمُ	on	عَلَى
to travel	سَافَرَ (م) يُسَافِرُ	tomorrow	غَدًا
to go	ذَهَبَ (م) يَذْهَبُ	close to	بِٱلْقُرْبِ مِنْ
to do	فَعَلَ (م) يَفْعَلُ	visit	زِيَارَة (ج) زِيَارَات
to want	أَرَادَ أَنْ (م) يُرِيدُ أَنْ	to visit	زَارَ (م) يَزُورُ
to reside, live	سَكَنَ (م) يَسْكُنُ	excellent	مُمْتَاز
to meet	إِلْتَقَى (م) يَلْتَقِي	with	مَعَ
hour	سَاعَة (ج) سَاعَات	which (+ noun)?	أَيّ؟
center	مَرْكَز (ج) مَرَاكِز	yes	نَعَمْ
language	لُغَة (ج) لُغَات	forbidden	مَمْنُوع
ten o'clock	أَلسَّاعَة ٱلْعَاشِرَة	when?	مَتَى؟
		see you	إِلَى ٱللِّقَاء

The letter م stands for the word مُضَارِع (*muḍari'*) meaning *present-future tense*.

Arabic verbs and their translation

In this textbook, Arabic verbs are introduced in the **third person singular past tense form.** Its English translation is provided in the infinitive form, as it is in the Arabic-English dictionary. For example: زَارَ (to visit), سَافَرَ (to travel). Although the English infinitive is not the literal translation of the Arabic verb, it expresses its conceptual meaning. Therefore, when a verb is part of a sentence, it should be translated according to its conjugated form (ignoring the infinitive structure). For example, in the sentence: زَارَ أَبِي بَيْرُوت, the translation is: "My father **visited** Beirut."

إِلَى ٱللِّقَاء . See you.

You can say إِلَى ٱللِّقَاء when leaving or when ending a phone call to indicate that you are looking forward to the next meeting. The reply is the same: إِلَى ٱللِّقَاء.

Exercise 37. Which word does not fit (in each group)?   تَمْرِين ٣٧ . جِدُوا ٱلشَّاذّ .

٢. أَيّ ، مَمْنُوع ، مُمْتَاز   ١. عَلَى ، مَتَى ، فِي

٣. مَرَاكِز ، لُغَات ، سَاعَات   ٤. يَذْهَبُ ، سَافَرَ ، يَسْكُنُ

تَمْرِين ٣٨. إِمْلَؤُوا ٱلْفَرَاغ بِٱلْكَلِمَة ٱلْمُنَاسِبَة.

Exercise 38. Fill in the blank with the appropriate word.

١. يُسَافِرُ كَرِيم غَدًا ــــــــــــ نِيو يُورك.   (فِي ، إِلَى ، عَلَى)

٢. يَسْكُنُ رَفِيقِي ــــــــــــ بُرُوكْلِين.   (فِي ، هَلْ ، عَلَى)

٣. أَهْلاً يَا كَرِيم. أَهْلاً ــــــــــــ يَا سَلِيم.   (بِكَ ، أَنْتَ ، بِكِ)

٤. ــــــــــــ تُسَافِرُ لِينْدَا إِلَى نِيو يُورك؟   (مَتَى ، أَيْنَ ، مَاذَا)

٥. ــــــــــــ يَفْعَلُ هُنَاكَ؟   (لِمَاذَا ، أَيْنَ ، مَاذَا)

٦. أَلُو، ــــــــــــ يَتَكَلَّمُ؟   (مِنْ ، مَنْ ، مَا)

٧. بِٱلْقُرْب ــــــــــــ مَكْتَبَة ٱلْكُونغرِيس   (مِنْ ، إِلَى ، فِي)

٨. ــــــــــــ ٱللِّقَاء غَدًا.   (فِي ، عَلَى ، إِلَى)

Exercise 39. Translate out loud.   تَمْرِين ٣٩. تَرْجِمُوا شَفَهِيًّا.

١. مَنْ يَتَكَلَّمُ؟   ٢. أَلْمَرْكَزُ ٱلْإِسْلامِيّ   ٣. إِلَى ٱللِّقَاء غَدًا.

٤. زِيَارَة مُمْتَازَة   ٥. فِي أَيّ سَاعَة؟   ٦. رَفِيقِي سَلْمَان

٧. أَلسَّلامُ عَلَيْكُمْ.   ٨. مَاذَا يَفْعَلُ هُنَاكَ؟   ٩. هٰذِهِ فِكْرَة مُمْتَازَة.

١٠. يَسْكُنُ فِي لُبْنَان.   ١١. هٰذَا مَمْنُوع.   ١٢. مَعَ مَنْ سَافَرَ؟

Listen to the conversation, then read it.   إِسْتَمِعُوا إِلَى ٱلْمُحَادَثَةِ ثُمَّ ٱقْرَؤُوهَا.

هٰذِهِ فِكْرَةٌ مُمْتَازَةٌ.

سَلِيم: أَلُو، أَلسَّلَامُ عَلَيْكُمْ.

كَرِيم: وَعَلَيْكُمُ ٱلسَّلَام.

سَلِيم: مَنْ يَتَكَلَّمُ؟ كَرِيم؟

كَرِيم: نَعَمْ، أَنَا كَرِيم.

سَلِيم: أَهْلاً يَا كَرِيم.

كَرِيم: أَهْلاً بِكَ يَا سَلِيم، أَنَا وَلِنْدَا سَنُسَافِرُ غَدًا إِلَى نِيُويُورك بِسَيَّارَتِي لِزِيَارَةِ (to visit) رَفِيقِي سَلْمَان، هَلْ تُرِيدُ أَنْ تَذْهَبَ مَعَنَا؟

سَلِيم: هٰذِهِ فِكْرَةٌ مُمْتَازَةٌ، وَأَيْنَ يَسْكُنُ رَفِيقُكَ سَلْمَان؟

كَرِيم: يَسْكُنُ فِي بْرُوكْلِين.

سَلِيم: وَمَاذَا سَنَفْعَلُ هُنَاكَ؟

كَرِيم: سَنَزُورُ ٱلْمَدِينَةَ وَسَنَذْهَبُ إِلَى ٱلْمَرْكَزِ ٱلْإِسْلَامِيّ هُنَاكَ.

سَلِيم: مُمْتَاز! وَأَيْنَ سَنَلْتَقِي؟ مَتَى؟ فِي أَيّ سَاعَة؟

كَرِيم: سَنَلْتَقِي غَدًا فِي ٱلسَّاعَةِ ٱلْعَاشِرَة فِي وَاشِنْطُن دِي سِي بِٱلْقُرْب مِنْ مَكْتَبَةِ ٱلْكُونغرِيس.

سَلِيم: شُكْرًا لَكَ يَا كَرِيم، إِلَى ٱللِّقَاء غَدًا.

كَرِيم: إِلَى ٱللِّقَاء.

سَنُسَافِرُ إِلَى نِيو يُورك.

We will travel to New York.

The verb نُسَافِرُ means: *we travel* (present tense) or *we will travel* (future tense).

The letter سَ which is added to the verb indicates that the verb is in the future tense.

تَمْرِين ٤٠. أَجِيبُوا شَفَهِيًّا ثُمَّ ٱكْتُبُوا ٱلْجَوَاب.

Exercise 40. Answer out loud, then write the answer.

١. مَنْ سَيُسَافِرُ إِلَى نِيو يُورك؟

_____

٢. مَنْ هُوَ سَلْمَان؟

_____

٣. أَيْنَ يَسْكُنُ سَلْمَان؟

_____

٤. مَنْ لِنْدَا؟

_____

في ٱلسَّاعَة ٱلْعَاشِرَة

When the definite article is added to a word that starts with the letter س, the ل

of the definite article is not pronounced in order to facilitate pronunciation.

Instead, the letter س takes شَدَّة:

سَاعَة   ⬅   أَلسَّاعَة

Note: There are additional 13 letters that behave in the same way.

Among them ل ن ز ر ذ د ث ت ش

These letters are called "Sun Letters."

تَمْرِين ٤١ . أَضيفُوا " أَلْ " لِلْكَلِمَات.

Exercise 41. Add the definite article to the words.

١. زَيْتُون ⬅ أَلزَّيْتُون

٢. ذَهَب _____

٣. زِيَارَة _____

٤. نُور _____

٥. سَلام _____

٦. دَرْس _____

٧. شَبَاب _____

٨. شَاي _____

٩. تَأْرِيخ _____

١٠. لُغَة _____

١١. سَاعَة _____

١٢. دَار _____

Exercise 42. Answer true or false.   تَمْرِين ٤٢ . أَجِيبُوا صَوَاب أَمْ خَطَأً.

false خَطَأ	true صَوَاب	
◯	◯	١. لِنْدَا لا تُسَافِرُ إِلَى نِيو يُورك مَعَ كَرِيم.
◯	◯	٢. سَلْمَان هُوَ رَفِيق كَرِيم.
◯	◯	٣. يَسْكُنُ كَرِيم وَسَلْمَان في بْرُوكلِين.
◯	◯	٤. مَكْتَبَةُ ٱلْكُونغرِيس في مَدِينَة نِيو يُورك.
◯	◯	٥. سَيُسَافِرُ كَرِيم مَعَ سَلِيم ولِنْدَا لِزِيَارَة سَلْمَان.
◯	◯	٦. سَيَلْتَقِي كَرِيم مَعَ سَلِيم غَدَاً في ٱلسَّاعَة ٱلْعَاشِرَة.

إِذا كُنْتَ كَذُوباً فَكُنْ ذَكُوراً.

'idha kunta kadhuuban fakun dhakuuran.

If you are a liar, have a good memory.

UNIT 4

تَعَلَّمُوا هٰذِهِ ٱلْمُفْرَدَات

Happy day to you	نَهَارُكَ سَعِيد	day time	نَهَار
age	عُمْر (ج) أَعْمَار	happy	سَعِيد
year	سَنَة (ج) سَنَوَات	ten	عَشْر
twins	تَوْأَمَان	It is a pleasure	تَشَرَّفْنَا

Listen to the conversation.

إِسْتَمِعُوا إِلَى ٱلْمُحَادَثَة .

أَخِي وَأُخْتِي تَوْأَمَانِ

دينا: نَهَارُكَ سَعِيد يَا أُسْتَاذ .

سمير: نَهَارُكِ أَسْعَد يَا دِينَا .

دينا: يَا أُسْتَاذ سمِير، هٰذِهِ أُسْرَتِي .

هٰذَا وَالِدِي سَلِيم وَهٰذِهِ وَالِدَتِي أَمَل .

سمير: أَهْلاً وَسَهْلاً، تَشَرَّفْنَا .

سَلِيم: تَشَرَّفْنَا بِكَ يَا أُسْتَاذ سَمِير .

أَمَل: أَهْلاً بِكَ يَا أُسْتَاذ.

دينا: وَهٰذا أَخِي. إِسْمُهُ مَرْوَان وعُمْرُهُ عَشْر سَنَوَات، وَهٰذِهِ أُخْتِي.

إِسْمُهَا نَوَال وَعُمْرُهَا أَيْضاً (*'aydan*) عَشْر سَنَوَات. أَخِي

وَأُخْتِي تَوْأَمَان.

سمير: أَهْلاً يَا مَرْوَان، أَهْلاً يَا نَوَال.

تَمْرِين ١. أَجِيبُوا شَفَهِيًّا.   Exercise 1. Answer out loud.

١. مَنْ هُوَ سَمِير؟   ٢. مَنْ هِيَ دينَا؟   ٣. مَنْ هِيَ نَوَال؟

٤. مَا ٱسْمُ والِدَتِكَ/والِدَتِكِ؟   ٥. مَا ٱسْمُ وَالِدكَ/وَالِدكِ؟

تَمْرِين ٢. أَحْضِرُوا صُورَة أُسْرَتِكُمْ وَقَدِّمُوا ٱلْأُسْرَة لِزُمَلائِكُمْ.

Exercise 2. Bring a picture of your family and present the family to your classmates.

Exercise 3. Circle the correct translation.   تَمْرِين ٣. أَحِيطُوا ٱلتَّرْجَمَةَ ٱلصَّحِيحَة .

He is ten years old. / She is ten years old.   ١. عُمْرُهُ عَشْرُ سَنَوَات .

This is my father Salim. / Salim is my father.   ٢. هٰذَا وَالِدِي سَلِيم .

Ten years / Ten hours   ٣. عَشْرُ سَاعَات

Today is a happy day. / A happy day to you.   ٤. نَهَارُكَ سَعِيد .

Nawal and Marwan are twins. / Nawal has a twin sister.   ٥. نَوَال وَمَرْوَان تَوْأَمَانِ .

Singular, dual and plural

The word تَوْأَمَان is dual. In Arabic there are three categories of numbers: **singular, dual, and plural.** Unlike English, there is a distinction between dual and plural. Whereas the plural in English means two or more, the plural in Arabic means three or more. For two people or things, Arabic has the dual form. The dual exists across the language in verbs, nouns, adjectives and pronouns. To summarize:

singular *mufrad* (مُفْرَد) indicates **one** person or one thing, for example: وَلَد

dual *muthanna* (مُثَنَّى) indicates **two** people or things, for example: وَلَدَان

plural *jam'* (جَمْع) indicates **three** or more people or things, for example: أَوْلاد

ḥaa   ح   ـ   ح   حَاء

ح sounds like an **h** with friction.

There is no English equivalent.

تَمْرِين ٤ . إِسْتَمِعُوا وَأَعِيدُوا ثُمَّ حَدِّدُوا حَرْفَ ٱلْحَاء.

Exercise 4. Listen and repeat, then identify the letter *ḥaa*.

١. مُحَمَّد   ٢. صَبَاحَ   ٣. حِمَار   ٤. حَال

Exercise 5. Write.   تَمْرِين ٥ . أُكْتُبُوا.

situation, condition   حَال

milk   حَلِيب

donkey   حِمَار

ḥaa in the middle of a word   أَلْحَاء فِي وَسَطِ ٱلْكَلِمَة

حـ

Praise be to God   أَلْحَمْدُ لله

liberty   أَلْحُرِّيَة

Excuse me (addressing *f. s.*)   إِسْمَحِي لِي

Muḥammad   مُحَمَّد

the donkey   أَلْحِمَار

ḥaa at the end of a word   أَلْحَاء فِ آخِرِ ٱلْكَلِمَة

not connected ح   connected ـح

salt   مِلْح

key   مِفْتَاح

apples (collective noun)   تُفَّاح

| The letters | ي ن ث ت ب | preceding | ح: |

فَتَحْنَا

1
2
3
4
5
6

A letter from this group preceding ح is written the same way that it is written when it precedes the letter م. The stroke that connects it to the ح must begin at the top of the letter and continue slightly diagonally downward to the left.

the sea   أَلْبَحْر

he opened   فَتَحَ

we   نَحْن

khaa   خ   ــخ   ــخـ   خاء

خ sounds like the German **ch** in "Ba**ch**."

There is no English equivalent.

تَمْرِين ٦. إِسْتَمِعُوا وَأَعِيدُوا ثُمَّ حَدِّدُوا حَرْفَ ٱلْخَاء.

Exercise 6. Listen and repeat, then identify the letter *khaa*.

٤. خَالِي   ٣. بِخَيْر   ٢. أُخْت   ١. أَخ

Exercise 7. Write.   تَمْرِين ٧. أُكْتُبُوا.

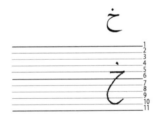

sister   أُخْت

spring   أَلْخَرِيف

brother   أَخ

أَخْ

```
1
2
3
4
5
6
7
8
9
10
11
```

history, date (calendar)   تَأْرِيخ

تَأْرِخ

```
1
2
3
4
5
6
7
8
9
10
11
```

تَمْرِين ٨ . إِقْرَؤُوا وَٱنْتَبِهُوا إِلَى ٱلْفَرْقِ بَيْنَ ٱلْحَاءِ وَٱلْخَاءِ.

Exercise 8. Read, paying attention to the difference between ح and خ.

bread خُبْز ٣.	uncle (*m.*) خَال ٢.	condition حَال ١.
to open فَتَحَ ٦.	key مِفْتَاح ٥.	m. name خَالِد ٤.
one وَاحِد ٩.	sea بَحْر ٨.	sister أُخْت ٧.

تَمْرِين ٩ . إِقْرَؤُوا ٱلْكَلِمَاتِ فِي ٱلتَّمْرِينِ ٱلسَّابِقِ لِزُمَلائِكُمْ وَٱطْلُبُوا مِنْهُمْ أَنْ

يَقُولُوا هَلْ تَحْتَوِي ٱلْكَلِمَةُ عَلَى حَرْفِ ٱلْحَاءِ أَمْ عَلَى حَرْفِ ٱلْخَاءِ.

Exercise 9. Read the words in the previous exercise to your classmates. Ask them to

indicate if the word contains the letter ح or the letter خ.

jiim   ج ـ جـ جـ جيم

ج sounds like the **j** in "joy."

تَمْرِين ١٠. إِسْتَمِعوا وأَعيدوا ثُمَّ حَدِّدُوا حَرْفَ ٱلْجيـم.

Exercise 10. Listen and repeat, then identify the letter *jiim*.

١. جَديد   ٢. جَامِعَة   ٣. وَاجِب   ٤. جَميل

Exercise 11. Write.   تَمْرِين ١١. أُكْتُبُوا.

ج   ـجـ   جـ

mosque   مَسْجِد

A title given to a Muslim after making the pilgramage to Mecca.   حَاجّ

تَمْرِين ١٢. صِلُوا ٱلْحُرُوف وَٱكْتُبُوا ٱلْكَلِمَات.

Exercise 12. Connect the letters to write the words.

_____ ◄—   ١. م + مَ + سْ + جِ + د

_____ ◄—   ٢. تَ + أ + رِ + ي + خ

_____ ◄—   ٣. جُ + و + ر + ج

_____ ◄—   ٤. جَ + ا + م + عَ + ة

_____ ◄—   ٥. بِ + خَ + يْ + ر

_____ ◄—   ٦. أَ + لْ + بَ + حْ + ر

Exercise 13. Read.   تَمْرِين ١٣. إِقْرَؤُوا.

١. تَ تَ ثَ   ٢. ثُ تُ ثُ   ٣. كُ قُ

٤. دَ ذَ   ٥. ذِ دِ ذِ   ٦. تُ فُ

٧. ثَ ذَ   ٨. غِ رِ   ٩. حُ خُ

١٠. غَ رَ   ١١. كَ قَ   ١٢. حَ خَ

١٣. ثَ ذَ   ١٤. ثِ ذِ   ١٥. غُ رُ

🔊

تَعَلَّمُوا هٰذِهِ ٱلْمُفْرَدَات

Bahrain	ٱلْبَحْرَيْن	brother	أخ (ج) إِخْوَة
hour, time	سَاعَة (ج) سَاعَات	sister	أُخْت (ج) أَخَوَات
Thursday	يَوْمُ ٱلْخَمِيس	how many, how much	كَمْ
uncle (maternal)	خَال	I have	لِي
uncle (paternal)	عَمّ	one	وَاحِد
university	جَامِعَة (ج) جَامِعَات	mosque	مَسْجِد (ج) مَسَاجِد

Exercise 14. Read.

تَمْرِين ١٤. إِقْرَؤُوا.

١. ‐ كَمْ أَخًا لَكَ؟
‐ لِي أخ وَاحِد.

٢. ‐ أَيْنَ تَدْرُسِينَ؟
‐ أَدْرُسُ في جَامِعَة ستانفورد.

٣. ‐ كَمْ أُخْتًا لَكَ؟
‐ لِي ثَلاث أَخَوَات.

٤. ‐ مَنْ هٰذَا؟
‐ هٰذَا أَخِي ٱلْكَبِير.

٥. ‐ كَمْ لُغَةً تَعْرِفُ؟
‐ أَعْرِفُ ثَلاث لُغَات.

٦. ‐ هَلْ هٰذَا عَمُّهَا؟
‐ نَعَمْ. هٰذَا عَمُّهَا أَحْمَد.

How many?   كَمْ؟

The word كَمْ is used to ask about the quantity of people and things. It is followed by *indefinite singular noun with double fatḥa,* تَنْوِينُ ٱلْفَتْح:

How many brothers do you (*f. s.*) have?   كَمْ أَخًا لَكِ؟

How many cars do you (*m. s.*) have?   كَمْ سَيَّارَةً لَكَ؟

Note: Double *fatḥa* is followed by silent *'alif* except when the word

ends with *taa marbuuṭa.*

Exercise 15. Solve the riddle.   تَمْرِين ١٥. حُلُّوا ٱللُّغْز.

لِنَوَال أَرْبَعَة إِخْوَة. لِكُلّ أَخ أُخْت.

كَمْ أَخًا وَكَمْ أُخْتًا فِي ٱلْأُسْرَة؟

حَلُّ ٱللُّغْز: صَفْحَة ١٥٩

ط ط ط ṭaa

ط sounds like an emphatic ت (stronger than **t** in "taught").

There is no English equivalent.

تَمْرِين ١٦ . إِسْتَمِعُوا وأَعِيدُوا ثُمَّ حَدِّدُوا حَرْفَ ٱلطَّاء.

Exercise 16. Listen and repeat, then identify the letter ṭaa.

١ . طَالِب   ٢ . مَطْعَم   ٣ . طَبِيب   ٤ . مَطَار

Exercise 17. Write.   تَمْرِين ١٧ . أُكْتُبُوا.

ط ١ ٢

student طَالِب

student طَالِب

breakfast فُطُور

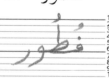

The tail of the letter preceded by ط must be lengthened slightly
to make room for the loop.

he fell سَقَطَ

تَمْرِينِ ١٨. إِقْرَؤُوا وَٱنْتَبِهُوا إِلَى ٱلْفَرْق بَيْنَ ٱلتَّاء وَٱلطَّاء.

Exercise 18. Read, paying attention to the difference between ت and ط.

Kuwait	٣. أَلْكُوَيْت	breakfast	٢. فُطُور	physician	١. طَبِيب
pilot	٦. طَيَّار	dot	٥. نُقْطَة	mistaken	٤. غَلْطَان
to repent	٩. تَابَ	airport	٨. مَطَار	Turkey	٧. تُرْكِيَا
to recover	١٢. طَابَ	to leave	١١. تَرَكَ	restaurant	١٠. مَطْعَم

تَمْرِينِ ١٩. إِقْرَؤُوا ٱلْكَلِمَات فِي ٱلتَّمْرِينِ ٱلسَّابِق لِزُمَلائِكُمْ وَٱطْلُبُوا مِنْهُمْ أَنْ

يَقُولُوا هَلْ تَحْتَوِي ٱلْكَلِمَة عَلَى حَرْف ٱلتَّاء أَمْ عَلَى حَرْفِ ٱلطَّاء.

Exercise 19. Read the words in the previous exercise to your classmates. Ask them
to indicate if the word contains the letter ت or the letter ط.

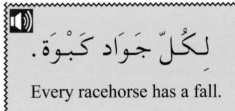

لِكُلّ جَوَاد كَبْوَة.

Every racehorse has a fall.

DHaa   ظ   ظاء

ظ sounds like an emphatic ذ.

There is no English equivalent.

تَمْرِين ٢٠. إِسْتَمِعُوا وَأَعيدُوا ثُمَّ حَدِّدُوا حَرْفَ ٱلظّاء.

Exercise 20. Listen and repeat, then identify the letter *DHaa*.

٤. ظُهْر   ٣. مَنْظَر   ٢. نَظيف   ١. عَظيم

Exercise 21. Write.   تَمْرِين ٢١. أُكْتُبوا.

ظ   ١   ٢

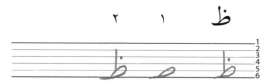

ظ is written exactly like the ط, except that it has a dot above the loop's highest point, on the right side of the perpendicular stroke.

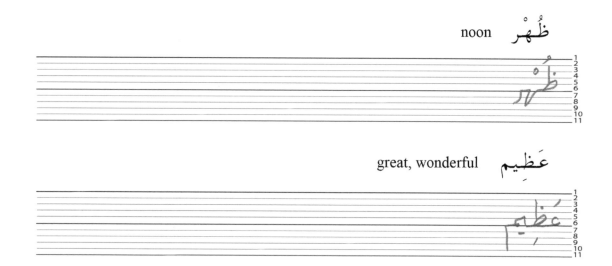

noon   ظُهْر

great, wonderful   عَظيم

تَمْرِين ٢٢ . إِقْرَؤُوا وَٱنْتَبِهُوا إِلَى ٱلْفَرْق بَيْنَ ٱلذَّال وَٱلظَّاء .

Exercise 22. Read, paying attention to the difference between ذ and ظ.

to look	٣. نَظَرَ	this, this is	٢. هٰذَا	To appear	١. ظَهَرَ
study	٦. مُذَاكَرَة	noon	٥. ظُهْر	to go	٤. ذَهَبَ
demonstration	٩. مُظَاهَرَة	professor	٨. أُسْتَاذ	great	٧. عَظِيم
view	١٢. مَنْظَر	shadow	١١. ظِلّ	student	١٠. تِلْمِيذ

تَمْرِين ٢٣ . إِقْرَؤُوا ٱلْكَلِمَات فِي ٱلتَّمْرِينِ ٱلسَّابِق لِزُمَلَائِكُمْ وَٱطْلُبُوا مِنْهُمْ أَنْ

يَقُولُوا هَلْ تَحْتَوِي ٱلْكَلِمَة عَلَى حَرْف ٱلذَّال أَمْ عَلَى حَرْف ٱلظَّاء .

Exercise 23. Read the words in the previous exercise to your classmates. Ask them to

indicate if the word contains the letter ذ or the letter ظ.

مَا حَكَّ جِلْدَكَ مِثْل ظِفْرِكَ .

No one can scratch your skin like your own nail.

Meaning: No one can help you better than you can help yourself.

şaad   صا   صـ   ص

ص sounds like an emphatic س .

(Stronger than the **s** in "sought").

There is no English equivalent.

تَمْرِين ٢٤ . إِسْتَمِعُوا وَأَعِيدُوا ثُمَّ حَدِّدُوا حَرْفَ ٱلصَّاد

Exercise 24. Listen and repeat, then identify the letter ṣaad.

١ . صَبَاح   ٢ . صَغِير   ٣ . مِصْر   ٤ . بَصَل

Exercise 25. Write.   تَمْرِين ٢٥ . أُكْتُبُوا.

ص   صـ

classroom   صَفّ

Egypt   مِصْر

thief   لِصّ

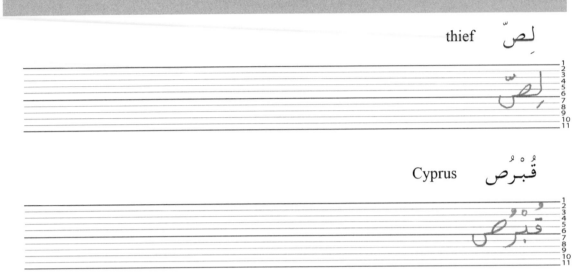

Cyprus   قُبْرُص

تَمْرِين ٢٦ . إِقْرَؤُوا وَٱنْتَبِهُوا إِلَى ٱلْفَرْق بَيْنَ ٱلسِّين وَٱلصَّاد .

Exercise 26. Read, paying attention to the difference between س and ص.

whip	سَوْط	٣.	picture	صُورَة	٢.	chapter (Qur'an)	سُورَة	١.

١. سُورَة chapter (Qur'an)   ٢. صُورَة picture   ٣. سَوْط whip

٤. صَوْت voice   ٥. عَسَل honey   ٦. بَصَل onion

٧. سَكَتَ to be silent   ٨. سَقَطَ to fall   ٩. صَادَ to hunt

١٠. سَادَ to govern   ١١. يَسِيرُ to move   ١٢. يَصِيرُ to become

تَمْرِين ٢٧ . إِقْرَؤُوا ٱلْكَلِمَات فِي ٱلتَّمْرِين ٱلسَّابِق لِزُمَلائِكُمْ وَٱطْلُبُوا مِنْهُمْ أَنْ يَقُولُوا هَلْ تَحْتَوِي ٱلْكَلِمَة عَلَى حَرْفِ ٱلسِّين أَمْ عَلَى حَرْفِ ٱلصَّاد .

Exercise 27. Read the words in the previous exercise to your classmates. Ask them to indicate if the word contains the letter س or the letter ص.

The words صَوْت (voice) and سَوْط (whip) sound exactly the same.

Emphatic consonants affect the sound of the whole word. The ت in

سَوْط sounds like ط because of the emphatic ص, and the س of صَوْت

sounds like ص because of the emphatic ط. In the word سُلْطَان

(sultan, ruler), the س sounds like ص because of the emphatic ط.

ḍaad   ضـ ض   ضاد

ض sounds like an emphatic د. It is stronger than **d** in "daughter."

There is no English equivalent.

تَمْرِين ٢٨. إِسْتَمِعُوا وَأَعِيدُوا ثُمَّ حَدِّدُوا حَرْفَ ٱلضَّاد

Exercise 28. Listen and repeat, then identify the letter *ḍaad*.

١. ضَابِط   ٢. أَبْيَض   ٣. رَمَضَان   ٤. تَفَضَّل

Exercise 29. Write.   تَمْرِين ٢٩. أُكْتُبُوا.

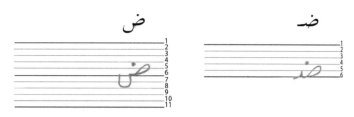

ض is written exactly like ص with a dot placed above the loop.

guest   ضَيْف

sick, patient (n.)   مَرِيض

officer   ضَابِط

تَمْرِين ٣٠. إِقْرَؤُوا وَٱنْتَبِهُوا إِلَى ٱلْفَرْقِ بَيْنَ ٱلضَّادِ وَٱلدَّال.

Exercise 30. Read, paying attention to the difference between ض and د.

beating, hitting	ضَرْب	٢.	path, trail	دَرْب	١.
officer	ضَابِط	٤.	principal	مُدِير	٣.
house	دَار	٦.	store	دُكَّان	٥.
ground, land	أَرْض	٨.	sick	مَرِيض	٧.
town, city, country	بَلَد	١٠.	white	أَبْيَض	٩.

تَمْرِين ٣١. إِقْرَؤُوا ٱلْكَلِمَاتِ فِي ٱلتَّمْرِينِ ٱلسَّابِقِ لِزُمَلَائِكُمْ. أُطْلُبُوا مِنْهُمْ أَنْ

يَقُولُوا هَلْ تَحْتَوِي ٱلْكَلِمَةُ عَلَى حَرْفِ ٱلضَّادِ أَمْ عَلَى حَرْفِ ٱلدَّال.

Exercise 31. Read the words in the previous exercise to your classmates. Ask them

to indicate if each word contains the letter ض or the letter د.

تَمْرِين ٣٢. صِلُوا ٱلْحُرُوف وَٱكْتُبُوا ٱلْكَلِمَات.

Exercise 32. Connect the letters to write the words.

١. عَ + ا + صِ + مَ + ة ⇐ _____

٢. أَ + لْ + مَ + رِ + ي + ض ⇐ _____

٣. مَ + سْ + جِ + د ⇐ _____

٤. ضُ + يُ + و + ف ⇐ _____

٥. أَ + بْ + يَ + ض ⇐ _____

٦. أَ + لْ + مَ + نْ + ظَ + ر ⇐ _____

٧. ضَ + ا + بِ + ط ⇐ _____

٨. بَ + طَ + ا + طَ + ا ⇐ _____

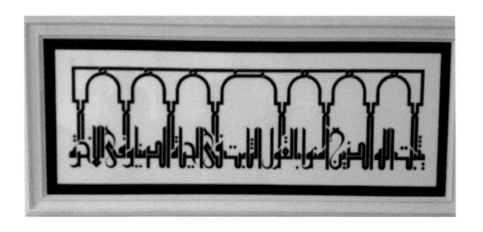

ٱلْـحُـرُوفُ ٱلْـعَـرَبِـيَّـة

The Arabic alphabet

أ ب ت ث ج ح خ ذ د ر ز س ش ص ض

ط ظ ع غ ف ق ك ل م ن ه و ي

1.   ة , ء , ى and لا are not included in the Arabic alphabet.

2.   Arabic letters can be used as numbers to delineate subsections. Rather than follow the order of the Arabic alphabet, however, they follow the order of the Hebrew alphabet. That is, the order is not

... ث ت ب أ

but ... د ج ب أ

To make the order easier to remember, Arabs group the letters into the following made-up words. The corresponding Hebrew letters are shown underneath the Arabic letters. There are no corresponding Hebrew letters for the last two:

أبجد	هوز	حطي	كلمن
אבגד	הוז	חטי	כלמנ

سعفص	قرشت	ثخذ	ضظغ
סעפצ	קרשת		

تَمْرِين ٣٣ . أَمَامَكُمْ أَسْمَاء لِلإِنَاث . إِنْسَخُوهَا حَسَبَ ٱلتَّرْتِيب ٱلأَبْجَدِيّ .

Exercise 33. The following are female names. Alphabetize them according to the Arabic alphabet.

إِلْهَام ؛ لَطِيفَة ؛ إِيمَان ؛ يُمْنَى ؛ رِيم ؛ نَوَال ؛

مَنَار ؛ مَهَا ؛ سَلِيمَة ؛ صَبَاح ؛ رَشِيدَة ؛

مُنَى ؛ نَدِيم ؛ حَنَان ؛ سَارَة ؛ أَمَل

تَمْرِين ٣٤ . أَمَامَكُمْ أَسْمَاء لِلذُّكُور . إِنْسَخُوهَا حَسَبَ ٱلتَّرْتِيب ٱلأَبْجَدِيّ .

Exercise 34. The following are male names. Alphabetize them according to the Arabic alphabet.

قَاسِم ؛ تَوْفِيق ؛ أَمِين ؛ بَسَّام ؛ حَسَن ؛ عَادِل

لُطْفِي ؛ خَالِد ؛ كَامِل ؛ سَلْمَان ؛ شَفِيق ؛ رَشِيد

عَبْدُ ٱللّٰه ؛ مُفِيد ؛ مَحْمُود ؛ فَارُوق ؛ إِلْيَاس

مَنْ عَلَّمَنِي حَرْفًا صِرْتُ لَهُ عَبْدًا .

He who teaches me one letter, I will be a slave to him.

The writing of *hamza*   كِتَابَةُ ٱلْهَمْزَة

The *hamza* could be written on three letters which serve as "chairs:" و , ا

and ـ / ى (without the two dots). It can also be written alone (without a

"chair") in the middle and at the end of a word. Examples:

داء (disease), أَسْئِلَة (questions), سُؤَال (a question), قِرَاءَة (reading).

تَمْرِين ٣٥ . إقْرَؤُوا.   Exercise 35. Read.

١. هَلْ عِنْدَكُمْ أَسْئِلَة يَا شَبَاب؟   ٢. عِنْدِي سُؤَال يَا أُسْتَاذ.

٣. إِلَى ٱللِّقَاء يَا مُنَى.   ٤. لَى ٱللِّقَاء يَا أُسْتَاذَة.

تَمْرِين ٣٦. أَمَامَكُمُ ٱلْمَثَل "مَنْ جَدَّ وَجَدَ." جِدُوا ٱلْكَلِمَات.

Exercise 36. In front of you is the proverb مَنْ جَدَّ وَجَدَ. Find the words.

He who makes every effort will find.

تَعَلَّمُوا هٰذِهِ ٱلْمُفْرَدات

statue	تِمْثَال	welcome	أَهْلاً وَسَهْلاً
freedom, liberty	حُرِّيَّة	please…	تَفَضَّل
public	عَامّ	it is a pleasure	تَشَرَّفْنَا
to want	أَرَادَ (م) يُرِيدُ	student	طَالِب (ج) طُلاب
restaurant	مَطْعَم (ج) مَطَاعِم	university	جَامِعَة (ج) جَامِعَات
east	شَرْق	to know	عَرَفَ (م) يَعْرِفُ
salad	سَلَطَة	after (time)	بَعْدَ
bread	خُبْز	food	أَكْل ، طَعَام
pita bread	خُبْز عَرَبِي	to visit	زَارَ (م) يَزُورُ
pastry (almonds/pistachios)	بَقْلاوة	morning	صَبَاح
roasted meat on a skewer	كَبَاب	fine, in good health	بِخَيْر
great	عَظِيم	good	خَيْر
film	فِيلْم (ج) أَفْلام	noon	ظُهْر

تَمْرِين ٣٧. أَحِيطُوا ٱلتَّرْجَمَةَ ٱلصَّحِيحَة.

Exercise 37. Circle the correct translation.

Statue of Liberty / freedom flag   ١. تِمْثَالُ ٱلْحُرِّيَّة

Georgetown University / Georgetown Center   ٢. جَامِعَة "جُورج تَاوُن"

an hour ago / after an hour   ٣. بَعْدَ سَاعَة

in the morning / in the evening   ٤. فِي ٱلصَّبَاح

the city station / the city center   ٥. مَرْكَزُ ٱلْمَدِينَة

the public library / the public books   ٦. أَلْمَكْتَبَةُ ٱلْعَامَّة

It is a pleasure meeting you. / I am honored to be here.   ٧. تَشَرَّفْنَا بِمَعْرِفَتِكُمْ.

a brother and a sister / a boy and a girl   ٨. أَخ وَأُخْت

after eating / before eating   ٩. بَعْدَ ٱلْأَكْل

a restaurant in the east / Middle Eastern restaurant   ١٠. مَطْعَم شَرْقِيّ

my paternal uncle and aunt / my maternal uncle and aunt   ١١. عَمِّي وَعَمَّتِي

at noon / in the afternoon   ١٢. بَعْدَ ٱلظُّهْر

Listen to the conversation, then read it.   إِسْتَمِعُوا إِلَى ٱلْمُحَادَثَة ثُمَّ ٱقْرَؤُوهَا .

أَهْلاً وَسَهْلاً

سَلْمَان: أَهْلاً يَا كَرِيم، أَهْلاً وَسَهْلاً، تَفَضَّلُوا .

كَرِيم: أَهْلاً بِكَ يَا سَلْمَان، هٰذِهِ لِنْدا وَهٰذَا سَلِيم .

سَلْمَان: أَهْلاً بِكِ يَا لِنْدا وَأَهْلاً بِكَ يَا سَلِيم .

هٰذَا أَخِي ٱلْكَبِير خَالِد هُوَ طَالِب فِي جَامِعَة كُولُومبِيَا

وَهٰذِهِ أُخْتِي خُلُود، وَهٰذَا خَالِي حُسَيْن وَهٰذِهِ عَمَّتِي

مَاجِدَة .

كَرِيم: تَشَرَّفْنَا بِمَعْرِفَتِكُمْ .

سَلْمَان: بَعْدَ ٱلْأَكْل سَنَذْهَبُ إِلَى ٱلسِّينَمَا فِي مَرْكَزِ ٱلْمَدِينَة .

كَرِيم: مُمْتَاز، أَنَا أُحِبُّ ٱلْأَفْلام كَثِيراً، وَمَاذَا سَنَفْعَلُ غَداً؟

سَلْمَان: فِي ٱلصَّبَاح سَنَذْهَبُ إِلَى جَامِعَة كُولُومبِيَا مَعَ أَخِي

خَالِد وَفِي ٱلظُّهْر سَنَزُورُ تِمْثالَ ٱلْحُرِّيَّة وَٱلْمَكْتَبَة

ٱلْعَامَّة .

كَرِيم: مُمْتَاز، وَنُرِيدُ أَيْضًا أَنْ نَأْكُلَ (to eat) فِي مَطْعَم شَرْقِيّ.

سَلْمَان: نَعَمْ، لِخَالِي مَطْعَم شَرْقِيّ فِي مَرْكَز بْرُوكْلِين وَسَنَأْكُلُ

هُنَاكَ ٱلْفَلَافِل وَٱلْكَبَاب وَٱلسَّلَطَة وَٱلْخُبْزَ ٱلْعَرَبِيّ وَٱلْبَقْلَاوَة.

كَرِيم: عَظِيم!

تَمْرِين ٣٨. أَجِيبُوا شَفَهِيًّا ثُمَّ ٱكْتُبُوا ٱلْأَجْوِبَة فِي دَفَاتِركُمْ.

Exercise 38. Answer out loud, then write the answers in your notebooks.

٢. مَنْ هُوَ حُسَيْن وَمَنْ هِيَ مَاجِدَة؟   ١. أَيْنَ تُوجَدُ (located) ٱلسِّينَمَا؟

٤. مَنْ هِيَ خُلُود؟   ٣. أَيْنَ يَدْرُسُ خَالِد؟

Exercise 39. True or false.   تَمْرِين ٣٩. صَوَاب أَمْ خَطَأً.

صَوَاب   خَطَأ

١. كَرِيم وَلِنْدَا وَسَلِيم يَزُورُونَ سَلْمَان.

٢. لِكَرِيم أَخ فِي بْرُوكْلِين ٱسْمُهُ سَلْمَان.

٣. يَدْرُسُ خَالِد فِي جَامِعَة كُولُومبِيَا فِي نِيو يُورْك.

٤. خُلُود هِيَ عَمَّة مَاجِدَة.

٥. كَرِيم يُحِبُّ ٱلْكَبَاب وَٱلسَّلَطَة وَٱلْخُبْزَ ٱلْعَرَبِيّ.

٦. يُوجَد (located) تِمْثَالُ ٱلْحُرِّيَّة فِي وَاشِنْطن دِي سِي.

هُوَ طَالِب

In Arabic, unlike English, there are sentences without a verb (or an auxiliary verb):

هُوَ طَالِب. ، هٰذِهِ أُسْرَتِي. ، هَانِي أُسْتَاذ. ، أَلْمَكْتَبَة كَبِيرَة.

In these sentences the first word is the subject and the second word is the predicate.

أَلظَّرْف　Adverbs

In the sentence .كَثِيرًا أُحِبُّ ٱلْأَفْلَام كَثِيرًا the word كَثِيرًا is an adverb. It modifies the

verb أُحِبُّ. Adverbs in Arabic take ـًا (تَنْوِينُ ٱلْفَتْح). Examples:

كَثِيرًا (a lot), قَلِيلًا (a little), طَبْعًا (by nature), شُكْرًا (thanks).

أَلضَّمَائِر　Pronouns

In Arabic there are three types of personal pronouns, just as there are in English:

Subject pronouns	أَلضَّمَائِرُ ٱلْمُنْفَصِلَة
Possessive pronouns	ضَمَائِرُ ٱلْمُلْكِيَّة
Object pronouns	ضَمَائِرُ ٱلنَّصْب

"**He** is a student." (*He* is a subject pronoun); "**His** house is big." (*His* is a
possessive pronoun); "Who saw **him**?" (*Him* is an object pronoun). Possessive
pronouns are attached to nouns, and object pronouns are attached to verbs. Now you
are going to learn the subject (personal) pronouns, which are independent words.

Subject Pronouns   أَلضَّمَائِرُ ٱلْمُنْفَصِلَة

In Arabic there are 12 subject pronouns. The singular and plural **first-person** pronouns (that is, "I" and "we") are the same in both masculine and feminine forms. However, the pronouns in **second** and **third** persons have distinct masculine and feminine forms. Note the following table:

we	نَحْنُ	I	أَنَا
you (*m. pl.*)	أَنْتُمْ	you (*m. s.*)	أَنْتَ
you (*f. pl.*)	أَنْتُنَّ	you (*f. s.*)	أَنْتِ
they (*m.*)	هُمْ	he	هُوَ
they (*f.*)	هُنَّ	she	هِيَ

Groups consisting of both men and women are considered masculine.

Dual subject pronouns

In Arabic there are two dual subject pronouns, and they serve for both

masculine and feminine forms:

You (*dual, m.& f.*)   –   أَنْتُمَا   ⟸   (أَنْتُمْ + ا)

They (*dual, m.& f.*)   –   هُمَا   ⟸   (هُمْ + ا)

The final silent *'alif* (ا) that marks the dual lengthens the *fatḥa*

preceding it, unlike a regular silent *'alif* (ا) at the end of a word (أَنَا).

تَمْرِين ٤٠ . إِمْلَؤُوا ٱلْفَرَاغَ بِٱلضَّمِيرِ ٱلْمُنَاسِب .

Exercise 40. Fill in the blank with the appropriate pronoun.

١. _____ يَدْرُسُ ٱلْهَنْدَسَة .   (هُوَ / هِيَ)

٢. _____ أُسْتَاذِي .   (هُوَ / أَنَا)

٣. يَا بِنْتِي أَيْنَ _____ ؟   (أَنْتَ / أَنْتِ)

٤. يَا سَلْمَان، هَلْ _____ كُوَيْتِيّ؟   (أَنْتِ / أَنْتَ)

٥. هٰذِهِ _____ مَدْرَسَةُ بِنْتِي .   (هِيَ / هُوَ)

٦. مَنْ _____ ؟ أَنَا مُنَى .   (أَنْتِ / هِيَ)

٧. نَبِيل طَالِب. ــــــــــ يَدْرُسُ في جَامِعَة بَيْرُوت. (أَنْتَ / هُوَ)

٨. سَاندرَا طَالِبَة. ــــــــــ تَدْرُسُ في جَامِعَة نيو يورك. (هُوَ / هِيَ)

٩. لِنْدا وأَمَل ونَادِيَة مِصْرِيَّات. ــــــــــ مِنْ مِصْر. (هُمْ / هُنَّ)

١٠. يا طُلاب، مِنْ أَيْنَ ــــــــــ ؟ (أَنْتُمْ / أَنْتُنَّ)

١١. ــــــــــ مِنْ مِصْر. (هُمْ / نَحْنُ)

تَمْرِين ٤١. يَتَكَلَّمُ رَامِي عَنْ نَفْسِهِ في الـ skype. إسْتَمِعُوا.

Exercise 41. Rami talks about himself on Skype. Listen.

أَلسَّلامُ عَلَيْكُمْ. إسْمِي رَامِي وأَسْكُنُ في مَدِينَة "لُونغ بِيتْش" في وِلايَة نيو يورك. أَنَا مُوَظَّف في بَنْك أَمْرِيكِيّ. لِي أَخ صَغِير وأُخْت كَبِيرَة. أُخْتِي طَالِبَة في جَامِعَة كولومبِيا وتَدْرُسُ ٱلْعَرَبِيَّة وٱلْهَنْدَسَة.

تَمْرِين ٤٢. قَدِّمْ نَفْسَكَ / نَفْسَكِ لِرَامِي. Exercise 42. Introduce yourself to Rami.

تَمْرِين ٤٣. مَاذَا تَعْرِفُونَ عَنْ رَامِي؟ أَجِيبُوا شَفَهِيًّا.

Exercise 43. What do you know about Rami? Answer out loud.

تَعَلَّمُوا هٰذِهِ ٱلْمُفْرَدَات

but	لٰكِنْ ، وَلٰكِنْ	sun	شَمْس
to like/love	أَحَبَّ (م) يُحِبُّ	moon	قَمَر
a lot	كَثِيرًا	mother	أُمّ (ج) أُمَّهَات
ball	كُرَة	history, date (calendar)	تَأْرِيخ
foot	قَدَم (ج) أَقْدَام	smart	شَاطِر
soccer	كُرَةُ ٱلْقَدَم	lazy	كَسْلان

تَمْرِين ٤٤ . أُكْتُبُوا كَلِمَات تَحْتَوِي عَلَى كُلّ مِنَ ٱلْجُذُور ٱلتَّالِيَة.

Exercise 44. Write words that contain each of the following roots.

٢. شطر _____   ١. أرخ _____

٤. حبب _____   ٣. كثر _____

٦. كسل _____   ٥. قدم _____

حَلُّ ٱللُّغْز – صَفْحَة ١٣٨

فِي ٱلأُسْرَة أَرْبَعَة إِخْوَة وَأُخْت وَاحِدَة.

تَمْرِين ٤٥. أَحِيطُوا ٱلتَّرْجَمَة ٱلصَّحِيحَة.

Exercise 45. Circle the correct translation.

Salman has a mother. / Salman's mother   ١. أُمّ سَلْمَان

Salman is lazy. / Salman does not study.   ٢. سَلْمَان كَسْلَان

The history professor / The history student   ٣. أُسْتَاذَةُ ٱلتَّأْرِيخ

basketball / soccer   ٤. كُرَةُ ٱلْقَدَم

Who are you (f. s.)? / Who are you (m. s.)?   ٥. مَنْ حَضْرَتُكِ؟

Exercise 46. Translate out loud.   تَمْرِين ٤٦. تَرْجِمُوا شَفَهِيًّا.

٣. طَالِب شَاطِر   ٢. أُسْتَاذَةُ ٱلْعَرَبِيَّة   ١. أَأَنْتَ سَلْمَان؟

٦. كُرَةُ ٱلْقَدَم   ٥. هُوَ لَا يَدْرُسُ.   ٤. إِبْنُكِ كَسْلَان.

٩. أُحِبُّ ٱلْعَرَبِيَّة كَثِيرًا.   ٨. أَدْرُسُ ٱلتَّأْرِيخ.   ٧. أَلشَّمْس وَٱلْقَمَر

أَلْكَسَل لَا يُطْعِمُ عَسَلًا.

Laziness does not feed you honey.

Listen to the conversation, then read it.   إِسْتَمِعُوا إِلى ٱلْمُحَادَثَة ثُمَّ ٱقْرَؤُوهَا .

سَلْمَان كَسْلَان

مَارِي: هَلْ حَضْرَتُكِ وَالِدَة سَلْمَان؟

أُمّ سَلْمَان: نَعَمْ، أَنَا أُمّ سَلْمَان . إِسْمِي أَدِيبَة وَمَنْ حَضْرَتُكِ؟

أَأَنْتِ أُسْتَاذَةُ ٱلتَّأْرِيخ؟

مَارِي: لا . أَنَا أُسْتَاذَةُ ٱلْعَرَبِيَّة . إِسْمِي مَارِي، تَشَرَّفْنَا .

أُمّ سَلْمَان: أَهْلاً، تَشَرَّفْنَا بِكِ يَا أُسْتَاذَة مَارِي .

مَارِي: إِبْنُكِ سَلْمَان طَالِب شَاطِر وَلٰكِنْ كَسْلان .

أُمّ سَلْمَان: نَعَمْ، سَلْمَان كَسْلَان . هُوَ يُحِبُّ ٱلْعَرَبِيَّة كَثِيراً وَلٰكِنْ لا يَدْرُسُ . أَنَا أَدْرُسُ وَوَالِدُهُ يَدْرُسُ وَأُخْتُهُ تَدْرُسُ وَلٰكِنْ هُوَ لا يَدْرُسُ . كُلَّ ٱلْيَوْم كُرَةُ ٱلْقَدَم وَٱلْكُومبيوتِر .

مَنْ حَضْرَتُكَ؟

حَضْرَتُكَ and حَضْرَتُكِ are respectful ways of addressing a man and a woman respectively.

Who are you, Sir?	مَنْ حَضْرَتُكَ؟
Who are you, Ma'am?	مَنْ حَضْرَتُكِ؟

Exercise 47. Answer out loud: yes or no.   تَمْرِين ٤٧ . أَجِيبُوا شَفَهِيًّا: نَعَمْ أَمْ لَا .

١ . هَلْ مَارِي هِيَ أُسْتَاذَةُ ٱلْفَرَنْسِيَّة؟

٢ . هَلْ دِينَا هِيَ أُخْت سَلْمَان؟

٣ . هَلْ سَلْمَان كَسْلَان؟

٤ . هَلْ سَلْمَان يُحِبُّ ٱلْعَرَبِيَّة؟

٥ . هَلْ أَدِيبَة هِيَ وَالِدَة سَلْمَان؟

٦ . هَلْ مَارِي تَدْرُسُ ٱلْعَرَبِيَّة؟

٧ . هَلْ مَارِي هِيَ أُمّ أَدِيبَة؟

٨ . هَلْ سَلْمَان يُحِبُّ كُرَةَ ٱلْقَدَم؟

"Sun and moon letters"　أَلْحُرُوفُ ٱلشَّمْسِيَّة وَٱلْقَمَرِيَّة

In Arabic there are fourteen letters before which the ل of the definite article (ال) is not pronounced. The ل is written, but it is silent. To make up for this, each of these fourteen letters receives a شَدَّة. These letters are called أَلْحُرُوفُ ٱلشَّمْسِيَّة ("sun letters"). All the other fourteen letters are called أَلْحُرُوفُ ٱلْقَمَرِيَّة ("moon letters"); the ل of the definite article before the moon letters *is* pronounced. Naming these letters after *sun* and *moon* is a mnemonic: The word شَمْس ("sun") starts with the letter ش, which is a sun letter, and the word قَمَر ("moon") starts with the letter ق, which is a moon letter.

The "sun letters" are:　أَلْحُرُوفُ ٱلشَّمْسِيَّة هِيَ:

س ش ن ل ت ث ط ظ ر ز ص ض د ذ

شَمْس ⟸ أَلشَّمْس ، سَلام ⟸ أَلسَّلام

The "moon letters" are:　أَلْحُرُوفُ ٱلْقَمَرِيَّة هِيَ:

أ ب ج ح خ ع غ ف ق ك م هـ و ي

قَمَر ⟸ أَلْقَمَر ، مَدِينة ⟸ أَلْمَدِينة

تَمْرِين ٤٨. أَضِيفُوا "أَلْـ" إِلَى ٱلْكَلِمَاتِ ٱلتَّالِيَة وَٱنْتَبِهُوا إِلَى ٱلْحُرُوفِ ٱلشَّمْسِيَّة.

Exercise 48. Add the definite article to the following words. Pay attention to the

"sun letters."

٢. طَالِب _____		١. دَرْس أَلدَّرْس	
٤. نَهَار _____		٣. مَرِيض أَلْمَرِيض	
٦. سَاعَة _____		٥. حُرِّيَّة _____	
٨. غَرْب _____		٧. تَأْرِيخ _____	
١٠. تِمْثَال _____		٩. أَكْل _____	
١٢. فِكْرَة _____		١١. صَبَاح _____	
١٤. جَامِعَة _____		١٣. مَطْعَم _____	

ضَرَبَنِي وَبَكَى سَبَقَنِي وَٱشْتَكَى.

He hit me and cried, and was ahead of me to complain.

UNIT 5

تَعَلَّمُوا هٰذِهِ ٱلْمُفْرَدَات

science	عِلْم (ج) عُلُوم	medicine	أَلطِّبّ، طِبّ
policy, diplomacy, politics	سِيَاسَة	Baghdad	بَغْدَاد
Political Science	أَلْعُلُومُ ٱلسِّيَاسِيَّة	which, what?	أَيّ؟
to do	عَمِلَ (م) يَعْمَل	what? (before a verb)	مَاذَا؟
Praise be to God	أَلْحَمْدُ لله	to teach	عَلَّمَ (م) يُعَلِّم

تَمْرِين ١. إِمْلَؤُوا ٱلْفَرَاغ بِٱلْكَلِمَة ٱلْمُنَاسِبة.

Exercise 1. Fill in the blank with the appropriate word.

١. _____ تَعْمَلُ يَا سَامِي؟   (أَيّ ، مَاذَا ، مَا)

٢. أَنَا طَالِب وَأَدْرُسُ _____ .   (ٱلْجَامِعَة ، ٱلْمَسَاء ، ٱلطِّبّ)

٣. مَاذَا _____ يَا أَمَل؟   (تُعَلِّمِينَ ، بَغْدَاد ، أَلْحَمْدُ لله)

Exercise 2. Translate out loud.   تَمْرِين ٢. تَرْجِمُوا شَفَهِيًّا.

١. مَاذَا تُعَلِّمِينَ؟   ٢. أَلْعُلُومُ ٱلسِّيَاسِيَّة   ٣. أَدْرُسُ ٱلطِّبّ

٤. فِي أَيّ جَامِعَة؟   ٥. فِي جَامِعَة بَغْدَاد   ٦. مَاذَا تَعْمَلُ؟

إِسْتَمِعُوا إِلَى أَلْمُحَادَثَة ثُمَّ أَقْرَؤُوهَا .

Listen to the conversation, then read it.

أَنَا طَالِبَة

بَسَّام: أَلسَّلَامُ عَلَيْكُمْ .

أَمَل: وَعَلَيْكُمُ أَلسَّلَام، كَيْفَ حَالُكَ يَا سَامِي؟

بَسَّام: أَلْحَمْدُ لله أَنَا بِخَيْر وَكَيْفَ حَالُكِ أَنْتِ يَا أَمَل؟

أَمَل: أَلْحَمْدُ لله، بِخَيْر .

بَسَّام: مَاذَا تُعَلِّمِينَ يَا أَمَل؟

أَمَل: لَا أُعَلِّمُ، أَنَا طَالِبَة .

بَسَّام: طَالِبَة؟

أَمَل: نَعَمْ .

بَسَّام: فِي أَيِّ جَامِعَة؟

أَمَل: فِي جَامِعَة بَغْدَاد وَأَدْرُسُ أَلْعُلُومَ أَلسِّيَاسِيَّة .

بَسَّام: عَظِيم!

أَمَل: وَمَاذَا تَعْمَلُ أَنْتَ يَا سَامِي؟

بَسَّام: أَنَا طَالِب وَأَدْرُسُ أَلطِّبّ .

أَمَل: أَيْنَ؟ فِي جَامِعَة بَغْدَاد؟

بَسَّام: لَا. أَنَا طَالِب فِي جَامِعَة بَيْرُوت.

أَمَل: مُمْتَاز، مَا شَاءَ ٱلله.

The word جَامِعَة means university. When this word is followed by another noun such as the name of the university, it creates a noun–noun phrase.

In this structure the ة in the word جَامِعَة is pronounced as ت (*jami'at* ...):

Beirut University	جَامِعَة بَيْرُوت
Baghdad University	جَامِعَة بَغْدَاد

Exercise 3. Answer.   تَمْرِين ٣. أَجِيبُوا.

٢. مَاذَا تَعْمَلُ أَمَل؟   ١. مَاذَا يَعْمَلُ بَسَّام؟

٤. فِي أَيّ جَامِعَة تَدْرُسُ أَمَل؟   ٣. مَاذَا تَعْمَلُ أَنْتَ؟ / مَاذَا تَعْمَلِينَ أَنْتِ؟

٦. مَاذَا يَدْرُسُ بَسَّام؟   ٥. فِي أَيّ جَامِعَة يَدْرُسُ بَسَّام؟

أَيّ ...

The question word أَيّ means, **which, what, what kind of...** .

It can be followed by both masculine or feminine nouns:

Which boy?	أَيّ وَلَد؟
Which girl?	أَيّ بِنْت؟

مَاذَا؟

The question word مَاذَا means **what?** It comes before verbs.

What do you (*m. s.*) do?	مَاذَا تَعْمَلُ؟
What do you (*f. s.*) do?	مَاذَا تَعْمَلِينَ؟
What do you (*m. s.*) study?	مَاذَا تَدْرُسُ؟
What do you (*f. s.*) study?	مَاذَا تَدْرُسِينَ؟

Exercise 4. Translate out loud.   تَمْرِين ٤ . تَرْجِمُوا شَفَهِيًّا.

1. - What do you do, Marwan (*m.*)?

   - I am a professor.

2. - Is Marwan a student?

   - No. He is a professor.

3. - Are you (*f. s.*) a student?

   - Yes, I am a student.

4. - Is Nur (*f.*) a professor?

   - No. She is a student.

5. - What do you do, Amal?

   - I am a student at Baghdad University.

6. - Are you (*m. s.*) a professor, Sami?

   - No. I am a student.

7. - What do you study, Amal?

   - I study Political Science.

8. - What do you study, Bassam?

   - I study medicine.

تَمْرِين ٥. مَاذَا تُرِيدُونَ أَنْ تَعْرِفُوا عَنْ بَسَّام وَأَمَل؟ إِسْأَلُوهُمَا.

Exercise 5. What do you want to know about بَسَّام and أَمَل؟ Ask them.

إِسْمِي أَمَل   إِسْمِي بَسَّام

يَاءُ ٱلنِّسْبَة   *nisba* adjectives

In the phrase أَلْكَاتِبُ ٱلْمِصْرِيّ (*the Egyptian writer*), the word ٱلْمِصْرِيّ is an adjective. It modifies the word أَلْكَاتِبُ. In Arabic, as in English, we can create adjectives from nouns. This is done by adding يّ – to singular nouns. (The last letter of the noun takes كَسْرَة followed by يّ.) This يّ – is called يَاءُ ٱلنِّسْبَة.

noun		adjective	adjective		noun
Day	⟹	**Daily**	يَوْمِيّ	⟸	يَوْم
Month	⟹	**Monthly**	شَهْرِيّ	⟸	شَهْر
Egypt	⟹	**Egyptian**	مِصْرِيّ	⟸	مِصْر

تَمْرِين ٦ . كَوِّنُوا صِفَات مِنَ ٱلْأَسْمَاءِ ٱلتَّالِيَة .

Exercise 6. Create adjectives from the following nouns.

	science عِلْم	.٢	لُبْنَانِيّ	Lebanon لُبْنَان	.١
_____	gold ذَهَب	.٤	_____	people شَعْب	.٣
_____	month شَهْر	.٦	_____	Messiah مَسِيح	.٥
_____	east شَرْق	.٨	_____	history تَأْرِيخ	.٧

---

1. If a noun ends in ا or يا or ة – drop these endings before adding يَاءُ ٱلنِّسْبَة .

فَرَنْسِيّ	⇐	فَرَنْسَا	.١
سُورِيّ	⇐	سُورِيَا	.٢
سِيَاسِيّ	⇐	سِيَاسَة	.٣

2. If a name of a city or a country starts with the definite article, **drop the definite article** before adding يَاءُ ٱلنِّسْبَة .

عِرَاقِيّ	⇐	أَلْعِرَاق	.٤
يَمَنِيّ	⇐	أَلْيَمَن	.٥

Note: In the word أَلْمَانِيَا (*Germany*) the أَلْ is part of the word and not the definite article. Therefore you should not drop it when adding يَاءُ ٱلنِّسْبَة

أَلْمَانِيّ	⇐	أَلْمَانِيَا	.٦

Exercise 7. Write according to the example.   تَمْرِين ٧. أُكْتُبُوا حَسَبَ ٱلْمِثَال.

مُؤَنَّث (feminine)	مُذَكَّر (masculine)	
يَوْمِيَّة	يَوْمِيّ	١. يَوْم (day)
ــــــــــــ	ــــــــــــ	٢. شَهْر (month)
ــــــــــــ	ــــــــــــ	٣. سِيَاسَة (politics)
ــــــــــــ	ــــــــــــ	٤. أَلْيُونَان (Greece)
ــــــــــــ	ــــــــــــ	٥. غَرْب (west)
ــــــــــــ	ــــــــــــ	٦. شَمَال (north)
ــــــــــــ	ــــــــــــ	٧. جَنُوب (south)
ــــــــــــ	ــــــــــــ	٨. شَرْق (east)
ــــــــــــ	ــــــــــــ	٩. سُورِيَا (Syria)
ــــــــــــ	ــــــــــــ	١٠. أَلْعِرَاق (Iraq)
ــــــــــــ	ــــــــــــ	١١. ثَقَافَة (culture)
ــــــــــــ	ــــــــــــ	١٢. أَمْرِيكَا (America)
ــــــــــــ	ــــــــــــ	١٣. أُسْبُوع (week)
ــــــــــــ	ــــــــــــ	١٤. عَالَم (world)

تَمْرِين ٨. قُولُوا شَفَهِيًّا حَسَبَ ٱلْمِثَال ثُمَّ ٱكْتُبُوا.

Exercise 8. Say out loud according to the example, then write.

١. هُوَ مِنْ مِصْر.   هُوَ مِصْرِيّ.   هِيَ مِنْ مِصْر.   هِيَ مِصْرِيَّة.

٢. هُوَ مِنْ سُورِيا. هُوَ _____   هِيَ مِنْ سُورِيا. هِيَ _____

٣. هُوَ مِنْ تُونِس. هُوَ _____   هِيَ مِنْ تُونِس. هِيَ _____

٤. هُوَ مِنَ ٱلْكُوَيْت. هُوَ _____   هِيَ مِنَ ٱلْكُوَيْت. هِيَ _____

٥. هُوَ مِنْ لِيبِيا. هُوَ _____   هِيَ مِنْ لِيبِيا. هِيَ _____

٦. هُوَ مِنْ قَطَر. هُوَ _____   هِيَ مِنْ قَطَر. هِيَ _____

٧. هُوَ مِنْ إِيرَان. هُوَ _____   هِيَ مِنْ إِيرَان. هِيَ _____

٨. هُوَ مِنَ ٱلْجَزَائِر. هُوَ _____   هِيَ مِنَ ٱلْجَزَائِر. هِيَ _____

The countries in the exercise above are feminine. The following are masculine:

أَلْعِرَاق ، لُبْنَان ، أَلأُرْدُنّ ، أَلْمَغْرِب ، أَلْيَمَن ، أَلسُّودَان

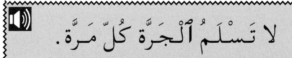

لا تَسْلَمُ ٱلْجَرَّة كُلّ مَرَّة.

The jar will not be safe every time.

تَعَلَّمُوا هٰذِهِ ٱلْمُفْرَدات

you (f. s.) want	تُرِيدِينَ	Please (addressing m. s.)	مِنْ فَضْلِكَ
after (time)	بَعْدَ	What time is it?	كَمِ ٱلسَّاعَة؟
religion	دِين (ج) أَدْيَان	ninth	تَاسِع (m.)، تَاسِعَة (f.)
to you, you have (m. s.)	لَكَ	eighth	ثَامِن (m.)، ثَامِنَة (f.)
to you, you have (f. s.)	لَكِ	exactly, sharp (time)	تَمَامًا
he was born	وُلِدَ	breakfast	فُطُور، إفْطَار
I was born	وُلِدْتُ	engineering	أَلْهَنْدَسَة، هَنْدَسَة
coffee	أَلْقَهْوَة، قَهْوَة	philosophy	أَلْفَلْسَفَة، فَلْسَفَة
now	أَلآن	Christian	مَسِيحِيّ (ج) مَسِيحِيُّونَ
where (place)	حَيْثُ	Muslim	مُسْلِم (ج) مُسْلِمُونَ
Friday	يَوْمُ ٱلْجُمْعَة	to return	رَجَعَ (م) يَرْجِعُ

تَمْرِين ٩ . أَحِيطُوا ٱلتَّرْجَمَةَ ٱلصَّحِيحَة .   Exercise 9. Circle the correct translation.

Please (addressing *m. s.*) / Please (addressing *f. s.*)   ١. مِنْ فَضْلِكَ

How many hours? / What time is it?   ٢. كَمِ ٱلسَّاعَة؟

Good afternoon. / Good morning.   ٣. صَبَاحُ ٱلْخَيْر

He is Russian. / He is a Christian.   ٤. هُوَ مَسِيحِيّ.

How are you (*m. s.*)? / How are you (*f. s.*)?   ٥. كَيْفَ حَالُكِ؟

This is a great idea. / This is a bad idea.   ٦. هٰذِهِ فِكْرَة مُمْتَازَة.

Do you (*f. s.*) want coffee? / Do you (*f. s.*) want tea?   ٧. هَلْ تُرِيدِينَ ٱلْقَهْوَة؟

God willing / Whatever God has given! (amazing!)   ٨. مَا شَاءَ ٱلله!

He has a boy in Morocco. / She was born in Morocco.   ٩. وُلِدَتْ فِي ٱلْمَغْرِب.

Good evening. / the evening is good.   ١٠. مَسَاءُ ٱلْخَيْر

Before breakfast / After breakfast   ١١. بَعْدَ ٱلْفُطُور

Engineering and computers / computer engineering   ١٢. هَنْدَسَةُ ٱلْكُمْبِيُوتِر

Listen to the conversation, then read it.   إِسْتَمِعُوا إِلَى ٱلْمُحَادَثَةِ ثُمَّ ٱقْرَؤُوهَا .

أَدْرُسُ هَنْدَسَةَ ٱلْكُمبِيُوتِر .

لِنْدَا :   مِنْ فَضْلِكَ يَا خَالِد، كَمِ ٱلسَّاعَةُ ٱلْآن؟

خَالِد :   أَلسَّاعَةُ ٱلثَّامِنَةُ تَمَامًا .

لِنْدَا :   شُكْرًا، وَمَتَى سَنَذْهَبُ إِلَى جَامِعَةِ كُولُومبِيَا؟

خَالِد :   فِي ٱلسَّاعَةِ ٱلتَّاسِعَة، بَعْدَ ٱلْفُطُور .

لِنْدَا :   مَاذَا تَدْرُسُ فِي ٱلْجَامِعَة؟

خَالِد :   أَدْرُسُ هَنْدَسَةَ ٱلْكُمبِيُوتِر وَٱلْعُلُومَ ٱلسِّيَاسِيَّة .

لِنْدَا :   مَا شَاءَ ٱلله!

خَالِد :   هَلْ أَنْتِ طَالِبَةٌ فِي ٱلْجَامِعَة؟

لِنْدَا :   نَعَمْ، أَدْرُسُ فِي ٱلْجَامِعَةِ ٱلْأَمْرِيكِيَّةِ فِي وَاشِنْطِن دِي سِي .

خَالِد :   وَمَاذَا تَدْرُسِينَ؟

لِنْدَا :   أَدْرُسُ ٱللُّغَةَ ٱلْعَرَبِيَّة وَٱلْفَلْسَفَة وَٱلدِّينَ ٱلْإِسْلامِيّ .

خَالِد :   مُمْتَاز! هَلْ أَنْتِ مُسْلِمَة؟

لِنْدَا :   لا، أَنَا مَسِيحِيَّة، وَأَنْتَ؟

خَالِد: أَنَا مُسْلِم.

لِنْدَا: هَلْ وُلِدْتَ فِي أَمْرِيكَا؟

خَالِد: نَعَم، وُلِدْتُ فِي نِيو يُورك. وَأَنْتِ؟

لِنْدَا: أَنَا وُلِدْتُ فِي لُوس أَنْجِلِيس.

خَالِد: هٰذِهِ مَدِينَة جَمِيلَة... هَلْ تُرِيدِينَ ٱلْقَهْوَة يَا لِنْدَا؟

لِنْدَا: هٰذِهِ فِكْرَة مُمْتَازَة، شُكْرًا لَكَ.

Exercise 10. Ask your classmates.   تَمْرِين ١٠. إِسْأَلُوا زُمَلَاءَكُمْ.

٢. مَاذَا تَدْرُسُ لِنْدَا؟   ١. مَاذَا يَدْرُسُ خَالِد؟

٤. أَيْنَ وُلِدَتْ لِنْدَا؟   ٣. أَيْنَ وُلِدَ خَالِد؟

٦. أَيْنَ ٱلْجَامِعَة ٱلْأَمْرِيكِيَّة؟   ٥. أَيْنَ جَامِعَة كُولُومبِيَا؟

تَمْرِين ١١. أُكْتُبُوا فِي دَفَاتِرِكُمْ ثَلَاثَة أَسْئِلَة عَنْ لِنْدَا وَخَالِد ثُمَّ أَجِيبُوا عَنْهَا.

Exercise 11. Write in your notebooks three questions about خَالِد and لِنْدَا

and answer them.

تَمْرين ١٢. حَدِّدُوا ٱلْجُمَلَ ٱلصَّحِيحَةَ عَنْ لِنْدَا وَخَالِد.

Exercise 12. Identify the correct sentences about لِنْدَا and خَالِد.

١. يَسْكُنُ خَالِد فِي مَدِينَةِ نِيو يورك.	١. تَسْكُنُ لِنْدَا فِي وِلَايَةِ نِيو يورك.
٢. يَدْرُسُ ٱلدِّينَ ٱلْإِسْلَامِيّ.	٢. تَدْرُسُ هَنْدَسَةَ ٱلْكُمْبِيُوتِر.
٣. خَالِد مُسْلِم.	٣. لِنْدَا مَسِيحِيَّة.
٤. خَالِد يُرِيدُ ٱلْقَهْوَة.	٤. لِنْدَا تُرِيدُ ٱلْقَهْوَة.
٥. وَالِد خَالِد أَمْرِيكِيّ.	٥. تَتَكَلَّمُ لِنْدَا مَعَ خَالِد فِي ٱلْمَسَاء.
٦. وُلِدَ خَالِد فِي جَامِعَةِ كُولُومبِيَا.	٦. وُلِدَتْ لِنْدَا فِي لُوس أَنْجِلِيس.

تَمْرِين ١٣. إِسْأَلُوا زُمَلَاءَكُمْ عَنْ مَكَانِ ٱلْوِلَادَةِ حَسَبَ ٱلْمِثَال.

Exercise 13. Ask your classmates about their place of birth according to the
     example.

أَيْنَ وُلِدْتَ يَا جُون؟   وُلِدْتُ فِي وِلَايَة ...   فِي مَدِينَة ...

أَيْنَ وُلِدْتِ يَا سَارَة؟   وُلِدْتُ فِي وِلَايَة ...   فِي مَدِينَة ...

What time is it?	كَمِ ٱلسَّاعَة؟

The question word كَمْ can also be used to ask about time, age and price.

What time is it?	كَمِ ٱلسَّاعَة؟
How old are you? (Literally: What is your age?)	كَمْ عُمْرُكَ؟
How much is the car? (Literally: What is the price of the car?)	كَمْ سِعْرُ ٱلسَّيَّارَة؟

Days of the week	أَيَّامُ ٱلْأُسْبُوع

Wednesday	يَوْمُ ٱلْأَرْبِعَاء	Sunday	يَوْمُ ٱلْأَحَد
Thursday	يَوْمُ ٱلْخَمِيس	Monday	يَوْمُ ٱلاثْنَيْنِ
Friday	يَوْمُ ٱلْجُمْعَة	Tuesday	يَوْمُ ٱلثَّلَاثَاء
		Saturday	يَوْمُ ٱلسَّبْت

Note: In speaking it is possible to omit the word يَوْم and to use only the
second word. Example: أَلْخَمِيس instead of يَوْمُ ٱلْخَمِيس.

Possessive pronouns　ضَمَائِرُ ٱلْمُلْكِيَّة

Personal possession (for example, "**my** mother" or "**her** father") is expressed by pronoun suffixes attached to the noun. Here are the possessive pronouns:

ours	نَا	(نَحْنُ)	my	ي ‍ـ	(أَنَا)
your (m. pl.)	كُمْ	(أَنْتُمْ)	your (m. s.)	كَ	(أَنْتَ)
your (f. pl.)	كُنَّ	(أَنْتُنَّ)	your (f. s.)	كِ	(أَنْتِ)
their (m.)	هُمْ	(هُمْ)	his	هُ	(هُوَ)
their (f.)	هُنَّ	(هُنَّ)	her	هَا	(هِيَ)

your (dual m.& f.)　كُمَا　(أَنْتُمَا)

their (dual m.& f.)　هُمَا　(هُمَا)

هٰذِهِ أُسْرَتِي .

هٰذَا وَالِدِي وَهٰذِهِ وَالِدَتِي

وَهٰذَا أَخِي وَهٰذِهِ أُخْتِي .

How do you attach a possessive pronoun suffix to a noun?

Add ُ — to the last letter of the noun (except for the first-person singular, which

takes —) and then attach the appropriate possessive pronoun suffix:

كِتَاب + هَا   ⟸   كِتَابُهَا *her book*

As you previously learned (U. 2, p. 78), when attaching a possessive pronoun to a

noun that ends with ة, the ة changes into ت :

مَدِينَة + هَا   ⟸   مَدِينَتُهَا *her city*

بَيْت + ضَمَائِرُ ٱلْمُلْكِيَّة

بَيْت + possessive pronouns

Dual	Pl.	S.
	بَيْتُنَا	بَيْتِي
بَيْتُكُمَا	بَيْتُكُم	بَيْتُكَ
	بَيْتُكُنَّ	بَيْتُكِ
بَيْتُهُمَا	بَيْتُهُم	بَيْتُه
بَيْتُهُمَا	بَيْتُهُنَّ	بَيْتُهَا

تَمْرِين ١٤. أَضِيفُوا ضَمَائِرَ ٱلْمُلْكِيَّة لِلْأَسْمَاءِ ٱلتَّالِيَة شَفَهِيًّا ثُمَّ ٱكْتُبُوا ٱلتَّصْرِيف.

Exercise 14. Attach possessive pronoun suffixes (as shown above) to the following nouns out loud, then write them.

٣. كُتُب   ٢. مَدِينَة   ١. دَار

There are other instances where — or — can be attached to the last letter of a noun before attaching the possessive pronoun suffix. This depends on the noun's grammatical function in the sentence and does not change the meaning.

She went to her home.   ذَهَبَتْ إِلَى بَيْتِهَا.

I saw her home.   رَأَيْتُ بَيْتَهَا.

تَمْرِين ١٥. أَضِيفُوا ضَمَائِرَ ٱلْمُلْكِيَّة حَسَبَ ٱلْمِثَال.

Exercise 15. Attach the possessive pronouns according to the example.

٢. هَدِيَّة (هُمَا) ــــــــــــ   ١. أَوْلَاد (أَنَا) أَوْلَادِي

٤. قَلْب (هُوَ) ــــــــــــ   ٣. سَيَّارَة (هِيَ) ــــــــــــ

٦. إِسْم (هِيَ) ــــــــــــ   ٥. أُسْتَاذ (نَحْنُ) ــــــــــــ

٨. رَفِيق (هُمْ) ــــــــــــ   ٧. فِكْرَة (أَنْتُمْ) ــــــــــــ

تَعَلَّمُوا هٰذِهِ ٱلْمُفْرَدَات

God willing	إِنْ شَاءَ ٱلله	I will see you (*m. s.*)	سَأَرَاكَ
way, road	طَرِيق (ج) طُرُق	soon	قَرِيبًا
Thank you very much	شُكْرًا جَزِيلاً	seventh	سَابِع، سَابِعَة
to convey, inform	بَلَّغَ (م) يُبَلِّغُ	half	نِصْف
Give my regards	بَلِّغْ سَلامِي	in the evening	مَسَاءً
See you	إِلَى ٱللِّقَاء	visit	زِيَارَة (ج) زِيَارَات
also	أَيْضًا	pretty, beautiful	جَمِيل
to enjoy	إِسْتَمْتَعَ (م) يَسْتَمْتِعُ	duty, homework	وَاجِب
		from me	مِنِّي

تَمْرِين ١٦. إِمْلَؤُوا ٱلْفَرَاغَ بِٱلْكَلِمَة ٱلْمُنَاسِبَة.

Exercise 16. Fill in the blank with the appropriate word.

١. نَحْنُ فِي _____ إِلَى وَاشِنْطن.   (ٱلطَّرِيق ، ٱلْوَاجِب ، ٱلصَّفّ)

٢. شُكْرًا _____ لَكَ مِنِّي وَمِنْ لِنْدَا.   (قَرِيبًا ، مَسَاءً ، جَزِيلاً)

٣. لا شُكْرَ عَلَى _____ .   (دَجَاج ، وَاجِب ، أَحْسَن)

٤. نَحْنُ _____ ٱسْتَمْتَعْنَا بِزِيَارَتِكُمْ.   (شُكْرًا ، قَرِيبًا ، أَيْضًا)

٥. سَأَرَاكَ فِي وَاشِنْطن _____ إِنْ شَاءَ ٱلله.   (قَرِيبًا ، زِيَارَة ، مِنِّي)

٦. بَلِّغْ _____ إِلَى ٱلْوَالِد وَٱلْوَالِدَة.   (سَأَرَاكَ ، سَلامِي ، نِصْف)

Exercise 17. Translate into English.   تَمْرِين ١٧. تَرْجِمُوا إِلَى ٱلْإِنْجْلِيزِيَّة.

٢. لا شُكْرَ عَلَى وَاجِب.   ١. شُكْرًا جَزِيلاً لَكَ.

٤. إِسْتَمْتَعْنَا بِزِيَارَتِكُمْ.   ٣. زِيَارَة جَمِيلَة

٦. بَلِّغْ سَلامِي.   ٥. إِنْ شَاءَ ٱلله.

٨. إِلَى ٱللِّقَاء.   ٧. سَأَرَاكَ قَرِيبًا.

١٠. أَلْعَمَّة مَاجِدَة   ٩. أَلْخَال حُسَيْن

Listen to the conversation, then read it.   إِسْتَمِعُوا إِلَى ٱلْمُحَادَثَةِ ثُمَّ ٱقْرَؤُوهَا .

سَأَرَاكَ قَرِيبًا إِنْ شَاءَ ٱلله

كَرِيـم: أَلُو، سَلْمَان؟

سَلْمَان: نَعَمْ يَا كَرِيم، أَيْنَ أَنْتُمْ؟

كَرِيـم: نَحْنُ فِي ٱلطَّرِيقِ إِلَى وَاشِنْطن، شُكْرًا جَزِيلاً لَكَ مِنِّي وَمِنْ لِنْدَا وَمِنْ سَلِيم عَلَى هٰذِهِ ٱلزِّيَارَةِ ٱلْجَمِيلَةِ لِنِيو يُورك .

سَلْمَان: لَا شُكْرَ عَلَى وَاجِب . نَحْنُ أَيْضًا ٱسْتَمْتَعْنَا بِزِيَارَتِكُمْ .

كَرِيـم: سَأَرَاكَ فِي وَاشِنْطن قَرِيبًا إِنْ شَاءَ ٱلله .

سَلْمَان: إِنْ شَاءَ ٱلله .

كَرِيـم: بَلِّغْ سَلَامِي إِلَى ٱلْوَالِد وَٱلْوَالِدَة وَٱلأَخ خَالِد، وَٱلأُخْت خُلُود، وَأَيْضًا إِلَى ٱلْخَال حُسَيْن وَٱلْعَمَّة مَاجِدَة .

سَلْمَان: شُكْرًا لَكَ وَإِلَى ٱللِّقَاء فِي وَاشِنْطن .

كَرِيـم: إِلَى ٱللِّقَاء .

لا شُكْر عَلَى وَاجِب.

A polite answer to شُكْرًا is: لا شُكْر عَلَى وَاجِب *There is no need for thanks; it is my duty.*

God willing.   إِنْ شَاءَ أَلله.

The statement إِنْ شَاءَ أَلله is used to acknowledge that things can happen only by the will of God (ALLaah). This statement is widely used in the Arab countries regarding any future plans or actions. Sometimes it can also express a polite rejection of one's request, since it is hard in the Arab culture to say "no" to a friend.

Exercise 18. True or false.   تَمْرِين ١٨. صَوَاب أَمْ خَطَأ.

خَطَأ	صَوَاب	
◯	◯	١. سَافَرَ كَرِيم إِلَى نِيو يُورك بِأَلْقِطَار (train).
◯	◯	٢. لِكَرِيم أَخ وَأُخْت.
◯	◯	٣. أَلْمُحَادَثَة هِيَ بَيْنَ كَرِيمَ وَسَلْمَان.
◯	◯	٤. خُلُود هِيَ وَالِدَة سَلْمَان.
◯	◯	٥. سَيَزُورُ سَلْمَان وَاشِنْطن يَوْمَ أَلثُّلاثَاء.
◯	◯	٦. مَاجِدَة هِيَ عَمَّة سَلْمَان.

The pronunciation of ل in أَللّٰه

You have noticed that in the phrase إِنْ شَاءَ ٱلله the ل in أَللّٰه is emphatic (similar to the sound of the l in law). This emphatic sound of the ل exists only in the word أَللّٰه. Here are some more examples:

What God has given! (Amazing).	١ . مَا شَاءَ ٱلله .
There is no god but God (ALLaah).	٢ . لَا إِلٰهَ إِلَّا ٱلله .
I swear by God the great!	٣ . وَٱلله ٱلْعَظِيم!
O God!	٤ . أَللّٰهُمَّ!
God forbid!	٥ . لَا سَمَحَ ٱلله!
God is the greatest.	٦ . ٱللهُ أَكْبَر .

Note: When the word أَللّٰه is preceded by كَسْرة the ل is pronounced regularly. Here are some examples:

Praise be to God.	١ . أَلْحَمْدُ لله .
God forbid!	٢ . أَعُوذُ بِٱلله!
In the name of God	٣ . بِسْمِ ٱلله
For God's sake, I beg you (m. s.).	٤ . بِٱلله عَلَيْكَ

Exercise 19. Fill in the blank.   تَمْرِين ١٩. إِمْلَؤُوا ٱلْفَرَاغَ.

> تِمْثَالَ ، فِيلْمًا ، جَامِعَةَ ، مَاجِدَةَ ، ٱلسَّاعَةَ
>
> ٱلْمَدِينَةِ ، ٱلْعَامَّةَ ، سَلْمَان ، إِلَى ، ٱلْكَبَاب

كَرِيم ولِنْدَا وَسَلِيم سَافَرُوا يَوْمَ ٱلْخَمِيس لِزِيَارَة ـــــــــــ فِي

بِرُوكْلِين وَتَعَرَّفُوا عَلَى أُسْرَتِهِ، عَلَى ٱلْأَخ خَالِد وَٱلْأُخْت خُلُود وَٱلْخَال

حُسَيْن وَٱلْعَمَّة ـــــــــــ. بَعْدَ ٱلْأَكْل ذَهَبُوا ـــــــــــ

ٱلسِّينَمَا فِي مَرْكَزِ ـــــــــــ وَشَاهَدُوا ـــــــــــ عَنْ

تَأْرِيخِ ٱلْإِسْلام. يَوْمَ ٱلْجُمْعَة ذَهَبُوا إِلَى مَانْهَاتِن وَزَارُوا ـــــــــــ

كُولُومْبِيَا حَيْثُ يَدْرُسُ خَالِد، ثُمَّ زَارُوا ـــــــــــ ٱلْحُرِّيَّة

وَٱلْمَكْتَبَة ـــــــــــ. وَفِي ٱلْمَسَاء، فِي ـــــــــــ

ٱلْخَامِسَة، ذَهَبُوا إِلَى مَطْعَم خَال سَلْمَان فِي مَرْكَز بِرُوكْلِين وَأَكَلُوا

هُنَاكَ ـــــــــــ وَٱلسَّلَطَة وَٱلْفَلَافِل وَٱلْخُبْزَ ٱلْعَرَبِيّ وَٱلْبَقْلَاوَة.

بَعْدَ هٰذِهِ ٱلزِّيَارَة ٱلْجَمِيلَة رَجَعَ كَرِيم ولِنْدَا وَسَلِيم إِلَى وَاشِنْطِن.

تَمْرِين ٢٠. إِمْلَؤُوا ٱلْفَرَاغ بِٱلْكَلِمَة ٱلْمُنَاسِبَة.

Exercise 20. Fill in the blank with the appropriate word.

١. لِخَالِي مَطْعَم شَرْقِيّ فِي ــــــــــ.   (ٱلْبَيْت ، ٱلْمَدِينَة ، ٱلظُّهْر)

٢. أَيْنَ ــــــــــ إِلَى ٱلْمَطْعَم؟   (ٱلطَّالِب ، ٱلظُّهْر ، ٱلطَّرِيق)

٣. أَكَلْنَا ٱلْفَلَافِل وَٱلْكَبَاب ــــــــــ.   (وَٱلسَّلَطَة ، وَٱلْمَطار ، وَٱلْبَنْك)

٤. هٰذَا ــــــــــ ٱلْكَبِير، خَالِد.   (وَالِدِي ، أُخْتِي ، أَخِي)

٥. هٰذَا خَالِي وَهٰذِه ــــــــــ.   (عَمِّي ، عَمَّتِي ، أُسْتَاذِي)

٦. بَلِّغْ ــــــــــ إِلَى ٱلْوَالِد وَٱلْوَالِدَة.   (أُسْتَاذِي ، سَلامِي ، عَمِّي)

٧. شَاهَدُوا ــــــــــ عَنْ تَأْرِيخِ ٱلْإِسْلام.   (شُكْرًا ، مَسَاءً ، فِيْلْمًا)

٨. زَارُوا ــــــــــ كُولُومبِيَا.   (جَامِعَة ، سَاعَة ، زِيَارَة)

Listen to the text, then read it.

إِسْتَمِعُوا إِلَى ٱلنَّصّ ثُمَّ ٱقْرَؤُوهُ.

دِينَا وَأُسْرَتُهَا

أَهْلاً. أَنَا دِينَا. أَنَا بِنْت أَمْرِيكِيَّة مِنْ أَصْل كُوَيْتِيّ. هٰذِهِ أُسْرَتِي. هٰذَا وَالِدِي زَكِيّ وَهٰذِهِ وَالِدَتِي كَوْثَر. وُلِدَ وَالِدِي بِٱلْكُوَيْت وَوُلِدَتْ وَالِدَتِي بِلُبْنَان. وَالِدِي طَبِيب أَسْنَان وَوَالِدَتِي مُهَنْدِسَة وتُدَرِّس ٱلْهَنْدَسَة في ٱلْجَامِعَة. لِأُسْرَتِي ثَلاثَة بُيُوت، بَيْت بِأَمْرِيكا وبَيْت بِٱلْكُوَيْت وبَيْت بِلُبْنَان.

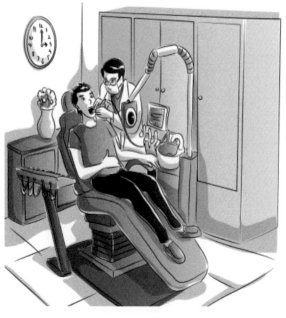

Exercise 21. Answer out loud: yes or no.   تَمْرِين ٢١. أَجِيبُوا شَفَهِيًّا: نَعَمْ أَمْ لَا.

٢. هَلْ دِينَا تَدْرُسُ ٱلْهَنْدَسَة؟   ١. هَلْ دِينَا كُوَيْتِيَّة؟

٤. هَلْ وَالِدَة دِينَا لُبْنَانِيَّة؟   ٣. هَلْ وَالِد دِينَا سُورِيّ؟

٦. هَلْ لِأُسْرَة دِينَا بَيْت بِلُبْنَان؟   ٥. هَلْ دِينَا هِيَ وَالِدَة زَكِيّ؟

٨. هَلْ زَكِيّ كَاتِب؟   ٧. هَلْ وَالِدَة دِينَا تُدَرِّسُ ٱلْهَنْدَسَة؟

بِنْت أَمْرِيكِيَّة مِنْ أَصْل كُوَيْتِيّ.

In the Arab world a person is identified as Kuwaiti or Egyptian according to the origin of his or her father. In the text دِينَا identifies herself as Kuwaiti.

This writer	هٰذَا ٱلْكَاتِب	⇐	this	هٰذَا ٱلـ ...
This is a writer.	هٰذَا كَاتِب	⇐	this is	هٰذَا ...

🔊 إِنْسَان بِلَا عَمَل كَشَجَرَة بِلَا ثَمَر.

A person without work is like a tree without the fruit.

Exercise 22. Read and translate out loud.   تَمْرِين ٢٢ . إقْرَؤُوا وَتَرْجِمُوا شَفَهِيًّا .

٢. هٰذَا ٱلدُّكْتُور مِنْ لُبْنَان .   ١. هٰذَا دُكْتُور .

٤. هٰذِه ٱلْهَدِيَّة جَمِيلَة .   ٣. هٰذِه هَدِيَّة .

٦. هٰذِه ٱلْأُسْتَاذَة جَدِيدَة .   ٥. هٰذِه أُسْتَاذَة .

٨. هٰذَا ٱلْكَاتِب لُبْنَانِيّ .   ٧. هٰذَا كَاتِب لُبْنَانِيّ .

١٠. هٰذَا ٱلْكَلْب كَبِير .   ٩. هٰذَا كَلْب كَبِير .

تَمْرِين ٢٣ . تَرْجِمُوا شَفَهِيًّا حَسَبَ ٱلْمِثَال ثُمَّ ٱكْتُبُوا ٱلتَّرْجَمَة فِي دَفَاتِرِكُمْ .

Exercise 23. Translate out loud according to the example, then write the translation
    in your notebooks.

This is my teacher (f.)   هٰذِه أُسْتَاذَتِي   This is my house. . هٰذَا بَيْتِي

1. This is her teacher.   1. This is our house.

2. This is our teacher.   2. This is his house.

3. This is their (dual m.) teacher.   3. This is your (m. pl.) house.

4. This is their (m.) teacher.   4. This is her house.

5. This is his teacher.   5. This is their (m. pl.) house.

6. This is your (f. pl.) teacher.   6. This is your (f. s.) house.

7. This is your (m. s.) teacher.   7. This is your (dual m.) house.

تَمْرِين ٢٤. تَرْجِمُوا شَفَهِيًّا ثُمَّ ٱكْتُبُوا ٱلتَّرْجَمَة.

Exercise 24. Translate out loud, then write the translation.

1. This is a writer (*f.*). _____

2. This writer (*f.*) is Lebanese. _____

3. This is an Egyptian professor (*m.*)._____

4. This gift is from my father. _____

5. Where is this professor from?_____

6. Is this your dog (*m.*)? _____

7. Yes. This is my dog. _____

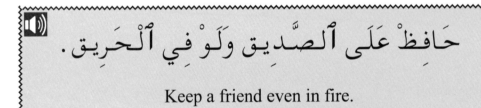

حَافِظْ عَلَى ٱلصَّدِيق وَلَوْ فِي ٱلْحَرِيق.

Keep a friend even in fire.

أَلْمَعْرِفَةُ وَٱلنَّكِرَةُ فِي ٱلْأَسْمَاءِ وَٱلصِّفَاتِ

Definite and indefinite nouns and adjectives

A noun can be either definite (مَعْرِفَة) or indefinite (نَكِرَة).

A noun is definite when:

1. It has the definite article: أَلْمَطْعَم ، أَلرِّسَالَة ، أَلطُّلَّاب

2. It has a possessive suffix: كِتَابُهُ ، بَيْتُنَا ، أُسْتَاذَتِي

3. It is the first noun of a noun-noun phrase إِضَافَة, in which the second
   noun is definite: بَيْتُ ٱلطَّالِب ، بِنْتُ خَالِد ، سَيَّارَةُ أُسْتَاذِنَا

4. It is a proper noun: أَلْقَاهِرَة، مِصْرِيًا ، إِبْرَاهِيم

5. It is preceded by the vocative يَ :   وَلَد يَ ا أُسْتَاذ

Note:

1. A noun cannot have more than one marker of definiteness. Therefore,
   you cannot add the definite article to a proper noun, to a noun that has a
   possessive suffix, or to the first noun in a noun-noun phrase, إِضَافَة.

2. In proper nouns such as أَلْعِرَاق, أَلْأُرْدُنّ, أَلْقُدْس, the definite article is
   part of the name, but still the أَلِف takes وَصْلَة if it is preceded by a
   letter or a word: إِلَى ٱلْعِرَاق

تَمْرِين ٢٥ . جِدُوا أَسْمَاء وَصِفَات مُعَرَّفَة فِي ٱلنَّصّ (صَفْحَة ١٨٤) وَحَدِّدُوا
نَوْعَ ٱلتَّعْرِيف .

Exercise 25. Find definite nouns and adjectives in the text (p. 184) and
   identify the kind of definition.

تَعَلَّمُوا هٰذِهِ ٱلْمُفْرَدَات

to call	إِتَّصَلَ بِ (م) يَتَّصِلُ بِ	then, and then	ثُمَّ
to drink	شَرِبَ (م) يَشْرَبُ	childhood	طُفُولَة
the coming, next	أَلْقَادِم	shadow	ظِلّ
to travel	سَافَرَ (م) يُسَافِرُ	we have, to us	لَنَا
museum	مَتْحَف (ج) مَتَاحِف	to eat	أَكَلَ (م) يَأْكُلُ
friend	صَدِيق (ج) أَصْدِقَاء	train	قِطَار
library	مَكْتَبَة (ج) مَكْتَبَات	soon	قَرِيبًا
philosophy	أَلْفَلْسَفَة ، فَلْسَفَة	Palestine	فِلَسْطِين
month	شَهْر (ج) شُهُور، أَشْهُر	high school	مَدْرَسَة ثَانَوِيَّة
		together	مَعًا

تَمْرين ٢٦. أَحِيطُوا ٱلتَّرْجَمَةَ ٱلصَّحِيحَة.

Exercise 26. Circle the correct translation

١.   كُلّ يَوْم خَمِيس
   On Thursday / Every Thursday

٢.   أَلْعُلُومُ ٱلسِّيَاسِيَّة
   Political Science / Sciences & Politics

٣.   مَدْرَسَة ثَانَوِيَّة
   Elementary school / High school

٤.   فِي ٱلصَّبَاح
   In the morning / In the evening

٥.   يَوْمُ ٱلثُّلاثَاء
   Tuesday / Monday

٦.   مِنْ أَصْل فِلَسْطِينِيّ
   Of Palestinian descent / From Palestine

٧.   فِي ٱلشَّهْرِ ٱلْقَادِم
   This month / Next month

٨.   أَلدِّينُ ٱلإِسْلامِيّ
   The Islamic religion / Islam and Judaism

٩.   سَنُسَافِرُ مَعًا.
   We traveled together. / We will travel together.

١٠. صَدِيق طُفُولَتِي
   My childhood friend / My childhood friends

١١. سَأَتَّصِلُ بِسَلْمَان.
   I called Salman. / I will call Salman.

١٢. إِنْ شَاءَ ٱلله.
   God willing. / What God has given! (Amazing).

Listen to the text, then read it.

إِسْتَمِعُوا إِلَى ٱلنَّصِّ ثُمَّ ٱقْرَؤُوهُ.

سَانْدْرَا وَصَدِيقَاتُهَا

إِسْمِي سَانْدْرَا وَأَسْكُنُ فِي مَدِينَةِ وَاشِنْطُن دِي سِي. كُلَّ يَوْمِ خَمِيسٍ فِي ٱلصَّبَاحِ أَذْهَبُ مَعَ صَدِيقَتِي لِيسَا وَصَدِيقَتِي لَطِيفَة إِلَى ٱلْجَامِعَة. نَحْنُ طَالِبَاتٌ فِي ٱلْجَامِعَةِ ٱلْأَمْرِيكِيَّة. أَنَا أَدْرُسُ ٱلْفَلْسَفَة وَٱلدِّينَ ٱلْإِسْلامِيَّ وَٱلْعَرَبِيَّةَ وَلِيسَا تَدْرُسُ ٱلْعُلُومَ ٱلسِّيَاسِيَّة وَٱللُّغَةَ ٱلْعَرَبِيَّةَ وَلَطِيفَة تَدْرُسُ ٱلْعَرَبِيَّةَ وَٱلتَّأْرِيخ. لَنَا أُسْتَاذَة مُمْتَازَة لِلُّغَةِ ٱلْعَرَبِيَّةِ ٱسْمُهَا رِيمَا. هِيَ تَسْكُنُ فِي نَفْسِ ٱلْمَدِينَةِ بِٱلْقُرْبِ مِنَ ٱلْجَامِعَة. رِيمَا أُرْدُنِّيَة مِنْ أَصْلٍ فِلَسْطِينِيّ. لِلْأُسْتَاذَة رِيمَا ثَلاثَةُ أَوْلاد وَهُمْ يَدْرُسُونَ فِي مَدْرَسَةٍ ثَانَوِيَّة. يَوْمَ ٱلثُّلاثَاء ذَهَبْنَا أَنَا ولِيسَا وَلَطِيفَة إِلَى مَكْتَبَةِ ٱلْكُونغْرِيسِ ثُمَّ أَكَلْنَا وَشَرِبْنَا فِي مَطْعَمِ شَرْقِيّ قَرِيبٍ مِنَ ٱلْجَامِعَة. فِي ٱلشَّهْرِ ٱلْقَادِم سَنُسَافِرُ مَعًا بِٱلْقِطَار، إِنْ شَاءَ ٱلله، إِلَى مَدِينَة نِيو يورك لِزِيَارَةِ ٱلْمَرْكَزِ ٱلْإِسْلامِيّ وَمَتْحَفِ ٱلْمِتْرُوبُولِتَان.

سَأَتَّصِلُ بِسَلْمَان صَدِيقِ طُفُولَتِي.

تَمْرِين ٢٧. جِدُوا ٱلتَّرْجَمَة فِي ٱلنَّصّ (صَفْحَة ١٩٦) ثُمَّ ٱنْسَخُوهَا.

Exercise 27. Find the translation in the text (p.196), then copy it.

1. We ate and drank. _____

2. On Tuesday _____

3. In the same city _____

4. Three children _____

5. Close to the university _____

6. High school _____

تَمْرِين ٢٨. أَجِيبُوا شَفَهِيًّا ثُمَّ ٱكْتُبُوا ٱلْأَجْوِبَة.

Exercise 28. Answer out loud, then write the answers.

١. أَيْنَ تَسْكُنُ سَانْدرَا؟ _____

٢. مَنْ هِيَ رِيمَا؟ _____

٣. أَيْنَ تُوجَدُ (located) مَكْتَبَةُ ٱلْكُونغرِيس؟

_____

٤. مَتَى ذَهَبَتْ سَانْدرَا إِلَى مَكْتَبَةِ ٱلْكُونغرِيس؟

_____

Exercise 29. Write questions to the answers.   تَمْرِين ٢٩. أُكْتُبُوا أَسْئِلَة لِلْأَجْوِبَة.

أَلسُّؤَال : _____

أَلْجَوَاب : لِلْأُسْتَاذَة رِيمَا ثَلاثَة أَوْلاد.

أَلسُّؤَال : _____

أَلْجَوَاب : سَلْمَان هُوَ صَدِيق طُفُولَة سَاندرَا.

أَلسُّؤَال : _____

أَلْجَوَاب : تَدْرُسُ سَاندرَا ٱلْفَلْسَفَة وَٱلدِّينَ ٱلْإِسْلامِيّ.

أَلسُّؤَال : _____

أَلْجَوَاب : تَسْكُنُ ٱلْأُسْتَاذَة رِيمَا فِي مَدِينَة وَاشِنْطُن بِٱلْقُرْب مِنَ ٱلْجَامِعَة.

أَلسُّؤَال : _____

أَلْجَوَاب : يُوجَدُ مَتْحَفُ ٱلْمترُوبُولِتَان فِي مَدِينَة نيو يورك.

لِلْأُسْتَاذَة رِيمَا ثَلَاثَة أَوْلَاد

When the preposition لِ is followed by الـ, the ١ of the definite article is dropped.

لِلـ ...   ⟸   لِ + أَلـ ...

لِلْأُسْتَاذَة   ⟸   لِ + أَلْأُسْتَاذَة

Note. If the noun itself starts with the letter لـ, then the whole definite article (ال) is dropped when لِ is added.

لِلُّغَة   ⟸   لِ + أَللُّغَة

لَنَا أُسْتَاذَة مُمْتَازَة لِلُّغَة أَلْعَرَبِيَّة.

Then, and then   ثُمَّ

The word ثُمَّ is used to express the order of events. Its meaning is *then, and then;* therefore, there is no need to add وَ to it.

ذَهَبْنَا إِلَى أَلْمَكْتَبَة ثُمَّ أَكَلْنَا وَشَرِبْنَا.

We went to the library, then we ate and drank.

أَكَلَ أَلطُّلَّاب أَلْفَلَافِل ثُمَّ شَرِبُوا أَلْقَهْوَة.

The students ate falafel, and then drank coffee.

The plural   أَلْجَمْع

The word أَوْلَاد is the plural of وَلَد. This kind of plural is called *broken*

plural (جَمْع تَكْسِير). It is made by "breaking" the singular form and

forming a new pattern (وَزْن) for the plural. Examples:

عِلْم (ج) عُلُوم ، دِين (ج) أَدْيَان ، أُسْتَاذ (ج) أَسَاتِذَة

In Arabic there is another kind of plural for nouns and adjectives: the sound

plural (أَلْجَمْعُ ٱلسَّالِم). It is made by adding a suffix to the singular.

For masculine humans only: ـِينَ or ـُونَ

مُهَنْدِس (ج) مُهَنْدِسُونَ / مُهَنْدِسِينَ

For feminine humans and things: ـَات

مَطَار (ج) مَطَارَات (airport) ، مُهَنْدِسَة (ج) مُهَنْدِسَات

If the noun ends with ة drop it and add ـَات

Exercise 30. Broken or sound plural?　تَمْرِين ٣٠. جَمْع تَكْسِير أَمْ جَمْع سَالِم؟

١. مَرْكَز (ج) مَرَاكِز ٢. لُغَة (ج) لُغَات

٣. طَالِبَة (ج) طَالِبَات ٤. صُورَة (ج) صُوَر

٥. سَيِّدَة (ج) سَيِّدَات ٦. حَافِلَة (ج) حَافِلات

٧. قَلْب (ج) قُلُوب ٨. مُوَظَّف (ج) مُوَظَّفُونَ/مُوَظَّفِينَ

٩. مَلِك (ج) مُلُوك ١٠. زِيَارَة (ج) زِيَارَات

١١. يَوْم (ج) أَيَّام ١٢. طَرِيق (ج) طُرُق

١٣. هَدِيَّة (ج) هَدَايَا ١٤. سَاعَة (ج) سَاعَات

١٥. سَيَّارَة (ج) سَيَّارَات ١٦. مَدِينَة (ج) مُدُن

١٧. جَامِعَة (ج) جَامِعَات ١٨. مُسْلِم (ج) مُسْلِمُونَ/مُسْلِمِينَ

Writing the date in Arabic   كِتَابَةُ ٱلتَّأْرِيخِ بِٱلْعَرَبِيَّةِ

Unlike in English, the date in Arabic is written from right to left. First write the number of the day, then write a slash (/), then to the left of that, write the number of the month. Finally put another slash (/) to the left of the month, and write the year. Remember that any number in Arabic that consists of more than one digit should be written from left to right. For example, December 12th, 1946:

١. ١٢ /

٢. ١٢/١٢

٤. ١٩٤٦/١٢/١٢

Y   M   D

١٩٤٦/١٢/١٢

Y   M   D

Exercise 31. Write the date in Arabic.   تَمْرِين ٣١. أُكْتُبُوا ٱلتَّأْرِيخَ بِٱلْعَرَبِيَّةِ.

1. October 7, 1954 _____   2. June 9, 1942 _____

3. Your date of birth _____   4. Your graduation date _____

5. Today's date _____

The tens　أَلْعَشَرَات

1. The tens from 20 to 90 have two endings: ‎ ‫ ـُ ون‬/ ‫ يـ ـ.‬ For example:

   ثَلاثُونَ　ثَلاثِينَ for 30. Which one you use depends on grammatical

   considerations that you will learn later.

2. In speaking it is common to omit the last vowel of these endings: For example,

   instead of saying ثَلاثُونَ you can say ثَلاثُون, and instead of سِتِّينَ you can

   say سِتِّين.

١٠	عَشَرَة
٢٠	عِشْرُونَ / عِشْرِينَ
٣٠	ثَلاثُونَ / ثَلاثِينَ
٤٠	أَرْبَعُونَ / أَرْبَعِينَ
٥٠	خَمْسُونَ / خَمْسِينَ
٦٠	سِتُّونَ / سِتِّينَ
٧٠	سَبْعُونَ / سَبْعِينَ
٨٠	ثَمَانُونَ / ثَمَانِينَ
٩٠	تِسْعُونَ / تِسْعِينَ
١٠٠	مِائَة / مِئَة

Double digit numbers 20-99

How to say two digit numbers that contain a ten and a "ones" digit, such as

22, 54, 78? Start with the ones digit and then "and" (وَ) and then the tens.

For example, the words "83 books" are said: ثَلاَثَة وَثَمَانُونَ كِتَابًا or

ثَلاَثَة وَثَمَانِينَ كِتَابًا (literally: three and eighty books). Choosing one way

or the other (ثَمَانِينَ or ثَمَانُونَ) depends on grammatical considerations.

There is no difference in meaning.

تَمْرِين ٣٢. إِقْرَؤُوا ٱلْأَعْدَاد.   Exercise 32. Read the numbers.

٧٣ ثَلاَثَة وَسَبْعُونَ		٢١ وَاحِد وَعِشْرُونَ	
٥٢ إِثْنَان وَخَمْسُونَ		٣٩ تِسْعَة وَثَلاثُونَ	

٧٥ .٤	٣٣ .٣	٨٧ .٢	٤٣ .١
٨١ .٨	٤٦ .٧	٩٨ .٦	٥٤ .٥
٧٦ .١٢	٩٩ .١١	٢٢ .١٠	٦٥ .٩

تَمْرِين ٣٣. إِخْتَارُوا خَمْسَة أَرْقَام مِنْ عِشْرِينَ إِلَى تِسْعَة وَتِسْعِينَ وَقُولُوهَا.

Exercise 33. Choose five numbers between 20 and 99 and say them.

تَمْرِين ٣٤. أَحيطُوا ٱلْعَدَدَ ٱلَّذي تَسْمَعُونَهُ.

Exercise 34. Circle the number that you hear.

٣٣	٦٢	٢٢	٦٦	٢٦	١.
٤١	٧١	٨١	٣١	٢١	٢.
٥٤	٤٥	٤٤	٥٥	٥١	٣.
٨٥	٨٤	٣٨	٢٨	٨٨	٤.
٥٠	٦٠	٧٠	٨٠	٩٠	٥.
٥٩	٩٩	٩٥	٤٩	٩٤	٦.
٣٥	٣٤	٣٣	٣٢	٣١	٧.
٥٢	٤٢	٣٢	٢٢	٢١	٨.

Solve the riddle.   حُلُّوا ٱللُّغْز.

كَبِير مِثْلُ ٱلْفِيل وَلٰكِنْ وَزْنُهُ صِفْر. مَا هٰذا؟

It is as big as an elephant but its weight is zero. What is it?

أَلْحَلّ في صَفْحَة ٢٢٨.

طَهَ حُسَيْن

أَديب وَنَاقِد مِصْري،

لُقِّبَ بِعَميدِ ٱلْأَدَبِ ٱلْعَرَبِيّ.

Egyptian author and critic, was called the
foremost representative of Arabic literature.

إِنَّ ٱلْجَامِعَةَ تَتَأَلَّفُ مِنْ طَالِبٍ حُرٍّ وَأُسْتَاذٍ حُرٍّ.

University consists of a free student and a free professor.

دُمُوعُ ٱلْحُبِّ.. قَطَرَاتٌ مِنْ نَهْرٍ فِي ٱلْجَنَّة.

The tears of love are drops from a river in Paradise.

تَمْرِين ٣٥. جِدُوا مَعْلُومَات عَنْ طَهَ حُسَيْن فِي ٱلْإِنْتِرْنِت.

Exercise 35. Find information about Taha Husain on the Internet.

UNIT 6

تَعَلَّمُوا هٰذِهِ ٱلْمُفْرَدَات 🔊

in the evening	مَسَاءً	to speak	تَكَلَّمَ (م) يَتَكَلَّمُ
husband	زَوْج (ج) أَزْوَاج	number	رَقْم (ج) أَرْقَام
grandfather	جَدّ (ج) أَجْداد	to invite	دَعَا (م) يَدْعُو
invitation	دَعْوَة (ج) دَعَوَات	to attend	حَضَرَ (م) يَحْضُرُ
distance	بُعْد	mosque	مَسْجِد (ج) مَسَاجِد
sixth	أَلسَّادِس	text	نَصّ (ج) نُصُوص
fifth	أَلْخَامِس	street	شَارِع (ج) شَوَارِع
nine	تِسْعَة	meal of breaking the fast	إفْطَار
cigarette	سِجَارة (ج) سَجَايِر	Imam (religious leader)	إمَام
phone	هَاتِف	to greet, salute	حَيَّا (م) يُحَيِّ
police	شُرْطَة	guest	ضَيْف (ج) ضُيُوف
to be	كَانَ (ج) يَكُونُ	address, title (book)	عُنْوَان (ج) عَنَاوِين

Exercise 1. Which word does not fit (in each group)؟   تَمْرِين ١. جِدُوا اَلشَّاذّ.

١. هَاتِف   اَلسَّادِس   اَلْخَامِس   ٢. إفْطَار   فُطُور   مُمْتَاز

٣. أَرْقَام   جَدّ   شَوَارِع   ٤. دَعَا   عُنْوَان   دَعْوَة

Exercise 2. Circle the correct translation.   تَمْرِين ٢. أَحِيطُوا اَلتَّرْجَمَة اَلصَّحِيحَة.

Who is talking? / Why are you talking?   ١. مَنْ يَتَكَلَّمُ؟

This year is a good year. / Happy New Year.   ٢. كُلّ عَام وَأَنْتَ بِخَيْر.

I invite you to the Iftar. / This is an invitation to the Iftar.   ٣. أَدْعُوكَ لِلإِفْطَار.

What time do you eat breakfast? / What time is the Iftar?   ٤. فِي أَيّ سَاعَة اَلإِفْطَار؟

At seven in the evening. / Every evening at seven.   ٥. فِي اَلسَّاعَة اَلسَّابِعَة مَسَاءً.

Your place is with us. / Please come to our place.   ٦. تَفَضَّلُوا عِنْدَنَا.

What is your address? / What is your title?   ٧. مَا هُوَ عُنْوَانُكَ؟

Where is the phone? / What is the phone number?   ٨. مَا رَقْمُ اَلْهَاتِف؟

In front of the mosque / The Imam of the mosque   ٩. إمَامُ اَلْمَسْجِد

١٠. أَنَا سَعِيد جِدًّا لِهٰذِهِ اَلدَّعْوَة.

I am very happy for this invitation. / I am very happy to invite you.

Listen to the conversation, then read it.   إِسْتَمِعُوا إِلَى ٱلْمُحَادَثَة ثُمَّ ٱقْرَؤُوهَا .

فِي أَيِّ سَاعَة ٱلْإِفْطَار؟

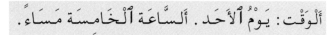

أَلْوَقْت: يَوْمُ ٱلْأَحَد . ٱلسَّاعَة ٱلْخَامِسَة مَسَاءً .

مَاجِد: أَلُو . . . ٱلسَّلَامُ عَلَيْكُمْ .

رَان: وَعَلَيْكُمُ ٱلسَّلَام . مَنْ يَتَكَلَّمُ؟

مَاجِد: أَنَا مَاجِد .

رَان: مَاجِد مِنْ نِيو جيرسِي؟

مَاجِد: نَعَمْ، مَاجِد مِنْ نِيو جيرسِي، كَيْفَ حَالُكَ يَا رَان؟

رَان: أَلْحَمْدُ لله بِخَيْر، رَمَضَان كَرِيم، يَا مَاجِد .

مَاجِد: عَلَيْنَا وَعَلَيْكُمْ .

رَان: كُلّ عَام وَأَنْتَ بِخَيْر .

مَاجِد: وَأَنْتَ بِخَيْر، أَدْعُوكَ أَنْتَ وَأُسْرَتَكَ يَوْمَ ٱلْخَمِيس لِلْإِفْطَار فِي بَيْتِنَا .

رَان: هٰذَا عَظِيم! شُكْرًا لَكَ يَا صَدِيقِي، فِي أَيِّ سَاعَة ٱلْإِفْطَار؟

مَاجِد: أَلْإِفْطَار فِي ٱلسَّاعَة ٱلسَّابِعَة مَسَاءً وَلٰكِنْ تَفَضَّلُوا عِنْدَنَا ٱلسَّاعَة ٱلسَّادِسَة .

ران: وَمَا عُنْوانُكَ؟ أَيْنَ تَسْكُنُ؟

مَاجِد: أَسْكُنُ فِي مَدِينَة كْلِيفْتُون فِي شَارِع فُولْتُون رقْم مِائَة وسَبْعِينَ.

ران: مَا رَقْمُ ٱلْهَاتِف؟

مَاجِد: صِفْر، أَرْبَعَة، ثَلَاثَة، وَاحِد، تِسْعَة، خَمْسَة، ثَمَانِيَة، إثْنَان، سَبْعَة، سِتَّة.

ران: مُمْتَاز، شُكْرًا، وَمَنْ سَيَكُونُ فِي ٱلْإِفْطَار؟

ماجِد: إمَامُ ٱلْمَسْجِد، وَخَالِي وَزَوْجَتُهُ وَٱلْأَوْلاد، وَعَمَّتِي وَزَوْجُهَا وَٱلْأَوْلاد، وَجَدِّي وَجَدَّتِي، وَضُيُوف وَأَنْتَ وَوَالِدُكَ وَوَالِدَتُكَ وَأُخْتُكَ.

ران: أَنَا سَعِيد جِدًّا لِهٰذِهِ ٱلدَّعْوَة، إلَى ٱللِّقَاء يَوْمَ ٱلْخَمِيس فِي ٱلسَّاعَة ٱلسَّادِسَة مَسَاءً، إنْ شَاءَ ٱلله.

ماجِد: إنْ شَاءَ ٱلله، إلَى ٱللِّقَاء.

ران: إلَى ٱللِّقَاء.

Exercise 3. Answer.

تَمْرين ٣. أَجِيبُوا.

١. كَيْفَ حَيَّا رَان صَدِيقَهُ مَاجِد فِي شَهْر رَمَضَان؟

_____

٢. مَا هُوَ عُنْوَان مَاجِد؟

_____

_____

٣. مَا عُنْوَانُكُمْ؟

_____

٤. مَنْ سَيَحْضُرُ ٱلْإِفْطَار فِي بَيْت مَاجِد؟

_____

_____

٥. أُكْتُبُوا ٱلْأَعْدَاد ٱلْمَذْكُورَة (mentioned) فِي هٰذِهِ ٱلْمُحَادَثَة.

_____

_____

_____

The month of Ramaḍan شَهْر رَمَضَان

According to the tenets of Islam, the Qur'an was first revealed to Prophet

Muhammad by the angel Gabriel during the month of Ramaḍan, on the "Night

of Destiny" (لَيْلَةُ ٱلْقَدْر). The month of Ramaḍan, the ninth month in the

Islamic calendar (أَلسَّنَة ٱلْهِجْرِيَّة), is a special time that includes worship,

reading the Qur'an, charitable acts, individual reflection and purification. It is

a religious obligation for Muslims from the age of 12 and older to fast from

sunrise to sunset as a symbol of their commitment to self-restraint. Muslims

eat a meal (أَلسَّحُور) before dawn, and they eat the meal that breaks the fast

(أَلإِفْطَار) at sunset. At the end of Ramaḍan, Muslims celebrate for three days

the Festival of Breaking the Fast (عِيدُ ٱلْفِطْر). Ramaḍan does not occur on a

fixed date every year, because it is celebrated according to the lunar calendar.

Fasting during the month of Ramaḍan is the fourth of the Five Pillars of Islam.

Muslims look forward to this month in which they seek to strengthen their

moral and spiritual values by strictly controlling their thoughts and actions.

رمضان كريم

In the month of Ramaḍan Muslims greet each other with the greeting

رَمَضَان كَرِيم. The answer to كُلّ عَام وَأَنْتَ بخَيْر or رَمَضَان كَرِيم

could be أَللّه أَكْرَم or رَمَضَان كَرِيم or عَلَيْنَا وَعَلَيْكُمْ.

تَمْرِين ٤ . إِمْلَؤُوا ٱلْفَرَاغِ بِٱلْكَلِمَة ٱلْمُنَاسِبَة .

Exercise 4. Fill in the blank with the appropriate word.

١. ـــــــــــــــ يَتَكَلَّمُ؟ (مِنْ ، مَنْ ، مِنْ ، إِلَى)

٢. كُلّ ـــــــــــــــ وَأَنْتُمْ بِخَيْر. (يَوْم ، عَام ، إِفْطَار)

٣. فِي ٱلسَّاعَة ٱلسَّادِسَة ـــــــــــــــ . (شُكْرًا ، أَهْلاً ، مَسَاءً)

٤. إِلَى ٱللِّقَاء ـــــــــــــــ ٱلْخَمِيس. (يَوْمَ ، شَهْر ، سَنَة)

٥. ـــــــــــــــ عُنْوَانُكِ؟ (لِمَاذَا ، مَا ، مَاذَا)

تَمْرِين ٥ . تَرْجِمُوا شَفَهِيًّا ثُمَّ ٱكْتُبُوا ٱلتَّرْجَمَة .

Exercise 5. Translate out loud, then write the translation.

1. How are you?   _____

    Thank God, I am fine.   _____

2. Where do you live?   _____

    I live in New Jersey.   _____

3. What is your address?   _____

    170 Fulton Street.   _____

4. What time is the 'iftar?   _____

    At seven o'clock in the evening._____

تَمْرِين ٦ . تَرْجِمُوا شَفَهِيًّا .   Exercise 6. Translate out loud.

١.   مَا هُوَ ٱلْعُنْوَان وَرَقْمُ ٱلْهَاتِف؟

٢.   كُلّ عَام وَأَنْتَ بِخَيْر .

٣.   إِلَى ٱللِّقَاء يَوْمَ ٱلْخَمِيس، إِنْ شَاءَ ٱلله .

٤.   أَلإِفْطَار فِي ٱلسَّاعَة ٱلسَّادِسَة مَسَاءً .

٥.   بَعْدَ ٱلإِفْطَار سَافَرَ جَدِّي وَجَدَّتِي فِي ٱلْحَافِلَة (bus) إِلَى نِيو يُورك .

تَمْرِين ٧ . إِسْأَلُوا زُمَلاءكُمْ عَنِ ٱلْوَقْت . إِسْتَعْمِلُوا ٱلأَجْوِبَة ٱلتَّالِيَة :

Exercise 7. Ask your classmates what time it is. Use the following answers:

أَلسَّاعَة ٱلثَّانِيَة   أَلسَّاعَة ٱلثَّالِثَة   أَلسَّاعَة ٱلسَّادِسَة   أَلسَّاعَة ٱلثَّامِنَة

تَمْرِين ٨ . وَصَلَتْ رِسَالَة نَصِّيَّة إِلَى مَاجِد . إِقْرَؤُوهَا .

Exercise 8. A text message arrived for Majid. Read it.

🔊

كُلّ عَام وَأَنْتُمْ بِخَيْر بِمُنَاسَبَة حُلُول شَهْر رَمَضَان ٱلْمُبَارَك .

إِبْنُ عَمِّكَ أَحْمَد .

أَجِيبوا: مَنْ بَعَثَ (sent) ٱلرِّسَالَة ٱلنَّصِّيَّة؟

The Noun　أَلِاسْم

1. A noun is a word that indicates a person, place, thing, or idea: مَاجِد ، بَغْدَاد ، دِين.

2. As you learned in Unit 1, all Arabic nouns are, either masculine or feminine.

   A few nouns are both. For example: سُوق (market) , طَرِيق (way, road),
   لِسَان (tongue), سِكِّين (knife).

3. As stated in Unit 4, nouns can be in the singular طَالِب (student), in the dual
   طَالِبَان / طَالِبَيْن (two students), or in the plural form طُلَاب (students);
   مُعَلِّمُونَ / مُعَلِّمِينَ (teachers).

4. A noun is presented in its indefinite masculine singular form: مُعَلِّم ، طَالِب.

5. Nouns can take prefixes: كَنَبِيل (like Nabil) , أَلْوَلَد and suffixes: بَيْتُهُ.

تَمْرِين ٩ . إِنْسَخُوا مِنَ ٱلنَّصِّ (صَفْحَة ٢١٠–٢٠٩) سِتَّة أَسْمَاء.

Exercise 9. Copy six nouns from the text (pp. 209-210).

.٢ _____		.١ _____
.٤ _____		.٣ _____
.٦ _____		.٥ _____

The Adjective أَلصِّفَة

1. An adjective is a word that modifies a noun: إِسْلَامِيّ ، كَبِير ، جَمِيل.

2. As in the case of nouns, an adjective is presented in its indefinite masculine

   singular form: جَمِيل.

3. An adjective must be in agreement with the noun it is modifying in number

   and gender, among other things. Therefore, the word "big" could be translated

   into Arabic using different forms: singular, dual or plural.

4. An adjective does not take possessive pronoun suffixes (my, his, her).

Exercise 10. Write six adjectives.   تَمْرِين ١٠ . أُكْتُبُوا سِتّ صِفَات .

_____ . ٢   _____ . ١

_____ . ٤   _____ . ٣

_____ . ٦   _____ . ٥

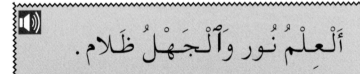

أَلْعِلْمُ نُور وَٱلْجَهْلُ ظَلَام .

Knowledge is light and ignorance is darkness.

إِسْم وَصِفَة

Noun-Adjective Phrase

In the phrase أَلـدّيـنُ ٱلإِسْلامِيُّ (*the Islamic religion*) the word

ٱلإِسْلامِيُّ is an adjective that modifies the word أَلـدّيـنُ. The adjective

in Arabic, unlike English, follows the noun it modifies and agrees with

it in gender, number, definiteness, and case ending (the vowel on the

last letter of the word. This will be taught in upcoming units).

the Islamic religion   أَلـدّينُ ٱلإِسْلامِيُّ

Both the noun and the adjective are definite, masculine and singular.

new students (f.)   طَالِبَات جَدِيدَات

Both the noun and the adjective are indefinite, feminine and plural.

Exercise 11. Read and translate.   تَمْرِيخن ١١ . إِقْرَؤُوا وَتَرْجِمُوا.

٢. فِي ٱلشَّهْرِ ٱلْقَادِم (next)	١. أَلسَّاعَةُ ٱلْخَامِسَة
٤. أَلْمَرْكَزُ ٱلإِسْلامِيُّ	٣. أَلـدّينُ ٱلإِسْلامِيُّ
٦. طَالِبَات جَدِيدَات	٥. أَللُّغَةُ ٱلْعَرَبِيَّة
٨. طُلَّاب مِصْرِيُّونَ	٧. أُسْتَاذَة مُمْتَازَة
١٠. مَدْرَسَة ثَانَوِيَّة	٩. مِنْ أَصْل فِلَسْطِينِيّ

أَلْعَدَدُ ٱلتَّرْتِيبِي — The ordinal numbers

sixth	أَلسَّادِس	first	أَلأَوَّل
seventh	أَلسَّابِع	second	أَلثَّانِي
eighth	أَلثَّامِن	third	أَلثَّالِث
ninth	أَلتَّاسِع	fourth	أَلرَّابِع
tenth	أَلْعَاشِر	fifth	أَلْخَامِس

Note: Ordinal numbers serve as adjectives and
are also used to indicate date and time.

أَلْوَقْت — The time

٧.	أَلسَّاعَةُ ٱلسَّابِعَة (وَٱلرُّبْع – 7:15)	١.	أَلسَّاعَةُ ٱلْوَاحِدَة
٨.	أَلسَّاعَةُ ٱلثَّامِنَة (وَٱلثُّلْث – 8:20)	٢.	أَلسَّاعَةُ ٱلثَّانِيَة
٩.	أَلسَّاعَةُ ٱلتَّاسِعَة (وَٱلنِّصْف – 9:30)	٣.	أَلسَّاعَةُ ٱلثَّالِثَة
١٠.	أَلسَّاعَةُ ٱلْعَاشِرَة	٤.	أَلسَّاعَةُ ٱلرَّابِعَة
١١.	أَلسَّاعَةُ ٱلْحَادِيَةَ عَشْرَةَ	٥.	أَلسَّاعَةُ ٱلْخَامِسَة
١٢.	أَلسَّاعَةُ ٱلثَّانِيَةَ عَشْرَةَ	٦.	أَلسَّاعَةُ ٱلسَّادِسَة

تَعَلَّمُوا هٰذِهِ ٱلْمُفْرَدَات

far	بَعِيد	Sir	سَيِّد (ج) سَادَة
far from	بَعِيد عَنْ	color	لَوْن (ج) أَلْوَان
in the distance	عَلَى بُعْد	red	أَحْمَر
to the left	إِلَى ٱلشِّمَال	white	أَبْيَض
straight	إِلَى ٱلأَمَام	street	شَارِع (ج) شَوَارِع
to the right	إِلَى ٱلْيَمِين	to know	عَرَفَ (م) يَعْرِف
holiday	عِيد (ج) أَعْيَاد	Excuse me. (addressing *m.*)	إِسْمَحْ لِي
Christmas	عِيدُ ٱلْمِيلاد	step	خُطْوَة (ج) خُطْوَات

Exercise 12. Translate into English.   تَمْرِين ١٢. تَرْجِمُوا إلى ٱلإِنْجْلِيزِيَّة.

٣. لَوْنُ ٱلْبَيْت أَحْمَر.   ٢. عِيدُ ٱلْمِيلاد   ١. إِسْمَحْ لِي.

٦. رَقْم مِائَة وَسَبْعُونَ   ٥. أَلْبَيْت بَعِيد.   ٤. إلى ٱلشِّمَال

٩. آسِف، لا أَعْرِف   ٨. إلى ٱلْيَمِين   ٧. أَلْبَيْتُ ٱلأَبْيَض

تَمْرِين ١٣. إِمْلَؤُوا ٱلْفَرَاغَ بِٱلْكَلِمَةِ ٱلْمُنَاسِبَة.

Exercise 13. Fill in the blank with the appropriate word.

١. هَلِ ٱلْبَيْت ــــــــــ ؟   (شَارِع ، بَعِيد ، خُطْوَة)

٢. إِلَى ٱلأَمَام ثُمَّ (then) ــــــــــ إِلَى ــــــــــ .   (ٱلْبَعِيد ، ٱلْعِيد ، ٱلْيَمِين)

٣. لَوْنُ ٱلْبَيْت ــــــــــ .   (أَبْيَض ، شَارِع ، سَيِّد)

٤. عَلَى ــــــــــ خُطْوَتَيْنِ مِنْ هُنَا.   (بَعِيد ، أَحْمَر ، بُعْد)

تَمْرِين ١٤. أُكْتُبُوا كَلِمَات تَحْتَوِي عَلَى كُلٍّ مِنَ ٱلْجُذُورِ ٱلتَّالِيَة وَقُولُوهَا.

Exercise 14. Write words that contain each of the following roots and say them.

٢. بعد ــــــــــــ   ١. لون ــــــــــــ

٤. شمل ــــــــــــ   ٣. سمح ــــــــــــ

٦. خطو ــــــــــــ   ٥. يمن ــــــــــــ

٨. حمر ــــــــــــ   ٧. شرع ــــــــــــ

Listen to the conversation, then read it.   إسْتَمِعُوا إلى ٱلْمُحَادَثَة ثُمَّ ٱقْرَؤُوهَا.

عَلَى بُعْد خُطْوَتَيْنِ مِنْ هُنَا

ألْوَقْت: يَوْمُ ٱلْخَمِيس. ألسَّاعَة ٱلرَّابِعَة وَٱلنِّصْف.

ران: إسْمَحْ لِي مِنْ فَضْلِكَ يَا سَيِّدِي.

— نَعَمْ، تَفَضَّلْ، مَاذَا؟

ران: أَيْنَ شَارِع "فُولْتُون؟"

— شَارِع "فُولْتُون"... أَيّ رَقْم؟

ران: رَقْم مِائَة وَسَبْعُونَ.

— آه، رَقْم مِائَة وَسَبْعُونَ... هَلْ هٰذَا بَيْتُ ٱلدُّكْتُور كَرِيم؟

ران: نَعَمْ، نَعَمْ، هَلِ ٱلْبَيْت بَعِيد؟

— لا. ألْبَيْت قَرِيب جِدًّا، عَلَى بُعْد خُطْوَتَيْنِ مِنْ هُنَا، بِٱلْقُرْبِ مِنْ مَرْكَزِ ٱلشُّرْطَة وَٱلْمَسْجِد.

ران: أَنَا لا أَعْرِف أَيْنَ مَرْكَزُ ٱلشُّرْطَة وَلا أَعْرِف أَيْنَ ٱلْمَسْجِد.

— إلَى ٱلأَمَام ثُمَّ إلَى ٱلْيَمِين ثُمَّ إلَى ٱلشِّمَال. لَوْنُ ٱلْبَيْت أَبْيَض وَأَحْمَر.

ران: شُكْرًا لَكَ وَرَمَضَان كَرِيم.

— ألله أكْرَم.

تَمْرِين ١٥. صَوَاب أَمْ خَطَأٌ.

Exercise 15. True or false.

صَوَاب   خَطَأ

١.   أَلْمَسْجِد قَرِيب مِنْ مَرْكَزِ ٱلشُّرْطَة.   ○   ○

٢.   لا يَعْرِفُ ٱلرَّجُل (man) أَيْنَ شَارِع "فُولْتُون".   ○   ○

٣.   إِسْمُ ٱلرَّجُل رَمَضَان كَرِيم.   ○   ○

٤.   يَسْكُنُ ٱلدُّكْتُور كَرِيم في شَارِع "فُولْتُون".   ○   ○

٥.   أَلْبَيْت عَلَى بُعْد خُطْوَتَيْنِ مِنْ هُنَا = أَلْبَيْت قَرِيب.   ○   ○

تَمْرِين ١٦. أَنْتُمُ ٱلآن في عَمَّان وَتَبْحَثُونَ عَنْ مَرْكَزِ ٱلشُّرْطَة. إِسْأَلُوا زُمَلاءَكُمْ ثُمَّ ٱكْتُبُوا ٱلْمُحَادَثَة.

Exercise 16. You are now in Amman and are looking for the police station.

Ask your classmates, and then write the conversation.

تَمْرِين ١٧. مَا أَلْوَانُ ٱلْعَلَمِ (flag) ٱلأُرْدُنِّيّ وَٱلْعَلَمِ ٱللُّبْنَانِيّ؟

Exercise 17. What are the colors of the Jordanian and the Lebanese flags?

أَبْيَض (white)	أَصْفَر (yellow)	أَحْمَر (red)
أَسْوَد (black)	أَزْرَق (blue)	أَخْضَر (green)

Exercise 18. Translate out loud.   تَمْرين ١٨. تَرْجِمُوا شَفَهِيًّا.

١. أَلْبَيْتُ ٱلأَبْيَض   ٢. إِسْمَحْ لِي مِنْ فَضْلِكَ.

٣. مَرْكَزُ ٱلشُّرْطَة   ٤. رَقْم مِائَة وَسَبْعُونَ

٥. أَلْعَلَمُ ٱلأَمْريكِيّ   ٦. إِنْ شَاءَ ٱلله.

٧. عَلَى بُعْد خُطْوَتَيْنِ مِنْ هُنَا   ٨. أَلسَّاعَة ٱلسَّادِسَة مَسَاءً

٩. إِلَى ٱلْيَمِين ثُمَّ إِلَى ٱلشِّمَال   ١٠. مَا هُوَ ٱلْعُنْوَان وَرَقْمُ ٱلْهَاتِف؟

إِسْمَحْ لِي مِنْ فَضْلِكَ.

Excuse me, please.

1. "Excuse me, please" is translated into Arabic according to gender and number:

 To address a male, use: إِسْمَحْ لِي مِنْ فَضْلِكَ.

 To address a female, use: إِسْمَحِي لِي مِنْ فَضْلِكِ.

 To address a group of people, use: إِسْمَحُوا لِي مِنْ فَضْلِكُمْ.

2. It is possible to use only the first part إِسْمَحْ لِي or only the second part مِنْ فَضْلِكَ:

إِسْمَحْ لِي يَا سَيِّدِي كَمِ ٱلسَّاعَة؟

مِنْ فَضْلِكَ يَا سَيِّدِي كَمِ ٱلسَّاعَة؟

مِنْ فَضْلِكَ يَا أُسْتَاذ ...

To ask your professor about the meaning of a word in Arabic, you can say:

من فَضْلِكَ يَا أُسْتَاذ، مَا مَعْنَى كَلِمَة "بَرْنَامَج"؟

Please, professor (m.), what is the meaning of the word "بَرْنَامَج"؟

If you want to ask how to say a certain word in Arabic, you can say:

إِسْمَحِي لِي مِنْ فَضْلِكِ يَا أُسْتَاذَة كَيْفَ نَقُول بِٱلْعَرَبِيَّة "hospital"؟

Excuse me, professor (f.) how do we say "hospital" in Arabic?

تَمْرِين ١٩. إِسْأَلُوا أُسْتَاذَكُمْ أَوْ أُسْتَاذَتَكُمْ عَنْ مَعْنَى ٱلْكَلِمَات ٱلتَّالِيَة:

Exercise 19. Ask your professor about the meanings of the following words:

٣. حَمْرَاء   ٢. تَجْرِبَة   ١. مَصْرِف

تَمْرِين ٢٠. إِسْأَلُوا أُسْتَاذَكُمْ أَوْ أُسْتَاذَتَكُمْ كَيْفَ تَقُولُونَ بِٱلْعَرَبِيَّة:

Exercise 20. Ask your professor how to say in Arabic:

1. I don't have ...   2. The pyramids   3. In my opinion

Solve the riddle.   حُلُّوا ٱللُّغْزَ.

🔊

فِي عِيدِ مِيلَادِهَا ٱلتَّاسِع قَالَ جَدّ سَارَة لِسَارَة:

يَا حَفِيدَتِي ٱلْعَزِيزَة (my beloved granddaughter)، أَلْيَوْمْ هُوَ عِيد

مِيلَادك (birthday) ٱلتَّاسِع. قَبْلَ سِتّ سَنَوَات كَانَ عُمْرِي

سِتَّة أَضْعَاف (times) عُمْرِك ٱلْيَوْمْ، فَمَا هُوَ عُمْرِي؟

(٥٤ سَنَة ، ٦٠ سَنَة ، ٧٢ سَنَة ، ٨٦ سَنَة)

تَمْرِين ٢١. تَرْجِمُوا شَفَهِيًّا ثُمَّ ٱكْتُبُوا ٱلتَّرْجَمَة فِي دَفَاتِرِكُمْ.

Exercise 21. Translate out loud, then write the translation in your notebooks.

1. - Excuse me, please (m. s.), what time is it?
    - Seven o'clock sharp. (تَمَامًا)

2. - Excuse me, please (f. s.), where is the police station?
    - Straight, then (ثُمَّ) to the right then to the left.

3. - In what university do you (f. s.) study?
    - I study at New York University.

4. - Excuse me, please (m. s.), where is Dr. Ahmad's house?
    - Sorry, I don't know.

5. - Excuse me, please (f. s.), where is King David Street?
    - To the left, then to the right.
    - Thank you very much. (جَزِيلاً)

مَنْعُ ٱلْتِقَاءِ ٱلسَّاكِنَيْنِ

Preventing two *sukuuns* in a row

(Auxiliary vowels)

In the sentence: هَلْ ٱلْبَيْت بَعِيد؟ the word هَلْ takes an auxiliary

vowel كَسْرَة to facilitate pronunciation.

The rule: أَلِف وَصْلَة before سُكُون changes into auxiliary

vowel كَسْرَة.

كَمْ ⬅ إِسْمَحْ لِي يَا سَيِّدِي كَمِ ٱلسَّاعَة؟

Two exceptions:

1. مِنْ before the definite article أَل takes فَتْحَة on the نْ.

مِنْ ⬅ مِنَ ٱلْبَيْت

2. In words that end with تُمْ ، كُمْ ، هُمْ ، هُمَا the م takes ضَمَّة.

أَنْتُمْ ⬅ هَلْ أَنْتُمُ ٱلطُّلَاب مِنْ مِصْر؟

تَمْرِين ٢٢. ضَعُوا ٱلْحَرَكَة ٱلْمُنَاسِبَة عَلَى ٱلْحَرْفِ ٱلَّذِي يَأْتِي قَبْلَ هَمْزَةِ
ٱلْوَصْل (أ).

Exercise 22. Add the appropriate vowel on the letter preceding 'alif waṣla.

١. وَصَلَتْ   –   وَصَلَتِ ٱلْأُسْتَاذَة إِلَى ٱلْجَامِعَة قَبْلَ سَاعَة.

٢. مِنْ   –   ذَهَبْنَا مِنَ ٱلْبَيْت فِي ٱلسَّاعَة ٱلسَّابِعَة.

٣. أَنْتُمْ   –   أَيْنَ أَنْتُمُ ٱلْآن (now)؟

٤. بَيْتُكُمْ   –   أَهٰذَا بَيْتُكُمُ ٱلْجَدِيد (new)؟

٥. مَنْ   –   مَنِ ٱسْمُهَا دِينَا؟   (Whose name is Dina?)

٦. أُكْتُبْ   –   أُكْتُبِ ٱلرِّسَالَة ٱلْيَوْم!   (أُكْتُبْ - Write! [you m. s.])

٧. عَنْ   –   إِسْأَلْ عَنِ ٱلْجَار قَبْلَ ٱلدَّار.   (إِسْأَلْ - Ask! [you m. s.])

٨. هَلْ   –   هَلِ ٱسْمُهَا إِيمَان؟

٩. قَرَأْتُمْ   –   مَتَى قَرَأْتُمُ ٱلْكِتَاب؟

١٠. خُذْ، مِنْ   –   خُذِ ٱلْكِتَاب مِنِ ٱبْنِي.   (خُذْ - Take! [you m. s.])

١١. كَمْ   –   كَمِ ٱلسَّاعَة؟

تَعَلَّمُوا هٰذِهِ ٱلْمُفْرَدَات

studies (learning)	دِرَاسَة	literature	أَدَب (ج) آدَاب
of course, certainly	طَبْعًا	party	حَفْلَة (ج) حَفَلات
year	عَام (ج) أَعْوَام	to teach	عَلَّمَ (م) يُعَلِّمُ
difficult, hard	صَعْب	late (*m.s.*)	مُتَأَخِّر
time	وَقْت (ج) أَوْقَات	school of (medicine)	كُلِّيَّة (ج) كُلِّيَّات
success	نَجَاح	Good evening	مَسَاءُ ٱلْخَيْر
new	جَدِيد (ج) جُدُد	conversation	مُحَادَثَة (ج) مُحَادَثَات
food	ٱلأَكْل ، أَكْل	Good morning	صَبَاحُ ٱلْخَيْر
as, likewise, just as	كَمَا	to meet	تَعَرَّفَ عَلَى (م) يَتَعَرَّفُ عَلَى
well	حَسَنًا	good	جَيِّد (ج) جَيِّدُونَ
delicious	لَذِيذ	word	كَلِمَة (ج) كَلِمَات
permission	إِذْن	place	مَكَان (ج) أَمَاكِن
half	نِصْف	another	آخَر (ج) آخَرُونَ

حَلُّ ٱللُّغْزِ صَفْحَة ٢٠٥: ظِلُّ ٱلْفِيل

تَمْرِين ٢٣. أَحِيطُوا ٱلتَّرْجَمَة ٱلصَّحِيحَة.

Exercise 23. Circle the correct translation.

What is your name (*m. s.*)? / What is your name (*f. s*)?　　١. مَا ٱسْمُ حَضْرَتِكِ؟

Every year is a good year. / Happy New Year.　　٢. كُلَّ عَام وَأَنْتَ بِخَيْرٍ.

What do you (*f. s.*) do? / What do you (*m. s.*) do?　　٣. مَاذَا تَعْمَلِينَ؟

Where is the university? / In which university?　　٤. فِي أَيِّ جَامِعَة؟

I teach French. / I teach Spanish.　　٥. أُعَلِّمُ ٱللُّغَة ٱلإِسْبَانِيَّة.

In the school of Medicine / This is a school of Medicine.　　٦. فِي كُلِّية ٱلطِّبّ

The school is dificult. / Difficult school　　٧. كُلِّيَّة صَعْبَة

God willing. / Whatever God has given! (Amazing!).　　٨. مَا شَاءَ ٱلله.

The good professors / The professors are very good.　　٩. أَلأَسَاتِذَة جَيِّدُونَ جِدًّا.

Thanks to you. / Thank you very much.　　١٠. شُكْرًا جَزِيلاً.

Exercise 24. Which word does not fit (in each group)?　　تَمْرِين ٢٤. جِدُوا ٱلشَّاذّ.

٢. حَفْلَة　لَذِيذ　مُمْتَاز　　　١. عِيد　مُحَادَثَة　عَام

٤. أَعْوَام　أَمَاكِن　جَيِّدُونَ　　　٣. حَفَلات　كَلِمَات　كُلِّيَّة

٦. مُتَأَخِّر　صَعْب　كُلِّيَّة　　　٥. وَقْت　أَدَب　صَعْب

Listen to the conversation, then read it.   إِسْتَمِعُوا إِلَى ٱلْمُحَادَثَة ثُمَّ ٱقْرَؤُوهَا .

كُلّ عَام وَأَنْتِ بِخَيْر .

ألْمَكَان: بَيْت أُسْرَة مَاجِد فِي نِيو جِيرْسِي .

ألْوَقْت: يَوْمُ ٱلْخَمِيس. ألسَّاعَة ٱلثَّامِنَة وَٱلنِّصْف .

ألْمُنَاسَبَة: شَهْر رَمَضَان – ألْإِفْطَار .

مَرْيَم: رَمَضَان كَرِيم .

ران: أَللهُ أَكْرَم، مَا ٱسْمُ حَضْرَتِك؟

مَرْيَم: أَنَا مَرْيَم، وَمَا ٱسْمُ حَضْرَتِكَ؟

ران: أَنَا رَان، تَشَرَّفْنَا .

مَرْيَم: تَشَرَّفْنَا بِكَ، كُلّ عَام وَأَنْتَ بِخَيْر .

ران: وَأَنْتِ بِخَيْر، مَاذَا تَعْمَلِينَ يَا مَرْيَم؟

مَرْيَم: أَنَا أُسْتَاذَة فِي ٱلْجَامِعَة .

ران: فِي أَيّ جَامِعَة؟

مَرْيَم: فِي جَامِعَة رَاتْجِيرس فِي نِيو جِيرْسِي. أَنَا أُسْتَاذَة مَاجِد .

ران: آه، أُسْتَاذَة مَاجِد، مَاذَا تُعَلِّمِينَ؟

مَرْيَم: أُعَلِّمُ ٱللُّغَة ٱلْإِسْبَانِيَّة وَٱلْأَدَب ٱلْإِسْبَانِيّ، وَأَنْتَ يَا رَان؟

ران: ‏ لا أُعَلِّمُ، أَنَا طَالِب .

مَرْيَم: ‏ في أَيّ كُلِّيَّة؟

ران: ‏ في كُلِّية ٱلطِّبّ في جَامِعَة نيو يورك .

مَرْيَم: مَا شَاءَ ٱلله! هٰذِه كُلِّيَّة صَعْبَة .

ران: ‏ صَعْبَة، وَلٰكِنْ أَنَا سَعِيد فِيهَا . أَلْأَسَاتِذَة في هٰذِهِ ٱلْكُلِّيَّة جَيِّدُونَ جِدًّا .

مَرْيَم: أَتَمَنَّى (to wish) لَكَ ٱلنَّجَاح فِي دِرَاسَتِكَ .

ران: ‏ شكرًا جَزِيلاً لَكِ .

مَرْيَم: حَسَنًا يَا ران، أُرِيدُ أَنْ أُسَلِّمَ عَلَى (to greet) ٱلآخَرِينَ، عَنْ إِذْنِكَ .

ران: ‏ تَفَضَّلِي، إِذْنُكِ مَعَكِ .

كُلُّ عَام وَأَنْتَ بِخَيْرٍ .   Happy New Year.

This greeting is said on religious and nonreligious holidays or on birthdays.

To a male: كُلّ عَامّ وَأَنْتَ بِخَيْر .   To a female: كُلّ عَام وَأَنْتِ بِخَيْر .

To a group (m. & f.): كُلّ عَامّ وَأَنْتُمْ بِخَيْر .

It is possible to greet one person using the plural. The answer is:

To a male: وَأَنْتَ بِخَيْر .   To a female: وَأَنْتِ بِخَيْر .

To a group (m. & f.): وَأَنْتُمْ بِخَيْر .

Exercise 25. Answer the questions.   تَمْرِين ٢٥ . أَجِيبُوا عَنِ ٱلْأَسْئِلَة .

١ . مَاذَا تَعْمَلُ مَرْيَم؟

_____

٢ . مَاذَا يَدْرُسُ رَان؟

_____

٣ . أَيّ لُغَة يَدْرُسُ مَاجِد فِي ٱلْجَامِعَة؟

_____

_____

٤ . مَا هُوَ ٱلْجَوَاب (answer) عَلَى: "عَنْ إِذْنِكَ؟"

_____

_____

With your (*m. s.*) permission   عَنْ إِذْنِك

If you are with a person or a number of people and you want to say good-bye in a polite way use the phrase:

عَنْ إِذْنِك (for *m. s.*);   عَنْ إِذْنِكِ (for *f. s.*);   عَنْ إِذْنِكُمْ (for *m. & f. pl.*).

The answer could be:

١ .   إِذْنُكَ مَعَكَ / إِذْنُكِ مَعَكِ .

٢ .   إِذْنُكَ مَعَكَ، مَعَ ٱلسَّلامَة / إِذْنُكِ مَعَكِ، مَعَ ٱلسَّلامَة .

٣ .   مَعَ ٱلسَّلامَة (Go with peace) .

Exercise 26. True or false.

تَمْرِين ٢٦. صَوَاب أَمْ خَطَأٌ.

صَوَاب   خَطَأ

⚪   ⚪   ١. مَرْيَم هِيَ أُسْتَاذَة رَان.

⚪   ⚪   ٢. مَرْيَم وَرَان يَدْرُسَانِ فِي نَفْسِ (same) ٱلْجَامِعَة.

⚪   ⚪   ٣. رَان طَالِب وَمَرْيَم أُسْتَاذَة.

⚪   ⚪   ٤. مَرْيَم أُسْتَاذَة فِي جَامِعَة نيو يورك.

⚪   ⚪   ٥. يَدْرُسُ رَان ٱلْأَدَبَ ٱلْإِنْجليزِيّ وَٱلطِّبّ فِي جَامِعَة نيو يورك.

⚪   ⚪   ٦. تَعَرَّفَ رَان عَلَى ٱلْأُسْتَاذَة مَرْيَم فِي بَيْت مَاجِد.

⚪   ⚪   ٧. أَلْأَسَاتِذة فِي كُلِّيَّة ٱلطِّبّ فِي جَامِعَة نيو يورك جَيِّدُونَ.

⚪   ⚪   ٨. كُلِّيَّةُ ٱلطِّبّ هِيَ كُلِّيَّة صَعْبَة.

🔊 عُصْفُور فِي ٱلْيَد خَيْر مِنْ عَشَرَة عَلَى ٱلشَّجَرَة.

A bird in the hand is better than ten in the tree.

تَمْرِين ٢٧ . أَكْمِلُوا تَلْخِيصَ ٱلْمُحَادَثَة (صفحة ٢٣٠ـ٢٣١) .

Exercise 27. Complete the summary of the conversation (pp. 230-231).

أَلْمُحَادَثَة هِيَ بَيْنَ ــــــــــــــــ وَ ــــــــــــــــ . مَرْيَم

هِيَ ــــــــــــــــ فِي ــــــــــــــــ رَاتْجِيرس فِي

نِيو جِيرسِي وَتُعَلِّمُ فِيهَا ــــــــــــــــ

وَ ــــــــــــــــ ــــــــــــــــ . رَان هُوَ

وَ ــــــــــــــــ فِي جَامِعَة نِيو يورك وَهُوَ

ــــــــــــــــ فِيهَا .

تَمْرِين ٢٨ . تَتَكَلَّمُ ٱلْأُسْتَاذَة مَرْيَم مَعَ مَاجِد فِي ٱلْجَامِعَة . تَكَلَّمُوا مَعَ
زُمَلائِكُمْ بَعْدَ أَنْ تَقْرَؤُوا ٱلنَّصّ ثُمَّ ٱكْتُبُوا ٱلْمُحَادَثَة فِي دَفَاتِرِكُمْ .

Exercise 28. Professor Mariam speaks with Majid at the university. Speak with
your classmates after reading the text, then write the conversation
in your notebooks.

يَوْمَ ٱلثُّلاثَاء بَعْدَ دَرْسِ ٱللُّغَةِ ٱلإِسْبَانِيَّةِ فِي ٱلْجَامِعَة تَكَلَّمَتِ ٱلْأُسْتَاذَة مَرْيَم
مَعَ مَاجِد وَشَكَرَتْهُ عَلَى ٱلإِفْطَارِ ٱلْجَمِيل وَقَالَتْ لَهُ إِنَّهَا ٱسْتَمْتَعَتْ كَثِيراً
بِٱلْأَكْلِ ٱللَّذِيذ . كَمَا قَالَتْ لَهُ إِنَّهَا تَعَرَّفَتْ عَلَى وَالِدِه وَوَالِدَتِه وَأُخْتِه ٱلصَّغِيرَة
وَأَيْضًا عَلَى ٱلإِمَام وَعَلَى صَدِيقِه رَان .

تَمْرِين ٢٩. أَنْتُمُ ٱلْآنَ فِي حَفْلَةٍ فِي ٱلْجَامِعَةِ ٱلْأَمْرِيكِيَّةِ فِي بَيْرُوت. تَعَرَّفُوا

عَلَى أَحَدِ ٱلطُّلَّابِ ثُمَّ ٱكْتُبُوا ٱلْمُحَادَثَةَ.

Exercise 29. You are now at a party at the American University in Beirut. Meet a

student, then write the conversation.

تَمْرِين ٣٠. لائِمُوا بَيْنَ ٱلْعَرَبِيَّةِ وَٱلْإِنجِلِيزِيَّةِ.

Exercise 30. Match the Arabic with the English.

a.	The Spanish language	——	١. إِسْتَمْتَعْنَا بِٱلْأَكْلِ.
b.	Happy New Year.	——	٢. أَللُّغَةُ ٱلْإِسْبَانِيَّة
c.	We enjoyed the food.	——	٣. أَكْلٌ لَذيذ
d.	How old are you (*f.*)?	——	٤. فِي نَفْسِ ٱلْجَامِعَة
e.	Excuse me, please (*f.*).	——	٥. كُلِّيَّةُ ٱلطِّبّ
f.	What is your name (*f.*)?	——	٦. لا شُكْرَ عَلَى واجِب.
g.	School of Medicine	——	٧. مَا ٱسْمُ حَضْرَتِكِ؟
h.	At the same university	——	٨. كُلّ عَام وَأَنْتَ بِخَيْر.
i.	Delicious food	——	٩. كَمْ عُمْرُكِ؟
j.	Don't mention it.	——	١٠. إِسْمَحِي لِي مِنْ فَضْلِكِ.

كُلّ

The quantifier كُلّ has two possible meanings depending on whether the noun following it is definite or not:

1. كُلّ + indefinite singular noun ⟹ **every, each**

      Every year كُلَّ عَام ; *Every student (f.)* كُلُّ طَالِبَة

2. كُلّ + definite singular or plural noun ⟹ **all, whole**

    The whole family كُلُّ ٱلْعَائِلَة ; *All the students* كُلُّ ٱلطُّلاب

3. Remember! كُلّ creates an إِضَافَة with the noun that follows it.

Exercise 31. Translate.   تَمْرِين ٣١. تَرْجِموا.

١.   كُلّ عَام وَأَنْتَ بِخَيْر.

٢.   كُلّ لِسَان إِنْسَان.

٣.   أَكَلَ رَان مِنْ كُلِّ شَيْء.

٤.   لِكُلّ سُؤَال جَوَاب.

٥.   تَعَرَّفْنَا عَلَى كُلِّ ٱلْأَسَاتِذَة وَٱلطُّلاب

٦.   أَعْرِفُ كُلَّ ٱلْكَلِمَاتِ ٱلْجَدِيدَة.

تَمْرِين ٣٢. تَرْجِمُوا شَفَهِيًّا ثُمَّ ٱكْتُبُوا ٱلتَّرْجَمَة في دَفَاتِرِكُمْ.

Exercise 32. Translate out loud, then write the translation in your notebooks.

1. All the time	2. Every year	3. All the conversations
4. Every holiday	5. All the professors	6. Every restaurant
7. Every father	8. All the food	9. All the languages

Exercise 33. Listen, then read.

تَمْرِين ٣٣. إِخْتَارُوا (choose) دَوْلَة عَرَبِيَّة وَٱبْحَثُوا عَنْهَا في ٱلْإِنْتَرْنِت :

مَا عَدَدُ ٱلسُّكَّان وَمَا هِيَ ٱلْعَاصِمَة (capital) وَمَا هِيَ ٱلدُّوَلُ

ٱلْمُجَاوِرَة (neighboring countries) وَمَنْ هُوَ ٱلْحَاكِم (ruler) وَمَا هِيَ

ٱلْعُمْلَة (currency) وَمَا هِيَ ٱللُّغَاتُ ٱلْمَحْكِيَّة (spoken) في هٰذِهِ

ٱلدَّوْلَة وَمَا أَلْوَانُ ٱلْعَلَم؟

مَنْ طَرَقَ ٱلْبَاب سَمِعَ ٱلْجَوَاب .

He who knocks on the door will hear the answer.

أَلْجَمْع غَيْرُ ٱلْعَاقِل

Non-human (nouns in the) plural

As stated earlier, an adjective must agree in number with the noun it modifies.

In the noun-adjective phrase أَلْكَلِمَاتُ ٱلْجَدِيدَة the adjective ٱلْجَدِيدَة (feminine singular) does not agree in number with the noun أَلْكَلِمَاتُ (plural feminine). A non-human noun in the plural is treated in Arabic as a **singular feminine**, regardless of the gender of the noun, in verbs (whether before or after the noun), adjectives and pronouns. Here are some examples:

The dogs barked all night.	١. نَبَحَتِ ٱلْكِلَابُ كُلَّ ٱللَّيْل.
These houses are big.	٢. هٰذِهِ ٱلْبُيُوت كَبِيرَة.
I wrote the words and studied them.	٣. كَتَبْتُ ٱلْكَلِمَات وَتَعَلَّمْتُهَا.
The United Nations	٤. أَلْأُمَم ٱلْمُتَّحِدَة
The United States	٥. أَلْوِلَايَاتُ ٱلْمُتَّحِدَة

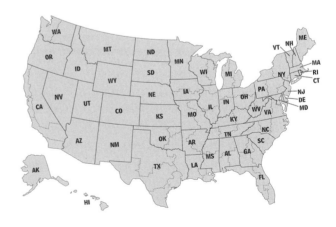

تَمْرِين ٣٤. إِمْلَؤُوا اَلْفَرَاغَ بِاَلْكَلِمَةِ اَلْمُنَاسِبَة.

Exercise 34. Fill in the blank with the appropriate word.

عَظِيم ، مُمْتَازَة ، كُلِّيَّة ، تَعَرَّفَ ، سَعِيدَة ، عَنْ ، اَلْإِنْجِلِيزِيَّة ، جَزِيلاً ، اَلنَّجَاح ، مُتَأَخِّر ، تُعَلِّمِينَ

١. هِيَ طَالِبَة فِي _____ اَلطِّبّ.

٢. أَتَمَنَّى لَكِ _____ فِي دِرَاسَتِكِ.

٣. أَنَا _____ ، عَنْ إِذْنِك. إِذْنُكَ مَعَكَ، مَعَ اَلسَّلامَة.

٤. طَبْعًا، هٰذِه جَامِعَة _____ .

٥. فِي أَيِّ جَامِعَة _____ ؟

٦. شُكْرًا _____ لَكِ.

٧. أُعَلِّمُ اَللُّغَةَ _____ وَاَلْأَدَبَ اَلْإِنْجِلِيزِيّ.

٨. هٰذا _____ ! هَلْ أَنْتِ _____ فِي هٰذِهِ اَلْجَامِعَة؟

٩. _____ رَان عَلَى اَلْأُسْتَاذَة مَرْيَم فِي دَار مَاجِد فِي نيو جِيرْسِي.

١٠. _____ إِذْنِكُمْ يَا شَبَاب. إِذْنُكَ مَعَكَ، مَعَ اَلسَّلامَة يَا أُسْتَاذ.

Pronunciation of ending vowels in speaking and reading aloud

1. In speaking or reading aloud you can pronounce a noun, a verb or an

   adjective as if a سُكُون is written on its last letter: كَبِير , سَأَل , بَيْت

2. As previously mentioned, a noun, a verb or an adjective that is followed

   by أ (هَمْزَةُ ٱلْوَصْل) must have a vowel on or beneath its last letter.

١. وَالِدَة سَمِير أَمْرِيكِيَّة مِنْ أَصْل سُورِيّ.

وَالِدَةُ ٱلطَّالِب أَمْرِيكِيَّة مِنْ أَصْل سُورِيّ.

٢. أَدْرُس فِي جَامِعَة نِيو يورك.

أَدْرُسُ ٱلطِّبّ فِي جَامِعَة نِيو يورك.

تَمْرِين ٣٥. إِسْأَلُوا زُمَلاءَكُمْ مَاذَا يَدْرُسُونَ. إِسْتَعْمِلُوا ٱلْقَائِمَةَ ٱلتَّالِيَةَ فِي أَجْوِبَتِكُمْ.

Exercise 35. Ask your classmates what they study. Use the following list to answer.

Commerce	أَلتِّجَارَة	History	أَلتَّأْرِيخ
Engineering	أَلْهَنْدَسَة	Economics	أَلاقْتِصَاد
Physics	أَلْفِيزِيَاء	Mathematics	أَلرِّيَاضِيَات
Law	أَلْحُقُوق	Chemistry	أَلْكِيمْيَاء
Philosophy	أَلْفَلْسَفَة	Religion	أَلدِّين

تَمْرِين ٣٦. أُكْتُبُوا أَرْبَع جُمَل حَسَبَ ٱلْمِثَال.

Exercise 36. Write four sentences according to the example.

١. أَنَا أَدْرُسُ ٱلْكِيمِيَاء وَدَان يَدْرُسُ ٱلْهَنْدَسَة وَدِينَا تَدْرُسُ ٱلْحُقُوق.

_____ ٢.

_____ ٣.

_____ ٤.

_____ ٥.

تَمْرِين ٣٧. تَرْجِمُوا شَفَهِيًّا ثُمَّ ٱكْتُبُوا ٱلتَّرْجَمَة فِي دَفَاتِرِكُمْ.

Exercise 37. Translate out loud, then write the translation in your notebooks.

1. Engineering and physics   2. At five o'clock sharp   3. With your permission

4. History and religion   5. All the students   6. Christmas party

7. The Philosophy professor   8. Of Egyptian origin   9. All day

تَمْرِين ٣٨. جِدُوا ثَلَاث جَامِعَات لُبْنَانِيَّة وَثَلَاث جَامِعَات مِصْرِيَّة فِي ٱلْإِنْتِرْنِت وَٱكْتُبُوا أَسْمَاءَهَا.

Exercise 38. Find three Lebanese universities and three Egyptian universities

on the Internet and write their names.

The root   أَلْجَذْر

Most words in Arabic—verbs, nouns, and adjectives—are derived from a root. Most of the roots consist of three consonants (radicals)—the trilateral root, أَلثُّلاثِيّ, but a few have four consonants, the quadrilateral root, أَلرُّبَاعِي. The root itself is not a word, but in many cases it does convey a general meaning. To produce a word (a verb, a noun, or an adjective), you need to insert the radicals into a pattern.

The pattern   أَلْوَزْن

The pattern itself is not a word. It contains everything that a word includes except the root. For example: When we take out the roots of the following words, we end up with the patterns.

pattern	root	word
ـَ ا ـ ـ ـَ	طلب	١. طَالِب
مُ ـ ـِّ ـ ـُ ون	علم	٢. مُعَلِّمُونَ
تَ ـ ـَ ـَّ ـ	كلم	٣. تَكَلَّمَ

The above patterns cannot be read. Therefore, when Arabic speakers want to say a pattern, they use the letters ف ع ل (فعل) as substitutes for the letters of the root. The first letter of the root (the first radical) is represented by the letter ف, the second radical is represented by the letter ع, and the third radical is represented by the letter ل.

Therefore, the pattern – – ا – would be said as فَاعِل, the pattern

مُ–ـَّ–ُ– ونَ would be said as مُفَعِّلُونَ, and the pattern تَ–ـَّ–ـَ would

be said as تَفَعَّلَ. These three letters فعل (read: *fa'ala*) are generic like x,

y and z in math and can represent any three letters.

Exercise 39. Complete the table.   تَمْرِين ٣٩. أَكْمِلُوا ٱللائِحَة.

أَلْكَلِمَة	أَلْجَذْر	أَلْوَزْن	
كَاتِب	كتب	– ـَ ا – ـِ – فَاعِل	١.
	كتب	مَ–ـْ–ـَ– مَفْعَل	٢.
	كتب	مَ–ـْ–ُ و– مَفْعُول	٣.
	بيت	– ـُ – ُ و– فُعُول	٤.
	صدق	– ـَ – ي – فَعِيل	٥.
	جمع	– ـَ ا – ـِ ة فَاعِلَة	٦.
	علم	أَ–ـْ–ـَ ا – أَفْعَال	٧.
	حدث	مُ–ـَ ا – ـَ ة مُفَاعَلَة	٨.

Root and pattern   أَلْـجَـذْر وَٱلْـوَزْن

Each root can be inserted into different patterns to create words that are related to the general meaning conveyed by the root. For example, the root كتب conveys the general meaning of *to write*. If we insert كتب into the patterns (مَفْـعُول) مَـ ـْ ـُ ـو and (فِعَال) ـِ ـَ ١ـ we get the words كِتَاب (book) and مَكْـتُوب (letter, written) respectively. Although letters are inserted between radicals (according to the pattern), the radicals must stay in the same order to maintain the same general meaning.

The following words share the root كتب

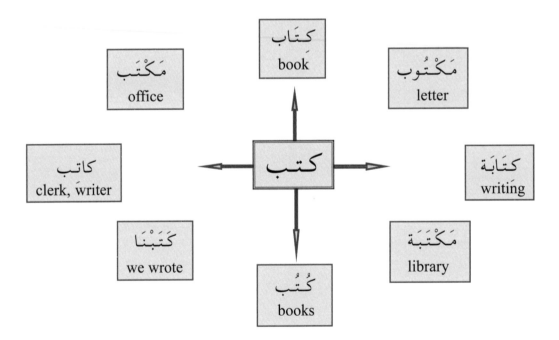

The following words share the root درس

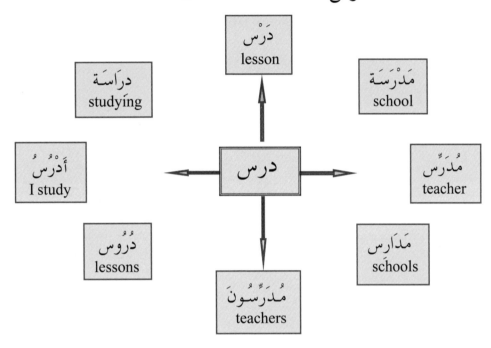

Exercise 40. What are patterns of the words?   تَمْرِين ٤٠ . مَا هِيَ أَوْزَانُ أَلْكَلِمَات؟

١. مَكْتَبَة **مَفْعَلَة**		٢. دُرُوس _____
٣. كِتَاب _____		٤. مَدَارِس _____
٥. مَكْتُوب _____		٦. مُدَرِّس _____
٧. كِتَابَة _____		٨. دِرَاسَة _____
٩. أُكْتُبُوا _____		١٠. مَدْرَسَة _____

تَمْرِين ٤١ . أُكْتُبُوا ٱلْجَذْرَ ٱلْمُشْتَرَك لِلْكَلِمَات .

Exercise 41. Write the common root of the words.

درس	دَرَسْتُ دَرَس	١. مَدْرَسَة
ــــــــــــــــــ	نَفْطُرُ فُطُور	٢. إفْطَار
ــــــــــــــــــ	كَلِمَات كَلام	٣. تَكَلَّمَ
ــــــــــــــــــ	أَعْرِفُ عَرَفْتُ	٤. تَعَرَّفْنَا
ــــــــــــــــــ	سَلام مُسْلِم	٥. إسْلام
ــــــــــــــــــ	أَلرَّابِع مُرَبَّع	٦. أَرْبَعَة
ــــــــــــــــــ	قَرَأْتِ أَقْرَأُ	٧. قِرَاءَة
ــــــــــــــــــ	مُشَاهَدَة شَاهِد	٨. شَاهَدْنَا

تَمْرِين ٤٢ . هٰذا هُوَ ٱلْجَذْر وَهٰذا هُوَ ٱلْوَزْن . أُكْتُبُوا ٱلْكَلِمَة .

Exercise 42. This is the root and this is the pattern. Write the word.

أَلْكَلِمَة	أَلْوَزْن	أَلْجَذْر	
سَافَرَ	فَاعَلَ	سفر	١.
ــــــــــــــــــ	أَفْعِلُ	عرف	٢.
ــــــــــــــــــ	تَفَعَّلَ	كلم	٣.
ــــــــــــــــــ	إفْتَعَلَ	قرب	٤.

مِنْ أَقْوَال ٱلْخَلِيفَة عُمَر بْنِ ٱلْخَطَّاب،

رَضِيَ ٱللهُ عَنْهُ:

Among the sayings of the Caliph Umar bnu–lkhaṭṭaab,

may Allah be pleased with him.

مَا نَدِمْتُ عَلَى سُكُوتِي مَرَّة

وَلَقَدْ نَدِمْتُ عَلَى ٱلْكَلام مِرَارًا .

I never regretted my silence
but I have often regretted my speech.

تَمْرِين ٤٣ . جِدُوا مَعْلُومَات عَنْ ٱلْخَلِيفَة عُمَر بْنِ ٱلْخَطَّاب فِي ٱلْإِنْتِرْنِت .

Exercise 43. Find information about أَلْخَلِيفَة عُمَر بْنُ ٱلْخَطَّاب on the Internet.

🔊

تَعَلَّمُوا هٰذِهِ ٱلْمُفْرَدَات

to grow	كَبُرَ (م) يَكْبُرُ	small, little	صَغِير (ج) صِغَار
similar to, like	مِثْل	to graduate	تَخَرَّجَ (م) يَتَخَرَّجُ
age, life	عُمْر (ج) أَعْمَار	class, grade	صَفّ (ج) صُفُوف
whenever, when	عِنْدَمَا	pupil, student	تِلْمِيذ (ج) تَلامِيذ
opinion	رَأْي (ج) آرَاء	to learn, study	تَعَلَّمَ (م) يَتَعَلَّمُ
		physician	طَبِيب (ج) أَطِبَّاء

تَمْرِين ١. إِمْلَؤُوا ٱلْفَرَاغَ بِٱلْكَلِمَةِ ٱلْمُنَاسِبَة.

Exercise 1. Fill in the blank with the appropriate word.

١. أَنَا تِلْمِيذَة فِي _____ ٱلْخَامِس. (ٱلْمَتْحَفِ ، ٱلصَّفِّ ، ٱلْقِطَارِ)

٢. مَاذَا سَتَدْرُسِينَ _____ تَكْبُرِينَ؟ (عِنْدَمَا ، أَمَامَ ، إِلَى)

٣. أَنَا طَالِب _____ مَاجِد. (عِنْدَمَا ، أَيْضاً ، مِثْل)

٤. أُرِيدُ أَنْ أَكُونَ _____ مِثْل وَالِدِي. (طَبِيبَة ، مَكْتَبَة ، طُفُولَة)

إِسْتَمِعُوا إِلَى ٱلْمُحَادَثَة ثُمَّ ٱقْرَؤُوهَا .   Listen to the conversation, then read it.

كَمْ عُمْرُكِ؟

أَلْمَكَان :   بَيْت أُسْرَة مَاجِد .

أَلْوَقْت :   يَوْمُ ٱلْخَمِيس . أَلسَّاعَة ٱلتَّاسِعَة تَمَامًا .

أَلْمُنَاسَبَة : شَهْر رَمَضَان – أَلْإِفْطَار .

رَان :   مَسَاءُ ٱلْخَيْر .

سَارَة :   مَسَاءُ ٱلنُّور، مَنْ حَضْرَتُكَ؟

رَان :   إِسْمِي رَان وَأَنَا صَدِيق مَاجِد، وَمَا ٱسْمُك؟

سَارَة :   أَنَا سَارَة أُخْت مَاجِد ٱلصَّغِيرَة .

رَان :   كَمْ عُمْرُكِ؟

سَارَة :   عَشْر سَنَوَات . وَكَمْ عُمْرُكَ؟

رَان :   عُمْرِي سِتَّة وَعِشْرُونَ عَامًا .

سَارَة :   هَلْ أَنْتَ طَالِب فِي ٱلْجَامِعَة مِثْل أَخِي مَاجِد؟

رَان :   نَعَمْ، أَنَا طَالِب مِثْلُهُ . فِي أَيّ صَفّ أَنْتِ؟

سَارَة :   أَنَا تِلْمِيذَة فِي ٱلصَّفِّ ٱلْخَامِس .

رَان :   وَمَاذَا سَتَدْرُسِينَ فِي ٱلْجَامِعَة عِنْدَمَا تَكْبُرِينَ؟

سَارَة :   سَأَدْرُسُ ٱلطِّبّ، أُرِيدُ أَنْ أَكُونَ طَبِيبَة مِثْل وَالِدِي، وَمَاذَا تَدْرُسُ أَنْتَ؟

رَان :   أَنَا أَدْرُسُ ٱلطِّبَّ .

سارة : مَا شَاءَ ٱلله! ومَتَى سَتَتَخَرَّجُ مِنَ ٱلْجَامِعَة؟

رَان :   سَأَتَخَرَّجُ هٰذِهِ ٱلسَّنَة .

سارة : وَسَتَكُونُ طَبِيبًا؟

رَان :   نَعَمْ، إِنْ شَاءَ ٱلله .

سارة : يَا مَاجِد، يَا مَاجِد، هَلْ رَان سَيَكُونُ طَبِيبًا هٰذِهِ ٱلسَّنَة ...؟

Exercise 2. Answer out loud.   تَمْرِين ٢ . أَجِيبُوا شَفَهِيًّا .

١. بَيْنَ مَنِ ٱلْمُحَادَثَة؟   ٢. مَنْ هِيَ سَارَة؟

٣. كَمْ عُمْر سَارَة؟   ٤. مَتَى سَيَتَخَرَّجُ رَان مِنَ ٱلْجَامِعَة؟

٥. كَمْ عُمْر رَان؟   ٦. مَاذَا يَعْمَلُ وَالِد مَاجِد؟

Exercise 3. What is your opinion?   تَمْرِين ٣ . ما رَأْيُكُمْ؟

١. هَلْ رَان عَرَبِيّ ...؟ هَلْ هُوَ مُسْلِم ... أَمْ مَسِيحِيّ ...؟

٢. أَيْنَ تَعَلَّمَ رَان ٱللُّغَة ٱلْعَرَبِيَّة؟

تَعَلَّمَ رَان ـ_____ في رَأْيِي،

like, similar to   مِثْل

The word مِثْل is a **noun** and must be followed by a noun or a pronoun. The vowel on the last letter could be *ḍamma, fatḥa,* or *kasra* (مِثْلُ , مِثْلَ or مِثْلِ) based on grammatical considerations.

I want to be a physician like my father.   أُرِيدُ أَنْ أَكُونَ طَبِيبَة مِثْلَ وَالِدِي .

I am a student like him.   أَنَا طَالِب مِثْلُهُ .

Prepositions   حُرُوفُ ٱلْجَرّ

A preposition links nouns, pronouns, and phrases to other words in a sentence and indicates the relationship between them. Prepositions in Arabic can be either separate words, such as عِنْدَ (*at the place of*), مَعَ (*with*), and أَمَام (*in front of*), or single-consonant prepositions, such as لِ (*to, to have*) and بِ (*in*), which are attached to the noun that follows them. Most prepositions can take pronoun suffixes (ضَمَائِر), for example,

مَعَكَ ⟸ مَعَ + كَ *with you (m. s.).* The pronouns attached to the prepositions take the same form as the possessive pronouns. A preposition followed by a noun is called a *prepositional phrase.* For example, بِٱلْبَيْت *in the house,* أَمَامَ ٱلْبَنْك *in front of the bank,* مِنْ سُورِيَا *from Syria.*

مَعَ + ضَمَائِر

with us	مَعَنَا	with me	مَعِي
with you (*m. pl.*)	مَعَكُمْ	with you (*m. s.*)	مَعَكَ
with you (*f. pl.*)	مَعَكُنَّ	with you (*f. s.*)	مَعَكِ
with them (*m. pl.*)	مَعَهُمْ	with him	مَعَهُ
with them (*f. pl.*)	مَعَهُنَّ	with her	مَعَهَا

with you (*m. and f. dual*) مَعَكُمَا

with them (*m. and f. dual*) مَعَهُمَا

لِ + ضَمَائِر

to us / we have	لَنَا	to me / I have	لِي
to you (*m. pl.*) / you have	لَكُمْ	to you (*m. s.*) / you have	لَكَ
to you (*f. pl.*) / you have	لَكُنَّ	to you (*f. s.*) / you have	لَكِ
to them (*m. pl.*) / they have	لَهُمْ	to him / he has	لَهُ
to them (*f. pl.*) / they have	لَهُنَّ	to her / she has	لَهَا

to you (*m. and f. dual*) / you (*m. and f. dual*) have لَكُمَا

to them (*m. and f. dual*) / they (*m. and f. dual*) have لَهُمَا

تَمْرِين ٤ . أَضِيفُوا ٱلضَّمَائِر لِحُرُوفِ ٱلْجَرّ شَفَهِيًّا ثُمَّ ٱكْتُبُوا ٱلتَّصْرِيف .

Exercise 4. Add pronouns to the prepositions out loud, then write the declension.

عِنْدَ   ،   أَمَام

تَمْرِين ٥ . حَوِّلُوا ٱلٱسْم إِلَى ٱلضَّمِيرِ ٱلْمُنَاسِب وَأَضِيفُوهُ إِلَى حَرْفِ ٱلْجَرّ

حَسَبَ ٱلْمِثَال .

Exercise 5. Replace the noun with the appropriate pronoun and add it to the
            preposition according to the example.

هَلْ تَحَدَّثْتَ مَعَ **ٱلطُّلَّاب**؟   ⬅   هَلْ تَحَدَّثْتَ **مَعَهُمْ**؟

١. فِي **ٱللُّغَة ٱلْعَرَبِيَّة** ــــــــــــــــ ٢٨ حَرْفًا .

٢. أَلْمَطْعَم أَمَامَ مَرْكَزِ **ٱلشُّرْطَة** (police station) ــــــــــــــــ .

٣. أَيْنَ ٱلْحَفْلَة؟   عِنْدَ **نَادِيَا** ــــــــــــــــ .

٤. زُرْتُ ٱلْأَهْرَام مَعَ **عَمِّي وَعَمَّتِي** ــــــــــــــــ .

٥. إِسْأَلُوا رَان عَنِ (about) **ٱلْأَسَاتِذَة** ــــــــــــــــ .

٦. تَكَلَّمَ مَاجِد مَعَ **أُمّ رَان** ــــــــــــــــ

٧. **لِهَانِي وَلَيْلَى** ــــــــــــــــ شَقَّة كَبِيرَة وَجَمِيلَة .

٨. مَاذَا سَتَدْرُسِينَ فِي **ٱلْجَامِعَة**؟ ــــــــــــــــ

تَعَلَّمُوا هٰذِهِ ٱلْمُفْرَدَات

yesterday	أَمْسِ	best	أَحْسَن
some	بَعْض	to do, act	فَعَلَ (م) يَفْعَلُ
tired	تَعْبَان	soft drinks	مَشْرُوبَات
oranges	بُرْتُقَال	member (of a family)	فَرْد (ج) أَفْرَاد
I was	كُنْتُ	family (extended)	عَائِلَة (ج) عَائِلَات
food	مَأْكُولَات	to play	لَعِبَ (م) يَلْعَبُ
sweets	حَلَوِيَّات	to cook	طَبَخَ (م) يَطْبُخُ
juice	عَصِير	kind, type	نَوْع (ج) أَنْوَاع
rice	أَرُزّ ، رُزّ	to meet	تَعَرَّفَ عَلَى (م) يَتَعَرَّفُ عَلَى
chickens	دَجَاج	to watch	شَاهَدَ (م) يُشَاهِدُ
meat	لَحْم	world	عَالَم
middle	مُنْتَصَف	to bring	أَحْضَرَ (م) يُحْضِرُ

تَمْرِين ٦ . إِمْلَؤُوا ٱلْفَرَاغ بِٱلْكَلِمَة ٱلْمُنَاسِبَة .

Exercise 6. Fill in the blank with the appropriate word.

١. وَلله ٱسْتَمْتَعْنَا _____ بِٱلإفْطَار . (ٱلْمَتْحَف ، شُكْرًا ، كَثِيرًا)

٢. تَعَرَّفْنَا عَلَى أَفْرَاد _____ مَاجِد . (صُفُوف ، عَائِلَة ، مَأْكُولات)

٣. _____ أَكْل فِي ٱلْعَالَم . (دَجَاج ، طَبَخَ ، أَحْسَن)

٤. بَعْدَ ٱلإفْطَار _____ ٱلتِّلْفَاز . (شَاهَدْنَا ، لَعِبْنَا ، فَعَلْنَا)

٥. رَجَعْتُ فِي _____ ٱللَّيْل . (عَصِير ، مُنْتَصَف ، أَمْسِ)

٦. لَعِبْنَا _____ ٱلْكُمْبِيُوتِر . (عَلَى ، فِي ، مِثْل)

Exercise 7. Translate into English.   تَمْرِين ٧ . تَرْجِمُوا إلى ٱلإنْجْلِيزِيَّة .

٢. كُلّ أَنْوَاعِ ٱلْمَأْكُولات   ١. إِسْتَمْتَعْنَا بِٱلأَكْل .

٤. عَصِيرُ ٱلْبُرْتُقَال   ٣. بَيْت صَدِيقِي

٦. تَعْبَان وَلٰكِنْ مَبْسُوط   ٥. كَيْفَ كَانَ ٱلإفْطَار؟

٨. لَعِبْنَا عَلَى ٱلْكُمْبِيُوتِر .   ٧. تَعَرَّفْنَا عَلَى ٱلأُسْتَاذَة .

١٠. أَحْسَن أَكْل فِي ٱلْعَالَم   ٩. فِي مُنْتَصَفِ ٱللَّيْل

Listen to the conversation, then read it. إِسْتَمِعُوا إِلَى ٱلْمُحَادَثَة ثُمَّ ٱقْرَؤُوهَا.

أَحْسَنُ أَكْلٍ فِي ٱلْعَالَم

ٱلْوَقْت: يَوْمُ ٱلْجُمْعَة. ٱلسَّاعَة ٱلثَّالِثَة وَٱلرُّبْع.

نَوال: أَيْنَ كُنْتَ أَمْسِ؟

ران: كُنْتُ فِي بَيْتِ صَدِيقِي مَاجِد فِي نِيُو جِيرْسِي لِلإِفْطَار.

نَوال: فِي نِيُو جِيرْسِي...؟ لِلإِفْطَار...؟ مَعَ مَنْ ذَهَبْتَ؟

ران: ذَهَبْتُ مَعَ وَالِدِي وَوَالِدَتِي وَأُخْتِي.

نَوال: وَكَيْفَ كَانَ ٱلإِفْطَار؟

ران: وَٱلله ٱسْتَمْتَعْنَا كَثِيراً بِٱلإِفْطَار وَتَعَرَّفْنَا

عَلَى أَفْرَاد عَائِلَة مَاجِد.

نَوال: وَكَيْفَ كَانَ ٱلأَكْل؟

ران: كَانَ ٱلأَكْل لَذِيذاً جِدًّا. أَحْسَنُ أَكْلٍ فِي ٱلْعَالَم.

نَوال: أَنَا أَيْضًا أُحِبُّ ٱلأَكْلَ ٱلْعَرَبِيّ. مَاذَا طَبَخُوا؟

ران: طَبَخُوا كُلَّ أَنْوَاعِ ٱلْمَأْكُولات: أَلأَرُزّ وَٱلدَّجَاج، وَٱلْكَبَاب، وَٱللَّحْم

وَأَحْضَرُوا ٱلسَّلَطَة، وَٱلْخُبْزَ ٱلْعَرَبِيّ وَٱلْحَلَوِيَّات وَٱلتَّمْر (dates)

وَعَصِيرَ ٱلْمَانْجُو وَعَصِيرَ ٱلْبُرْتُقَال.

نوال: وَمَاذَا فَعَلْتَ بَعْدَ ٱلْإِفْطَار؟

ران: بَعْدَ ٱلْإِفْطَار أَنَا وَمَاجِد شَاهَدْنَا ٱلتِّلْفَاز وَلَعِبْنَا عَلَى ٱلْكُمْبِيُوتِر،

وَأَبُو مَاجِد وَبَعْضُ ٱلضُّيُوف ذَهَبُوا إِلَى ٱلْمَسْجِد لِلصَّلَاة.

نوال: وَمَتَى رَجَعْتَ إِلَى ٱلْبَيْت؟

ران: رَجَعْتُ فِي مُنْتَصَفِ ٱللَّيْل تَعْبَان وَلٰكِنْ مَبْسُوط.

تَمْرِين ٨. أَجِيبُوا.   Exercise 8. Answer.

١. هَلْ ذَهَبَتْ أُخْت رَان إِلَى بَيْت مَاجِد فِي نِيو جِيرْسِي؟

_____

٢. مَاذَا فَعَلَ رَان بَعْدَ ٱلْإِفْطَار؟

_____

٣. مَتَى رَجَعَ رَان وَأُسْرَتُهُ إِلَى ٱلْبَيْت؟

_____

٤. أَكْمِلُوا: عِنْدَمَا ذَهَبَ أَبُو مَاجِد وَبَعْضُ ٱلضُّيُوف إِلَى ٱلْمَسْجِد، أَنَا وَمَاجِد

_____ ٱلتِّلْفَاز وَ _____ عَلَى ٱلْكُمْبِيُوتِر.

Exercise 9. Answer.   تَمْرِين ٩. أَجِيبُوا.

١.   أَيْنَ كُنْتَ؟

كُنْتُ ـــــــــــــــــــــــــــــــــــــ

٢.   إِلَى أَيْنَ سَافَرْتَ؟

سَافَرْتُ ـــــــــــــــــــــــــــــــــ

٣.   مَعَ مَنْ سَافَرْتَ؟

سَافَرْتُ ـــــــــــــــــــــــــــــــــ

Exercise 10. Write questions for the answers.   تَمْرِين ١٠. أُكْتُبُوا أَسْئِلَة لِلْأَجْوِبَة.

١.   أَلسُّؤَال: مَاذَا ـــــــــــــــــــــــــــــــــ ؟

أَلْجَوَاب: أَكَلْتُ ٱلْكَبَاب وَٱلْأُرُزّ وَٱلسَّلَطَة.

٢.   أَلسُّؤَال: إِلَى أَيْنَ ـــــــــــــــــــــــــ ؟

أَلْجَوَاب: ذَهَبَ أَبُو مَاجِد وَبَعْضُ ٱلضُّيُوف بَعْدَ ٱلْإِفْطَار إِلَى ٱلْمَسْجِد لِلصَّلاة.

٣.   أَلسُّؤَال: مَتَى ـــــــــــــــــــــــــــــــ ؟

أَلْجَوَاب: رَجَعَ رَان إِلَى ٱلْبَيْت فِي مُنْتَصَفِ ٱللَّيْل.

The prayer أَلصَّلَاة

One of the most important commandments of Islam is the prayer. Muslims pray

five times a day, facing Mecca (مَكَّة ٱلْمُكَرَّمَة) in Saudi Arabia. Prayer is

always recited in Arabic. A Muslim can pray anywhere and in private, but

according to Prophet Muhammad the reward is greater for a congregational

prayer at the mosque. At noon on Friday a central prayer with a large

congregation is held in the Mosque (مَسْجِد). The prayer is the second of the

five pillars of Islam and begins with the words أَللهُ أَكْبَر, *God is the greatest.*

تَمْرِين ١١. إِبْحَثُوا فِي ٱلْإِنترِنِت عَنْ أَرْكَانِ ٱلْإِسْلَام ٱلْخَمْسَة.

Exercise 11. Look on the Internet for the Five Pillars of Islam. (Write their
names in Arabic and English and be ready to introduce one of
them in the classroom.)

١. _____

٢. _____

٣. _____

٤. _____

٥. _____

The verb in the past tense أَلْفِعْلُ ٱلْمَاضِي

The verb in the past tense أَلْفِعْلُ ٱلْمَاضِي indicates an action that occurred in the past. For example: كَتَبَ (he wrote), تَعَلَّمْنَا (we studied). In أَلْمَاضِي, the subject (doer of an action) is indicated by a suffix attached to the verb through conjugation. For example, in the verb كَتَبْتُ the suffix تُ is indicative of the subject pronoun أَنَا (I). In the verb تَعَلَّمْنَا the suffix نَا is indicative of the subject pronoun نَحْنُ (we). Therefore, you do not need to use separate subject pronouns when conjugating verbs, because the subject is already included within the verb. Here is the full conjugation of أَلْمَاضِي in the singular and plural.

تَصْرِيفُ ٱلْفِعْلِ ٱلْمَاضِي

We wrote	(نَحْنُ) كَتَبْنَا	I wrote	(أَنَا) كَتَبْتُ
You (m. pl.) wrote	(أَنْتُمْ) كَتَبْتُمْ	You (m. s.) wrote	(أَنْتَ) كَتَبْتَ
You (f. pl.) wrote	(أَنْتُنَّ) كَتَبْتُنَّ	You (f. s.) wrote	(أَنْتِ) كَتَبْتِ
They (m. pl.) wrote	(هُمْ) كَتَبُوا	He wrote	(هُوَ) كَتَبَ
They (f. pl.) wrote	(هُنَّ) كَتَبْنَ	She wrote	(هِيَ) كَتَبَتْ

تَمْرِين ١٢. صَرِّفُوا شَفَهِيًّا ثُمَّ ٱكْتُبُوا ٱلتَّصْرِيف فِي دَفَاتِرِكُمْ.

Exercise 12. Conjugate out loud, then write the conjugation in your notebooks.

سَكَنَ ، ذَهَبَ ، دَرَسَ

أَلْمُثَنَّى فِي ٱلْفِعْلِ ٱلْمَاضِي   The dual in the past tense

The dual is created by adding ا to:

١. (أَنْتُمْ) كَتَبْتُمْ + ا ← أَنْتُمَا كَتَبْتُمَا   You (m. and f. dual) wrote

٢. (هُوَ) كَتَبَ + ا ← هُمَا كَتَبَا   They (m. dual) wrote

٣. (هِيَ) كَتَبَتْ + ا ← هُمَا كَتَبَتَا   They (f. dual) wrote

Unlike the regular silent أَلِف at the end of a word, the silent أَلِف that indicates the dual lengthens the فَتْحَة preceding it.

تَمْرِين ١٣. حَدِّدُوا ٱلْفِعْلَ ٱلْمَاضِي وَضَمِيرَهُ ثُمَّ تَرْجِمُوا ٱلْجُمَل إِلَى ٱلْإِنْجِلِيزِيَّة.

Exercise 13. Identify the verb in the past tense and its pronoun, then translate the sentences into English.

١. جَلَسَتْ نُور فِي غُرْفَتِهَا وَلَعِبَتْ عَلَى ٱلْكُمْبِيُوتِر.

٢. سَافَرْنَا فِي ٱلصَّبَاح وَرَجَعْنَا إِلَى ٱلْبَيْت فِي مُنْتَصَفِ ٱللَّيْل.

٣. تَخَرَّجَا مِنَ ٱلْجَامِعَة مُنْذُ سَنَة.

٤ . لِمَاذَا مَا سَافَرْتُنَّ فِي ٱلصَّيْفِ إِلَى ٱلْمَغْرِب؟

٥ . ذَهَبُوا إِلَى طَبِيبِ ٱلْأَسْنَانِ وَمَا رَجَعُوا حَتَّى (until) ٱلآن .

All verbs in Arabic in أَلْمَاضِي are conjugated in the same way and have the same suffixes. The basic form of أَلْمَاضِي is the third person masculine singular (he) which has no suffix.

تَصْرِيفُ ٱلْفِعْلِ ٱلْمَاضِي

	نَحْنُ ـــــــ نَا		أَنَا ـــــــ تُ
أَنْتُمَا ـــــــ تُمَا	أَنْتُمْ ـــــــ تُمْ		أَنْتَ ـــــــ تَ
	أَنْتُنَّ ـــــــ تُنَّ		أَنْتِ ـــــــ تِ
هُمَا ـــــــ ا	هُمْ ـــــــ وا		هُوَ ـــــــ
هُمَا ـــــــ تَا	هُنَّ ـــــــ نَ		هِيَ ـــــــ تْ

تَمْرِين ١٤ . صَرِّفُوا شَفَهِيًّا ثُمَّ ٱكْتُبُوا ٱلتَّصْرِيفَ فِي دَفَاتِرِكُمْ.

Exercise 14. Conjugate out loud, then write the conjugation in your notebooks.

هُوَ:   سَكَنَ ،   تَخَرَّجَ ،   سَافَرَ ،   إِسْتَأْجَرَ (he rented)

تَمْرِين ١٥. قُولُوا ٱلْفِعْلَ ٱلْمُنَاسِب شَفَهِيًّا ثُمَّ ٱكْتُبُوه.

Exercise 15. Say the appropriate verb out loud, then write it.

١. فِي ٱلصَّيْف ــــــــــــــ مَعَ أُسْرَتِي إِلَى فَرَنْسَا.   (سَافَرَ – أَنَا)

٢. أَيْنَ ــــــــــــــ يَا شَبَاب؟   (سَكَنَ – أَنْتُمْ)

٣. كَيْفَ ــــــــــــــ مَعَهُ؟   (تَكَلَّمَ – أَنْتَ)

٤. ــــــــــــــ فِي مَطْعَم لُبْنَانِيّ.   (أَكَلَ – نَحْنُ)

٥. ــــــــــــــ عَلَى ٱلْأُسْتَاذِ ٱلْجَدِيد.   (تَعَرَّفَ – هُمْ)

٦. إِلَى أَيْنَ ــــــــــــــ أَمْسِ؟   (ذَهَبَ – أَنْتِ)

٧. مَاذَا ــــــــــــــ فِي ٱلْإِفْطَار؟   (أَكَلَ – أَنْتُمَا)

٨. ــــــــــــــ ٱلشَّقَّة بِسَبَبِ ٱلْمَنْظَرِ ٱلْجَمِيل.   (إِسْتَأْجَرَ – هُمْ)

٩. هَلْ ــــــــــــــ بَعْدَ ٱلتَّخَرُّج إِلَى ٱلْأُرْدُنّ؟   (سَافَرَ – هُمَا)

١٠. مَتَى ــــــــــــــ ران وَأُسْرَتُهُ إِلَى ٱلْبَيْت؟   (رَجَعَ – هُوَ)

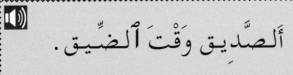

أَلصَّديِق وَقْتَ ٱلضِّيقِ.

A friend in need is a friend indeed.

نَفْيُ ٱلْمَاضِي   Negation of the past tense

To negate ٱلْمَاضِي put مَا before the verb:

We didn't eat and didn't drink.   مَا أَكَلْنَا وَمَا شَرِبْنَا.

تَمْرِين ١٦. إِخْتَارُوا ٱلتَّرْجَمَةَ ٱلصَّحِيحَةَ بِٱلْعَرَبِيَّة.

Exercise 16. Choose the correct Arabic translation.

1. We didn't know his name.   ب. مَا عَرَفْتِ ٱسْمَهُ.   أ. مَا عَرَفْنَا ٱسْمَهُ.

2. They (*m.*) rented the apartment.   ب. إِسْتَأْجَرُوا ٱلشَّقَّة.   أ. إِسْتَأْجَرْتُنَّ ٱلشَّقَّة.

3. We spoke with him yesterday.   ب. تَكَلَّمْنَا مَعَهُ أَمْسِ.   أ. تَكَلَّمْنَ مَعَهُ أَمْسِ.

4. Did you (*dual*) eat?   ب. هَلْ أَكَلَا؟   أ. هَلْ أَكَلْتُمَا؟

5. She traveled a year ago.   ب. سَافَرْتِ مُنْذُ سَنَة.   أ. سَافَرَتْ مُنْذُ سَنَة.

6. When did you (*f. pl.*) return?   ب. مَتَى رَجَعْتُمْ؟   أ. مَتَى رَجَعْتُنَّ؟

إِمْدَحْ صَدِيقَكَ عَلَنًا وَعَاتِبْهُ سِرًّا.

Praise your friend openly and criticize him secretly.

تَمْرِين ١٧ .   قُولُوا شَفَهِيًّا حَسَبَ ٱلْمِثَال ثُمَّ ٱكْتُبُوا ٱلْجُمَل فِي دَفَاتِرِكُمْ.

Exercise 17. Say aloud according to the example, then write the sentences
in your notebooks.

١. هُو: إِسْتَأْجَرَ شَقَّة صَغِيرَة.

أَنَا: إِسْتَأْجَرْتُ شَقَّة صَغِيرَة.

نَحْنُ ، هُمَا (f.) ، أَنْتُمْ ، هُمْ ، أَنْتَ

٢. هُو: تَخَرَّجَ مِنَ ٱلْجَامِعَة قَبْلَ سَنَة.

أَنْتِ ، هِيَ ، هُمَا (m.) ، أَنْتُمَا ، هُنَّ

٣. هُو: إِتَّصَلَ بِٱلْأُسْتَاذَة أَمْسِ.

هُمْ ، أَنْتَ ، أَنْتُمَا ، أَنَا ، أَنْتُنَّ

Verbs that require prepositions

While some verbs do not require a preposition after them (to connect to the

object), other verbs do. For example, the verb إِسْتَأْجَرَ (to rent) does not

require a preposition, إِسْتَأْجَرَ شَقَّة He rented an apartment. The verbs

تَخَرَّجَ مِنَ ٱلْجَامِعَة require prepositions: إِتَّصَلَ and تَخَرَّجَ He graduated

from the university, إِتَّصَلَ بِٱلْأُسْتَاذَة He called the professor (f.).

Exercise 18. Complete the sentences.   تَمْرين ١٨. أَكْمِلُوا ٱلْجُمَل.

١. مَاذَا أَكَلْتِ يَا مَرْيَم؟ أَكَلْتُ _____

٢. _____ رَجَعْتُ إِلَى ٱلْبَيْت

٣. _____ بَعْدَ ٱلْإِفْطَار

٤. مَتَى سَافَرْتَ يَا ران؟ سَافَرْتُ _____

٥. أَيْنَ كُنْتِ يَا شِيرَا؟ كُنْتُ _____

٦. أَنَا مَا عَرَفْتُ أَيْنَ _____

٧. تَعَرَّفَتْ مُنَى عَلَى _____

٨. أين سَكَنَتْ نَوال؟ سَكَنَتْ _____

٩. إِتَّصَلَ مَاجِد بِٱلْأُسْتَاذَة _____

١٠. هَلْ أَكَلْتُمَا ٱلْعَشَاء (dinner)؟ نَعَمْ، _____

تَعَلَّمُوا هٰذِهِ ٱلْمُفْرَدَات

that (followed by subject)	أَنَّ	thankfullness, thanks	شُكْر
that I	أَنَّنِي، أَنِّي	food	أَلطَّعَام، طَعَام
that you (m. s.)	أَنَّكَ	thing, something	شَيْء (ج) أَشْيَاء
well mannered, educated	مُؤَدَّب	to feel (that...)	شَعَرَ أَنَّ (م) يَشْعُرُ أَنَّ
smartest	أَشْطَر	duty, assignment	وَاجِب

تَمْرِين ١٩. إِمْلَؤُوا ٱلْفَرَاغ بِٱلْكَلِمَة ٱلْمُنَاسِبة.

Exercise 19. Fill in the blank with the appropriate word.

١. لا _____ عَلَى وَاجِب. (طَعَام ، شُكْر ، أَشْطَر)

٢. سَارَة هِيَ بِنْت _____ وَشَاطِرَة. (طُفُولَة ، مُؤَدَّب ، مُؤَدَّبَة)

٣. مَرْيَم هِيَ _____ بِنْت فِي ٱلْعَالَم. (أَشْطَر ، مُؤَدَّبَة ، مِثْل)

٤. _____ أَنَّنِي أَتَكَلَّمُ مَعَ طَالِبَة فِي ٱلْجَامِعَة. (شَيْء ، أَلطَّعَام ، شَعَرْتُ)

٥. كَيْفَ كَانَ _____ . (أَلطَّعَام ، ٱلْمَكْتَبَة ، أَشْطَر)

Listen to the conversation, then read it.

إِسْتَمِعُوا إِلَى ٱلْمُحَادَثَة ثُمَّ ٱقْرَؤُوهَا.

لا شُكْرَ عَلَى وَاجِب

أَلْوَقْت: يَوْمُ ٱلْجُمْعَة. أَلسَّاعَة ٱلْخَامِسَة وَٱلنِّصْف.

ران: أَلُو

ماجد: أَهْلاً يَا ران.

ران: أَهْلاً يَا مَاجِد، وَٱللَّه أَنَا وَأُسْرَتِي ٱسْتَمْتَعْنَا أَمْس كَثِيرًا بِٱلإِفْطَارِ ٱلْجَمِيل، شُكْرًا جَزِيلاً لَكَ (thank you very much) يَا مَاجِد.

ماجد: لا شُكْرَ عَلَى وَاجِب. نَحْنُ أَيْضًا ٱسْتَمْتَعْنَا بِزِيَارَتِكُمْ. هَلْ تَعَرَّفْتَ عَلَى أُسْتَاذَتِي مَرْيَم؟ هِيَ أَحْسَن أُسْتَاذَة فِي ٱلْجَامِعَة.

ران: نَعَم. تَعَرَّفْتُ عَلَيْهَا وَتَعَرَّفْتُ أَيْضًا عَلَى سَارَة، بِنْت مُؤَدَّبَة وَشَاطِرَة، مَا شَاءَ ٱللَّه! شَعَرْتُ أَنَّنِي أَتَكَلَّمُ مَعَ طَالِبَة فِي ٱلْجَامِعَة.

ماجد: سَارَة أُخْتِي هِيَ أَشْطَر بِنْت فِي نِيو جِيرْسِي، وَكَيْفَ كَانَ ٱلطَّعَام؟

ران: كَانَ ٱلأَكْل لَذِيذًا جِدًّا. أَكَلْتُ مِنْ كُلِّ شَيْء، أَحْسَن أَكْل فِي ٱلْعَالَم.

ماجد: شُكْرًا، أَنَا سَعِيد أَنَّكَ ٱسْتَمْتَعْتَ بِٱلطَّعَام.

ران: سَأَرَاكَ قَرِيبًا فِي نِيو يُورْك إِنْ شَاءَ ٱللَّه.

ماجد: إِنْ شَاءَ ٱللَّه.

Exercise 20. True or false?   تَمْرِين ٢٠. صَوَاب أَمْ خَطَأٌ؟

صَوَاب   خَطَأ

○	○	١. لِرَان أُخْت صَغِيرَة ٱسْمُهَا سَارَة.
○	○	٢. سَارَة بِنْت مُؤَدَّبَة وَشَاطِرَة.
○	○	٣. يَتَكَلَّمُ رَان مَعَ مَاجِد بِٱلْهَاتِف.
○	○	٤. مَاجِد وَسَارَة أَخ وَأُخْت.
○	○	٥. كَانَ ٱلإِفْطَار يَوْمَ ٱلْخَمِيس في الصَّبَاح.
○	○	٦. أَكَلَ رَان مِنْ كُلِّ شَيْء.
○	○	٧. تَعَرَّفَ رَان عَلَى أُخْت سَارَة.
○	○	٨. رَجَعَ مَاجِد إِلَى ٱلْبَيْت يَوْمَ ٱلْخَمِيس في مُنْتَصَفِ ٱللَّيْل.
○	○	٩. كَانَ ٱلأَكْل في ٱلإِفْطَار لَذِيذاً.

تَمْرِين ٢١. تَرْجِمُوا شَفَهِيًّا ثُمَّ ٱكْتُبُوا ٱلتَّرْجَمَة.

Exercise 21. Translate out loud, then write the translation.

1. - Thank you (*m. s.*) very much.
   - Don't mention it.

2. - How was the food?
   - The food was delicious.

3. - Did you (*f. s.*) meet my sister Sarah?
   - Yes, I met Sarah. She is a smart girl.

4. - I will see you (*m. s.*) soon, God willing.
   - God willing.

The Forms أَوْزَانُ ٱلْأَفْعَال

The verbs in Arabic come in different groups: **Forms** (or patterns أَوْزَان). A Form
(a pattern, وَزْن) is a particular grouping of verbs that have the same features
(vowels, شَدَّة, or additional letters) added to the root, and a specific pattern for
أَلْمَصْدَر [verbal noun (gerund) derived from the verb]. The Forms are used to
classify verbs by these additional features. Each Form has a name and a number
and can be called by either one. For example, you can call Form 1:
وَزْن فَعَلَ or أَلْوَزْنُ ٱلْأَوَّل. In Arabic there are ten Forms.

The names of the Forms أَسْمَاءُ ٱلْأَوْزَان

The name of a **Form** is created by replacing the root (the three radicals) of a
verb in the **third person masculine singular** in أَلْمَاضِي, with the generic
radicals - فعل. For example, the verb كَتَبَ is third person singular in
أَلْمَاضِي: replace its three radicals (كتب) with the generic radicals فعل and
you get the name of the Form - فَعَلَ [Form 1]. Verbs like نَزَلَ, فَتَحَ and
دَرَسَ that share the same features (pattern), belong to this Form. Another
example, the verb سَافَرَ is third person singular in أَلْمَاضِي. Replace its three
radicals (سفر) with the generic radicals فعل and you get the name of the Form
- فَاعَلَ. Verbs like عَاوَنَ and قَابَلَ , شَاهَدَ that share the same features
(pattern), belong to this Form [Form 3].

أَلأَوْزَان: أَلْمَاضِي وَٱلْمُضَارِع وَٱلْمَصْدَر

	أَلْمَصْدَر	أَلْمُضَارِع	أَلْمَاضِي
1. Form 1*	(different patterns)	يَفْعُلُ	فَعَلَ
2. Form 2	تَفْعِيل	يُفَعِّلُ	فَعَّلَ
3. Form 3	مُفَاعَلَة/فِعَال	يُفَاعِلُ	فَاعَلَ
4. Form 4	إفْعَال	يُفْعِلُ	أَفْعَلَ
5. Form 5	تَفَعُّل	يَتَفَعَّلُ	تَفَعَّلَ
6. Form 6	تَفَاعُل	يَتَفَاعَلُ	تَفَاعَلَ
7. Form 7	إنْفِعَال	يَنْفَعِلُ	إنْفَعَلَ
8. Form 8	إفْتِعَال	يَفْتَعِلُ	إفْتَعَلَ
9. Form 9**	إفْعِلال	يَفْعَلُّ	إفْعَلَّ
10. Form 10	إسْتِفْعَال	يَسْتَفْعِلُ	إسْتَفْعَلَ

* In وَزْن فَعَلَ (Form 1) there are verbs that take فَتْحَة, ضَمَّة or كَسْرَة in their second radical in أَلْمُضَارِع and أَلْمَاضِي. For example:

نَزَلَ يَنْزِلُ or شَرِبَ يَشْرَبُ or كَبُرَ يَكْبُرُ.

** Form 9 is not productive; meaning, no new verbs could be created using this pattern.

تَمْرِينٌ ٢٢. أُكْتُبُوا أَرْبَعَ جُمَلٍ بِٱلْإِنْجِليزيَّةِ تَتَعَلَّقُ بِٱلْأَوْزَان.

Exercise 22. Write four sentences in English regarding to the Forms.

Example: In Forms 2 and 5 the second radical has a شَدَّة.

1. _____

2. _____

3. _____

4. _____

Exercise 23. Write the names of the Forms.   تَمْرِينٌ ٢٣. أُكْتُبُوا أَسْمَاءَ ٱلْأَوْزَان.

أَلْوَزْن	أَلْجَذْر	أَلْفِعْل		أَلْفِعْل	أَلْجَذْر	أَلْوَزْن
_____	علم	٢. عَلَّمَ		تَبَادَلَ	بدل	تَفَاعَلَ ١.
_____	برك	٤. بَارَكَ		_____	أجر	إسْتَأْجَرَ ٣.
_____	شرب	٦. شَرِبَ		_____	خرج	أخْرَجَ ٥.
_____	متع	٨. إسْتَمْتَعَ		_____	سفر	سَافَرَ ٧.
_____	خرج	١٠. تَخَرَّجَ		_____	شرك	إشْتَرَكَ ٩.

تَمْرِين ٢٤. أُكْتُبُوا أَرْقَامَ ٱلْأَوْزَان حَسَبَ ٱلْمِثَال.

Exercise 24. Write the numbers of the Forms according to the example.

> ٱلْأَوَّل ، ٱلثَّانِي ، ٱلثَّالِث ، ٱلرَّابِع ، ٱلْخَامِس
> ٱلسَّادِس ، ٱلسَّابِع ، ٱلثَّامِن ، (ٱلتَّاسِع) ، ٱلْعَاشِر

١. سَكَتَ أَلْوَزْنُ (1) ٱلْأَوَّل
٢. إِنْسَحَبَ ٱلْوَزْنُ _____

٣. أَحْضَرَ ٱلْوَزْنُ _____
٤. عَلَّمَ أَلْوَزْنُ _____

٥. شَاهَدَ أَلْوَزْنُ _____
٦. تَذَكَّرَ أَلْوَزْنُ _____

٧. تَبَادَلَ أَلْوَزْنُ _____
٨. إِشْتَرَكَ أَلْوَزْنُ _____

٩. تَعَرَّفَ أَلْوَزْنُ _____
١٠. أَرْسَلَ أَلْوَزْنُ _____

١١. لَعِبَ أَلْوَزْنُ _____
١٢. تَخَرَّجَ أَلْوَزْنُ _____

١٣. إِنْقَطَعَ أَلْوَزْنُ _____
١٤. شَعَرَ أَلْوَزْنُ _____

١٥. تَعَلَّمَ أَلْوَزْنُ _____
١٦. إِسْتَمْتَعَ أَلْوَزْنُ _____

تَمْرِين ٢٥. أُكْتُبُوا ٱلْفِعْل حَسَبَ ٱلْوَزْن وَٱلْجَذْرِ.

Exercise 25. Write the verbs according to the pattern and the root.

ألْفِعْل	ألْجَذْر	ألْوَزْن		ألْفِعْل	ألْجَذْر	ألْوَزْن
_____	شرك	٢. يَفْتَعِلُ		يَتَخَرَّجُ	خرج	١. يَتَفَعَّلُ
_____	فهم	٤. يَفْعَلُ		_____	جوب	٣. يُفَاعِلُ
_____	سلم	٦. يُفَعِّلُ		_____	أجر	٥. يَسْتَفْعِلُ
_____	شهد	٨. يُفَاعِلُ		_____	حضر	٧. يُفْعِلُ
_____	لعب	١٠. يَفْعَلُ		_____	عرف	٩. يَتَفَعَّلُ

تَمْرِين ٢٦. أُكْتُبُوا ٱلْأَفْعَال بِٱلْمُضَارِعِ حَسَبَ ٱلْمِثَال.

Exercise 26. Write the verbs in the present-future tense according to the example.

_____ ٢. إِنْسَحَبَ	يُعَلِّمُ	١. عَلَّمَ
_____ ٤. سَافَرَ	_____	٣. أَحْضَرَ
_____ ٦. تَكَلَّمَ	_____	٥. تَعَرَّفَ
_____ ٨. أَرْسَلَ	_____	٧. إِسْتَأْجَرَ
_____ ١٠. شَعَرَ ‒ُ *	_____	٩. شَاهَدَ

* The dash and the فَتْحَة above it represent the second radical in the present-future tense (ٱلْمُضَارِع).

أَسْمَاءُ حُرُوفِ ٱلْجَذْرِ
Names of the root's radicals (letters)

The first radical of the root is called: فَاءُ ٱلْفِعْل

The second radical of the root is called: عَيْنُ ٱلْفِعْل

The third radical of the root is called: لَامُ ٱلْفِعْل

The three radicals are written as a word (connected) without vowels.

They are pronounced as if each letter has a فَتْحَة (*shahada* شَهـد).

تَمْرِين ٢٧ . إِمْلَؤُوا ٱلْفَرَاغِ.

Exercise 27. Fill in the blank.

١. عَيْنُ ٱلْفِعْل في "دَخَلْتُمْ" ‎_____ ٢. فَاءُ ٱلْفِعْل في "أَنْزل" ‎_____

٣. لَامُ ٱلْفِعْل في "تَشْرَبِينَ" ‎_____ ٤. عَيْنُ ٱلْفِعْل في "شَاهَدْنَ" ‎_____

تَمْرِين ٢٨ . قُولُوا ٱلْجَذْر وَٱلضَّمِير شَفَهِيًّا حَسَبَ ٱلْمِثَال.

Exercise 28. Say out loud the root and the pronoun according to the example.

يَجْلِسُ ⟸ ٱلْجَذْر: جلس ، ٱلضَّمِير: هُوَ

١. سَافَرْتُمْ ٢. تَبْحَثِينَ ٣. أَتَكَلَّمُ ٤. نَظَرْنَا ٥. تَدْخُلُ

٦. سَكَنَّ ٧. أَرْسَلْتَ ٨. تَفْهَمِينَ ٩. تَعَرَّفْتُ ١٠. تَسْتَأْجِرُونَ

تَمْرِين ٢٩. أُكْتُبُوا ٱلْمَاضِيَ وَٱلْمُضَارِعَ حَسَبَ ٱلْمِثَال.

Exercise 29. Write the past tense and the present-future tense according to the example.

خصص ٥ ⟸ تَخَصَّصَ يَتَخَصَّصُ

١. شهد – Form ٣	٢. كلم – Form ٥	٣. برك – Form ٣
٤. درس – Form ٢	٥. سحب – Form ٧	٦. عون – Form ٦
٧. نقل – Form ٨	٨. رسل – Form ٤	٩. قبل – Form ١٠

تَعَلَّمُوا هٰذِهِ ٱلْمُفْرَدَات

to take place	دَارَ (م) يَدُورُ	apartment	شَقَّة (ج) شُقَق
tooth	سِنّ (ج) أَسْنان	quarter	رُبْع (ج) أَرْبَاع
		noon	ظُهْر

إِسْتَمِعُوا إِلَى ٱلْمُحَادَثَة ثُمَّ ٱقْرَؤُوهَا .

Listen to the conversation, then read it.

أَيْنَ ران؟

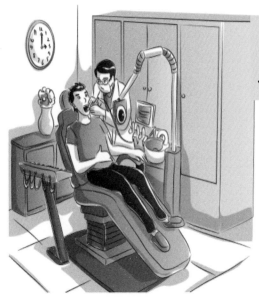

ٱلْمَكَان : شَقَّة عَائِلَة ران فِي نيو يورك .

ٱلْوَقْت : ٱلسَّاعَة ٱلثَّالِثَة وَٱلرُّبْع بَعْدَ ٱلظُّهْر .

مَاجِد : أَلُو، مَرْحَبًا .

أُمّ ران : أَهْلاً .

مَاجِد : هَلْ رَان فِي ٱلْبَيْت؟

أُمّ ران : لا . مَنْ حَضْرَتُكَ؟

مَاجِد : أَنَا صَدِيقُهُ مَاجِد مِنْ نيو جِيرْسِي .

أُمّ ران : أَهْلا، أَهْلا يَا مَاجِد .

مَاجِد : أَهْلاً بِك . مِنْ فَضْلِك هَلْ تَعْرِفِينَ إِلَى أَيْنَ ذَهَبَ؟

أُمّ ران : ذَهَبَ إِلَى طَبِيب ٱلْأَسْنَان مُنْذُ سَاعَة .

مَاجِد : وَهَلْ قَالَ مَتَى سَيَرْجِعُ؟

أُمّ ران : فِي ٱلسَّاعَة ٱلرَّابِعَة وَٱلنِّصْف .

مَاجِد : هَلْ سَيَرْجِعُ إِلَى شَقَّتِه ٱلْجَدِيدَة؟

أُمّ ران : نَعَمْ .

مَاجِد: سَأَذْهَبُ إِلَيْهِ فِي ٱلْمَسَاء.

أُمّ ران: هَلْ تَعْرِفُ عُنْوَانَ ٱلشَّقَّة؟

مَاجِد: نَعَمْ أَعْرِفُهُ، شُكْرًا لَك.

أُمّ ران: لا شُكْرَ عَلَى وَاجِب.

تَمْرِين ٣٠. أَجِيبُوا شَفَهِيًّا ثُمَّ ٱكْتُبُوا ٱلْأَجْوِبَة.
Exercise 30. Answer out loud, then write the answers.

١. إِلَى أَيْنَ ذَهَبَ ران؟ _____

٢. مَتَى سَيَرْجِعُ؟ _____

٣. إِلَى أَيْنَ سَيَذْهَبُ مَاجِد فِي ٱلْمَسَاء؟ _____

تَمْرِين ٣١. تَرْجِمُوا شَفَهِيًّا ثُمَّ ٱكْتُبُوا ٱلتَّرْجَمَة.
Exercise 31. Translate out loud, then write the translation.

1. Who is Majid? _____

2. Who are you (f. s.) ? _____

3. Majid is Rahn's friend. _____

4. Rahn went to the dentist. _____

Exercise 32. True or false.   تَمْرِين ٣٢. صَوَاب أَمْ خَطَأٌ؟

صَوَاب   خَطَأ

○   ○   ١. تَكَلَّمَ مَاجِد مَعَ أُمّ رَان.

○   ○   ٢. إتَّصَلَ مَاجِد بِرَان فِي ٱلسَّاعَة ٱلثَّالِثَة.

○   ○   ٣. رَان وَمَاجِد صَدِيقَان.

○   ○   ٤. تَكَلَّمَ رَان مَعَ أُخْت مَاجِد.

○   ○   ٥. لِرَان شَقَّة جَدِيدَة.

○   ○   ٦. لَا يَعْرِفُ مَاجِد عُنْوَان شَقَّة رَان.

○   ○   ٧. ذَهَبَ رَان فِي ٱلسَّاعَة ٱلثَّانِيَة وَٱلرُّبْع إِلَى طَبِيب ٱلأَسْنَان.

تَمْرِين ٣٣. رَجَعَ رَان إِلَى شَقَّتِه ٱلْجَدِيدَة فِي "إِيطَالِيَا ٱلصَّغِيرَة" فِي مَانْهَاتِن فِي ٱلسَّاعَة ٱلرَّابِعَة وَٱلنِّصْف، وَٱتَّصَلَ بِصَدِيقِه مَاجِد. وَلَٰكِنَّ مَاجِد مَا كَانَ فِي ٱلْبَيْت فَتَكَلَّمَ مَعَ وَالِدِه. تَكَلَّمُوا مَعَ زُمَلائِكُمْ ثُمَّ ٱكْتُبُوا ٱلْمُحَادَثَة فِي دَفَاتِرِكُمْ.

Exercise 33. Rahn returned to his new apartment in "Little Italy" in Manhattan at 4:30 and called his friend Majid. Majid was not at home so Rahn spoke with his father. Speak with your classmates, then write the conversation in your notebooks.

تَمْرِين ٣٤. قُولُوا ٱلسَّاعَة وَمَاذَا حَدَثَ فِي هٰذِهِ ٱلسَّاعَة؟

Exercise 34. Say the time and what happened at each hour?

Changes in pronouns هُمَا ، هُنَّ ، هُمْ ، ـهُ

The suffix pronouns ـهُ ، هُمْ ، هُنَّ ، هُمَا change into هُمَا ، هُنَّ ، هُمْ ، ـهُ
after:

١. كَسْرَة ـِ :   بِهِ ،   بِهِمْ ،   بِهِنَّ ،   بِهِمَا

٢. يَاء with سُكُون ـيْ : إِلَيْهِ ، إِلَيْهِمْ ، إِلَيْهِنَّ ، إِلَيْهِمَا

٣. silent يَاء ـي :   فِيهِ ،   فِيهِمْ ،   فِيهِنَّ ،   فِيهِمَا

We enjoyed it very much.   إِسْتَمْتَعْنَا بِهِ كَثِيرًا.

The house is big. It has four bedrooms.   أَلْبَيْت كَبِير. فِيهِ أَرْبَع غُرَف نَوْم.

Did you (f. s.) send the letter to them?   هَلْ أَرْسَلْتِ ٱلرِّسَالَة إِلَيْهِمْ؟

حُرُوفُ ٱلْجَرّ

فِي in   ، بِ in

Dual	Pl.	S.	Dual	Pl.	S.
	بِنَا	بِي	فِيَّ	فِينَا	فِيَّ
بِكُمَا	بِكُمْ	بِكَ	فِيكُمَا	فِيكُمْ	فِيكَ
	بِكُنَّ	بِكِ	فِيكُنَّ	فِيكِ	
بِهِمَا	بِهِمْ	بِهِ	فِيهِمَا	فِيهِمْ	فِيهِ
بِهِمَا	بِهِنَّ	بِهَا	فِيهِمَا	فِيهِنَّ	فِيهَا

Pay attention to the changes in the pronouns.

تَمْرِين ٣٥. غَيِّرُوا ٱلضَّمِير شَفَهِيًّا حَسَبَ ٱلْمِثَال ثُمَّ ٱكْتُبُوا ٱلْجُمَل.

Exercise 35. Change the pronoun out loud according to the example, then

write the sentences.

*He thinks about **him** a lot.*   ١. يُفَكِّرُ فِيهِ (هُوَ) كَثِيرًا.

أَنْتُمْ   هُمْ   هِيَ   أَنْتِ   هُنَّ   هُمَا

*I called **him** an hour ago.*   ٣. إِتَّصَلْتُ بِهِ (هُوَ) قَبْلَ سَاعَة.

هُمَا   هِيَ   أَنْتُنَّ   أَنْتُمْ   هُمْ   أَنْتُمَا

لَدَى ، عَلَى ، إِلَى

The prepositions إِلَى (to) end with أَلِف مَقْصُورَة. (at) لَدَى ،(on) عَلَى

When a suffix pronoun is added to them, the أَلِف مَقْصُورَة changes into يْ.

إِلَى + نَا ← إِلَيْنَا , عَلَى + كَ ← عَلَيْكَ , لَدَى + كُمْ ← لَدَيْكُمْ

إِلَى + ضَمَائِر

dual	Pl.	S.
	إِلَيْنَا	إِلَيَّ
إِلَيْكُمَا	إِلَيْكُمْ	إِلَيْكَ
	إِلَيْكُنَّ	إِلَيْكِ
إِلَيْهِمَا	إِلَيْهِمْ	إِلَيْهِ
إِلَيْهِمَا	إِلَيْهِنَّ	إِلَيْهَا

Pay attention to the changes in the pronouns.

تَمْرِين ٣٦. أَضِيفُوا ٱلضَّمَائِرَ لِحَرْفَيِ ٱلْجَرّ "لَدَى" وَ"عَلَى" شَفَهِيًّا وَكِتَابِيًّا.

Exercise 36. Add pronouns to both prepositions لَدَى and عَلَى out loud and

in writing.

تَمْرِين ٣٧. غَيِّرُوا ٱلضَّمِيرَ شَفَهِيًّا حَسَبَ ٱلْمِثَالِ ثُمَّ ٱكْتُبُوا ٱلْجُمَل.

Exercise 37. Change the pronoun out loud according to the example, then
write the sentences.

١. سَيُرْسِلُونَ ٱلرِّسَالَةَ **إِلَيْهِ** (هُوَ) غَدًا.   *They will send **him** the letter tomorrow.*

هِيَ   نَحْنُ   أَنْتُمْ   أَنَا   هُمْ   أَنْتُمَا

٢. تَعَرَّفْنَا **عَلَيْهِ** (هُوَ) في ٱلْجَامِعَة.   *We met **him** at the university.*

أَنْتُنَّ   هُمْ   أَنْتُمْ   هِيَ   هُمَا   هُوَ

تَمْرِين ٣٨. إِمْلَؤُوا ٱلْفَرَاغَ بِحَرْفِ ٱلْجَرِّ ٱلْمُنَاسِب.

Exercise 38. Fill in the blank with the appropriate preposition.

مَعَ	قَبْلَ	بِـ	إِلَى	عَلَى	في

١. ذَهَبَ ران _____ ٱلسَّاعَةَ ٱلثَّانِيَة وَٱلرُّبْع _____ _____ طَبِيبِ ٱلْأَسْنَان.

٢. إِسْتَمْتَعْنَا كَثِيرًا _____ ٱلإِفْطَار وَتَعَرَّفْنَا _____ أَفْرَاد عَائِلَة مَاجِد.

٣. ذَهَبْتُ _____ وَالِدِي وَوَالِدَتِي وَأُخْتِي _____ نيو جيرسي.

٤. تَعَرَّفَتْ مَرْيَم _____ أُخْت مَاجِد.

٥. وَصَلَتِ ٱلْأُسْتَاذَة _____ ٱلْجَامِعَة _____ سَاعَة.

🔊

تَعَلَّمُوا هٰذِهِ ٱلْمُفْرَدَات

rug, carpet	سَجَّادَة (م) سَجَاجِيد	room	غُرْفَة (ج) غُرَف
wall	حَائِط (ج) حِيطَان	sleep	نَوْم
picture	صُورَة (ج) صُوَر	noon	ظُهْر
wife	زَوْجَة (ج) زَوْجَات	Congratulations!	مَبْرُوك!
summer	صَيْف	view	مَنْظَر (ج) مَنَاظِر
Let's go!	هَيَّا بِنَا!	great	رَائِع
kitchen	مَطْبَخ (ج) مَطَابِخ	to rent	إِسْتَأْجَر (م) يَسْتَأْجِرُ
hungry	جَوْعَان	gift, present	هَدِيَّة (ج) هَدَايَا
thirsty	عَطْشَان	Open!	إِفْتَحْ!
pyramid	هَرَم (ج) أَهْرَام	because of	بِسَبَب

🔊

لِلْحِيطَان آذَان .

Walls have ears.

تَمْرِين ٣٩. أُكْتُبُوا كَلِمَات تَحْتَوِي عَلَى كُلٍّ مِنَ ٱلْجُذُورِ ٱلتَّالِيَة.

Exercise 39. Write words that contain each of the following roots.

٢. سبب	_____	١. عطش	_____
٤. أجر	_____	٣. سجد	_____
٦. نظر	_____	٥. برك	_____
٨. صور	_____	٧. فتح	_____
١٠. هرم	_____	٩. زوج	_____

Exercise 40. Which word does not fit (in each group)?   تَمْرِين ٤٠. جِدُوا ٱلشَّاذّ.

٢. صُوَر غُرَف حِيطَان	١. صَغِير عَشَاء رَائِع
٤. تَخَرَّج مَنْظَر إِسْتَأْجَر	٣. سَجَّادَة حَائِط بَعْدَ
٦. مَطْبَخ مَنَاظِر هَدَايَا	٥. أَهْرَام جَوْعَان أَسْنَان

Exercise 41. Translate out loud.   تَمْرِين ٤١. تَرْجِمُوا شَفَهِيًّا.

٣. بَعْدَ ٱلتَّخَرُّج	٢. هَدِيَّة جَمِيلَة	١. غُرْفَةُ ٱلنَّوْم
٦. هَيَّا بِنَا!	٥. صُورَةُ ٱلأَهْرَام	٤. أَلْمَنْظَر رَائِع.
٩. جَوْعَان وعَطْشَان	٨. عَمِّي وزَوْجَتُهُ	٧. شَقَّة جَدِيدَة

إِسْتَمِعُوا إِلَى ٱلْمُحَادَثَة ثُمَّ ٱقْرَؤُوهَا .   Listen to the conversation, then read it.

فِي شَقَّة رَان ٱلْجَدِيدَة

أَلْمَكَان: شَقَّة رَان ٱلْجَدِيدَة فِي "إِيطَالِيَا ٱلصَّغِيرَة" فِي مَانْهَاتِن .

أَلْوَقْت: أَلسَّاعَة ٱلسَّابِعَة وَٱلرُّبْع مَسَاءً .

مَاجِد: شَقَّتُكَ جَمِيلَة يَا رَان، مَبْرُوك! مَا شَاءَ ٱلله!

رَان: بَارَكَ ٱللهُ فِيكَ .

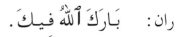

مَاجِد: غُرْفَةُ ٱلنَّوْم كَبِيرَة وَٱلْمَنْظَر رَائِع!

رَان: إِسْتَأْجَرْتُ هٰذِه ٱلشَّقَّة بِسَبَب ٱلْمَنْظَر .

مَاجِد: تَفَضَّلْ، هٰذِه هَدِيَّة صَغِيرَة لِلشَّقَّة ٱلْجَدِيدَة . إِفْتَحْهَا ...

رَان: آه، سَجَّادَة حَائِط ...، هٰذِه ٱلسَّجَّادَة جَمِيلَة جِدًّا! هَلْ هِيَ مِنْ

مِصْر؟

مَاجِد: نَعَمْ، وَلٰكِنْ كَيْفَ عَرَفْتَ؟

رَان: مِنْ صُورَة ٱلْأَهْرَام . هَلْ زُرْتَ ٱلْأَهْرَام؟

مَاجِد: نَعَمْ . كُنْتُ فِي مِصْر مَعَ عَمِّي وَزَوْجَتِه قَبْلَ أَرْبَعَة أَشْهُر وَزُرْنَا

ٱلْأَهْرَام فِي ٱلْجِيزَة .

ران: عَظِيم! أَنَا أَيْضًا سَأُسَافِرُ إِلَى مِصْر فِي ٱلصَّيْف، بَعْدَ ٱلتَّخَرُّج

إِنْ شَاءَ ٱلله، مَعَ ٱلأُسْتَاذ هَانِي... هَيَّا بِنَا إِلَى ٱلْمَطْبَخ يَا مَاجِد،

أَنَا جَوْعَان وعَطْشَان.

بِسَبَب   Because of

After the word بِسَبَب comes a noun or a phrase (not a sentence):

بِسَبَب ٱلْمَنْظَر   Because of the view

بِسَبَب can take pronouns: بِسَبَبِكَ *because of you* (m. s.)

تَمْرِين ٤٢. أَجِيبُوا شَفَهِيًّا ثُمَّ ٱكْتُبُوا ٱلأَجْوِبَة.

Exercise 42. Answer out loud, then write the answers.

١. أَيْنَ دَارَتْ هٰذِه ٱلْمُحَادَثَة؟

_____

٢. مَتَى زَارَ مَاجِد وَعَمُّهُ ٱلأَهْرَام؟

_____

٣. أَيْنَ تُوجَدُ (located) ٱلأَهْرَام؟

_____

٤. مَا هِيَ هَدِيَّة مَاجِد لِرَان؟

_____

تَمْرِين ٤٣ . يَتَّصِل مَاجِد بِصَدِيقِه أَمْجَد وَيَتَكَلَّمُ مَعَهُ عَنْ شَقَّة ران ٱلْجَدِيدَة .

تَكَلَّمُوا مَعَ رُمَلائِكُمْ ثُمَّ ٱكْتُبُوا ٱلْمُحَادَثَة فِي دَفَاتِرِكُمْ .

Exercise 43. Majid calls his friend Amjad and speaks with him about Rahn's

new apartment. Speak with your classmates, then write the

conversation in your notebooks.

Congratulations!   مَبْرُوك !

The word مَبْرُوك, is used to congratulate a person or a group of people on
various occasions such as weddings, births, passing exams, successfully
finishing projects, receiving a promotion, or upon graduation. It is also used to
congratulate a person upon buying something new. The proper response would
be:

١ . بَارَكَ ٱللهُ فِيكَ (لِلْمُذَكَّر m.)   ٢ . بَارَكَ ٱللهُ فِيكِ (لِلْمُؤَنَّث f.)

٣ . بَارَكَ ٱللهُ فِيكُمْ (لِلْجَمْع pl.)

The Pyramids   أَلأَهْرَام

While the Pyramids were built for a common purpose, they varied
considerably in size. The largest Pyramids are located in Giza, not far from
Cairo. The largest and most famous of them is the Pyramid of Khufu. The
Egyptians built the Pyramids on the west bank of the Nile because they
believed that the kingdom of the dead was found in the west, where the sun
sets. The pyramid shape is designed to enable a convenient and smooth ascent
to heaven.

تَمْرِين ٤٤ . إِمْلَؤُوا ٱلْفَرَاغ بِٱلْكَلِمَة ٱلْمُنَاسِبَة .

Exercise 44. Fill in the blank with the appropriate word.

١. هٰذِهِ ٱلشَّقَّة ـــــــــــــــــــــ .   (مَبْسُوطَة ، جَمِيلَة ، لَذِيذَة)

٢. ـــــــــــــــــــــ ٱلنَّوْم فِي هٰذِهِ ٱلشَّقَّة كَبِيرَة . (غُرْفَة ، حَائِط ، سَجَّادَة)

٣. هٰذِهِ ـــــــــــــــــــــ ٱلْمَطْعَمِ ٱللُّبْنَانِيّ . (صُورَة ، حَائِط ، عَشَاء)

٤. هَلْ ـــــــــــــــــــــ ٱلأَهْرَام؟   (أَسْتَأْجَرْتِ ، تَخَرَّجْتِ ، زُرْتِ)

٥. أَنَا ـــــــــــــــــــــ وَأُرِيدُ ٱلْفَلَافِل . (عَطْشَان ، جَوْعَان ، رَائِع)

٦. إِسْتَأْجَرْتُ ٱلشَّقَّة بِسَبَبِ ـــــــــــــــــــــ .(ٱلأَسْنَان ، ٱلأَهْرَام ، ٱلْمَنْظَر)

٧. سَتُسَافِرُ مَرْيَم إِلى مِصْر فِي ٱلصَّيْف، بَعْدَ ـــــــــــــــــــــ .

(ٱلنَّوْم   ٱلتَّخَرُّج   ٱلْعَشَاء)

تَمْرِين ٤٥. أَلصِّفَتَانِ "جَوْعَان" وَ"عَطْشَان" هُمَا عَلَى وَزْنِ "فَعْلَان." كَوِّنُوا كَلِمَات مِنَ ٱلْجُذُورِ ٱلتَّالِيَة عَلَى هٰذَا ٱلْوَزْن وَجِدُوا مَعْنَاهَا فِي ٱلْإِنْتِرْنِت.

Exercise 45. The two adjectives جَوْعَان and عَطْشَان use the pattern of فَعْلَان.

Write words from the following roots on this pattern (adding ـَان ─

at the end of each root) and find their meanings on the Internet.

٢. برد _____	١. تعب _____
٤. غلط _____	٣. خرب _____
٦. كسل _____	٥. زعل _____
٨. نعس _____	٧. فرح _____
١٠. حرر (حَرْرَان) ⟸ حَرَّان *	٩. غضب _____

رْ + رَ ⟸ رَّ *

إِذَا عُرِفَ ٱلدَّاء عُرِفَ ٱلدَّوَاء.

If the disease is diagnosed the cure will be known (found).

جُبْرَان خَلِيل جُبْرَان

فَنَّان لُبْنَانِيّ وَشَاعِر وَكَاتِب

إِذَا قَالَ ٱلشِّتَاء إِنَّ ٱلرَّبِيع فِي قَلْبِي

فَمَنْ يُصَدِّقُ ٱلشِّتَاء؟

When the winter says the spring is in my heart,

who believes the winter?

تَمْرِين ٤٦ . جِدُوا مَعْلُومَات عَنْ جُبْرَان خَلِيل جُبْرَان فِي ٱلْإِنْترْنِت .

Exercise 46. Find information about Jubran Khalil Jubran on the Internet.

تَمْرِين ٤٧ . جِدُوا مَعْلُومَات عَنْ لُبْنَان فِي ٱلْإِنترنت بِمَا فِيهَا ٱلْعَاصِمَة وَعَدَدُ
ٱلسُّكَّان وَٱلْعُمْلَة ونِظَامُ ٱلْحُكْم وَٱلدِّين وَٱلدُّوَل ٱلْمُجَاوِرَة وَمُدُن
مَرْكَزِيَّة وَٱللُّغَة ٱلرَّسْمِيَّة .

Exercise 47. Find information about Lebanon on the Internet including the
capital, population, currency, regime, religion, neighboring
countries, important cities and official language.

UNIT 8

تَعَلَّمُوا هٰذِهِ ٱلْمُفْرَدَات

because	لأَنَّ	soup	شُورْبَة
because I	لأَنَّني	tomato	طَمَاطَة، طَمَاطِم
how?	كَيْفَ؟	country	دَوْلَة (ج) دُوَل
that	ذٰلكَ	by the way	عَلَى فِكْرَة
How is that?	كَيْفَ ذٰلكَ؟	culture	حَضَارَة (ج) حَضَارَات
		very	جِدًّا

تَمْرين ١. إِمْلَؤُوا ٱلْفَرَاغ بِٱلْكَلِمَة ٱلْمُنَاسِبَة.

Exercise 1. Fill in the blank with the appropriate word.

١. هٰذِهِ ـــــــــــــــ لَذيذة جِدًّا.   (ٱلدَّوْلَة ، ٱلْحَضَارَة ، ٱلشُّورْبَة)

٢. ـــــــــــــــ فِكْرَة، لِمَاذَا تَدْرُسُ ٱلْعَرَبِيَّة؟   (في ، عَلَى ، إلَى)

٣. أَدْرُسُ ٱلْعَرَبِيَّة ـــــــــــــــ أُحِبُّهَا (I like it).   (لأَنَّني ، ذٰلكَ ، لأَنَّ)

٤. هَلْ وُلِدَ في ـــــــــــــــ عَرَبِيَّة؟   (فِكْرَة ، دَوْلَة ، شُورْبَة)

٥. يُسَافِرُ إلَى مِصْر وَٱلأُرْدُن وَـــــــــــــــ.   (ٱلْحَضَارَة ، ٱلدَّوْلَة ، ٱلْمَغْرِب)

Listen to the conversation, then read it.   إِسْتَمِعُوا إِلَى ٱلْمُحَادَثَة ثُمَّ ٱقْرَؤُوهَا .

كَمْ لُغَة يَعْرِفُ وَالِدُكَ؟

أَلْمَكَان : شَقَّة ران فِي نيو يورك .

أَلْوَقْت : أَلسَّاعَة ٱلثَّامِنَة تَمَامًا .

ماجد : هٰذِهِ ٱلشُّورْبَة لَذِيذَة جِدًّا .

ران : مَا ٱسْمُهَا بِٱلْعَرَبِيَّة؟

ماجد : شُورْبَة دَجَاج مَع أَرُزّ .

ران : أَنَا أُحِبُّ هٰذِهِ ٱلشُّورْبَة كَثِيرًا وَأَيْضًا أُحِبُّ شُورْبَةَ ٱلطَّمَاطِم .

ماجد : عَلَى فِكْرَة يَا ران، لِمَاذا تَدْرُسُ ٱلْعَرَبِيَّة؟

ران : لِأَنَّنِي أُحِبُّ هٰذِهِ ٱللُّغَة كَثِيرًا وَأُحِبُّ ٱلْحَضَارَةَ ٱلْعَرَبِيَّة، وَأَيْضًا

وَالِدِي يَعْرِفُ هٰذِهِ ٱللُّغَة .

ماجد : كَيْفَ ذٰلِكَ؟ هَلْ وُلِدَ فِي دَوْلَة عَرَبِيَّة؟

ران : لا . وُلِدَ هُنَا فِي أَمْرِيكَا فِي مَدِينَة وَاشْنْطُن دِي سِي . هُوَ دَرَسَ

ٱلْعَرَبِيَّة فِي ٱلْمَدْرَسَة ٱلثَّانَوِيَّة ثُمَّ فِي ٱلْجَامِعَة، وَيُسَافِرُ كَثِيرًا

إِلَى مِصْر وَٱلْأُرْدُنّ وَٱلْمَغْرِب وَقَطَر وَعُمَان .

ماجد : كَمْ لُغَة يَعْرِفُ وَالِدُكَ؟

ران: يَعْرِفُ أَرْبَع لُغَات . ٱلإِنجليزِيَّة وَٱلْعَرَبِيَّة وَٱلْفَرَنْسِيَّة وَٱلْإِسْبَانِيَّة .

ماجد : رَائِع! مَا شَاءَ ٱلله! كُلَّ لِسَان إِنْسَان!

Exercise 2. True or false.   تَمْرِين ٢ . صَوَاب أَمْ خَطَأ؟

🔊

صَوَاب خَطَأ

١ . وُلِدَتْ وَالِدَة ران فِي دَوْلَة عَرَبِيَّة .   ○ ○

٢ . يَعْرِفُ ران أَرْبَع لُغَات .   ○ ○

٣ . يَدْرُسُ ران ٱلْعَرَبِيَّة لِأَنَّهُ يُحِبُّ ٱللُّغَة وَٱلْحَضَارَة .   ○ ○

٤ . يُسَافِرُ وَالِد ران كَثِيرًا إِلَى مِصْر وَسُورِيَا .   ○ ○

٥ . يُحِبُّ مَاجِدُ شُورْبَةَ ٱلدَّجَاج مَعَ ٱلأَرُزّ .   ○ ○

٦ . دَرَسَ وَالِد رَان ٱلْعَرَبِيَّة فِي ٱلْمَدْرَسَة ٱلثَّانَوِيَّة .   ○ ○

٧ . يُحِبُّ رَان شُورْبَةَ ٱلطَّمَاطِم .   ○ ○

٨ . وُلِدَ أَبُو ران فِي وِلَايَة وَاشِنْطُن دي سي .   ○ ○

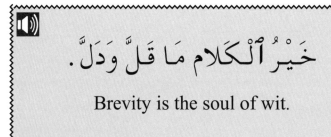

🔊

خَيْرُ ٱلْكَلام مَا قَلَّ وَدَلَّ .

Brevity is the soul of wit.

Exercise 3. Ask your classmates.   تَمْرِين ٣ . إِسْأَلُوا زُمَلاءَكُمْ.

1. In which city were you born?   فِي أَيّ مَدِينَة وُلِدْتَ / وُلِدْتِ؟

2. Does your father know Arabic?   هَلْ يَعْرِفُ وَالِدُكَ / وَالِدُكِ ٱلْعَرَبِيَّة؟

3. Does your mother know Spanish?   هَلْ تَعْرِفُ وَالِدَتُكَ / وَالِدَتُكِ ٱلإِسْبَانِيَّة؟

تَمْرِين ٤ . إِسْأَلُوا زُمَلاءَكُمْ أَرْبَعَة أَسْئِلَة عَنْ وَالِد ران . أُكْتُبُوا ٱلأَسْئِلَة وَٱلأَجْوِبَة.

Exercise 4. Ask your classmates four questions regarding Rahn's father.

       Write the questions and the answers.

١ . أَلسُّؤَالُ ٱلأَوَّل : _____

أَلْجَوَاب : _____

٢ . أَلسُّؤَالُ ٱلثَّاني : _____

أَلْجَوَاب : _____

٣ . أَلسُّؤَالُ ٱلثَّالِث : _____

أَلْجَوَاب : _____

٤ . أَلسُّؤَالُ ٱلرَّابِع : _____

أَلْجَوَاب : _____

Because   لِأَنَّ

After the word لِأَنَّ comes a sentence that starts with a noun

or a pronoun that is attached to لِأَنَّ:

مَا ذَهَبَ ران إِلَى ٱلْجَامِعَة ٱلْيَوْم لِأَنَّ ٱلْأُسْتَاذ هَاني مَرِيض.

Rahn did not go to the university today because Professor Hani is sick.

يَدْرُسُ ران ٱلْعَرَبِيَّة لِأَنَّهُ يُحِبُّ ٱللُّغَة وَٱلْحَضَارة.

Rahn studies Arabic because he likes the language and the culture.

pronouns + لِأَنَّ

because we	لِأَنَّنَا	because I	لِأَنِّي / لِأَنَّنِي
because you (*m. pl.*)	لِأَنَّكُمْ	because you (*m. s.*)	لِأَنَّكَ
because you (*f. pl.*)	لِأَنَّكُنَّ	because you (*f. s.*)	لِأَنَّكِ
because they (*m. pl.*)	لِأَنَّهُمْ	because he	لِأَنَّهُ
because they (*f. pl.*)	لِأَنَّهُنَّ	because she	لِأَنَّهَا

because you (*m. and f. dual*) لِأَنَّكُمَا

because they (*m. and f. dual*) لِأَنَّهُمَا

تَمْرِين ٥ . إِمْلَؤُوا ٱلْفَرَاغَ . إِخْتَارُوا "لِأَنَّ" أَوْ "بِسَبَبِ."

Exercise 5. Fill in the blank. Choose لِأَنَّ (because) or بِسَبَبِ (because of).

١. أُحِبُّ هٰذَا ٱلْمَطْعَم _____ ٱلْأَكْلَ فيه لَذيذ .

٢. ذَهَبَ ران إِلَى طَبيبِ ٱلْأَسْنَان _____ ٱلْوَجَع (pain) .

٣. يَدْرُسُ ران ٱلْعَرَبِيَّة _____هُ يُحِبُّ ٱللُّغَة وَٱلْحَضَارَة .

٤. إِسْتَأْجَرَ ران ٱلشَّقَّة في مانهاتن _____ ٱلْمَنْظَرِ ٱلْجَميل .

٥. مَا ذَهَبَ سامي إِلَى ٱلْحَفْلَة _____ ناديا مَا ذَهَبَتْ .

٦. مَا ذَهَبُوا إِلَى ٱلْجَامِعَة ٱلْيَوْم _____ ٱلطَّقْسِ ٱلْمُثْلِج .
(the snowy weather)

تَمْرِين ٦ . إِسْأَلُوا زُمَلاءَكُمُ ٱلْأَسْئِلَة ٱلتَّالِيَة . إِخْتَارُوا ٱلْجَوَابَ ٱلْمُنَاسِب .

Exercise 6. Ask your classmates the following questions. Choose the appropriate answer.

خَمْس لُغَات	أَرْبَع لُغَات	ثَلاث لُغَات	لُغَتَيْنِ	لُغَة وَاحِدَة

١. كَمْ لُغَة تَعْرِفُ / تَعْرِفينَ؟ أَعْرِفُ _____

٢. كَمْ لُغَة يَعْرِفُ وَالِدُكَ / وَالِدُكِ؟ يَعْرِفُ _____

٣. كَمْ لُغَة تَعْرِفُ وَالِدَتُكَ / وَالِدَتُكِ؟ تَعْرِفُ _____

Exercise 7. Translate.   تَمْرِين ٧ . تَرْجِمُوا.

1. How many languages do you (*m. s.*) know?

_____

2. How many brothers and sisters do you (*f. s.*) have?

_____

3. How many universities are in this state?

_____

4. How many books did you (*m. pl.*) read this week (أُسْبُوع)?

_____

تَمْرِين ٨ . أُكْتُبُوا أَسْمَاءَ خَمْس دُوَل عَرَبِيَّة تَبْدَأُ بِ – أَلْ...

Exercise 8. Write the names of five Arab countries that start with the definite article.

_____ . ٢   _____ . ١

_____ . ٤   _____ . ٣

_____ . ٥

أَلصَّبْر مِفْتَاحُ ٱلْفَرَج.

Patience is the key to relief.

تَمْرِين ٩ . أُكْتُبُوا أَسْمَاءَ ٱلدُّوَلِ بِٱللُّغَةِ ٱلْعَرَبِيَّة.

Exercise 9. Write in Arabic the names of the countries.

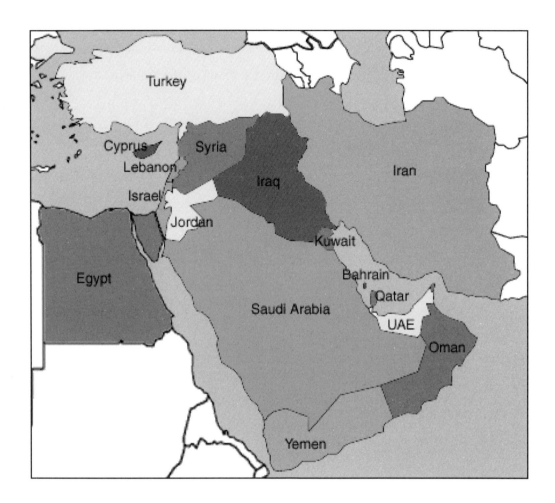

_____

_____

_____

_____

تَمْرِين ١٠. أَمَامَكُمْ أَسْمَاء جَرَائِد عَرَبِيَّة. إِبْحَثُوا عَنِ ٱلدَّوْلَة ٱلَّتِي تَصْدُرُ فِيهَا

كُلّ جَرِيدَة ثُمَّ ٱكْتُبُوا ٱسْمَ ٱلدَّوْلَة.

Exercise 10. Here are names of some Arabic newspapers. Find out the country in which

each paper is published, then write the name of the country.

١. جَرِيدَةُ ٱلشَّرْقِ ٱلأَوْسَط تَصْدُرُ في _____

٢. جَرِيدَةُ أَخْبَارِ ٱلْيَوْم تَصْدُرُ في _____

٣. جَرِيدَةُ ٱلأَهْرَام تَصْدُرُ في _____

٤. جَرِيدَةُ ٱلرَّافِدَيْن تَصْدُرُ في _____

٥. جَرِيدَةُ ٱلنَّهَار تَصْدُرُ في _____

تَمْرِين ١١. أُكْتُبُوا أَسْمَاءَ ٱلدُّوَل ٱلْمُجَاوِرَة لِلْعِرَاق وَٱلسُّعُودِيَّة؟

Exercise 11. Write the names of the countries bordering Iraq and Saudi Arabia.

أَلدُّوَلُ ٱلْمُجَاوِرَة لِلْعِرَاق هي : _____

_____

أَلدُّوَلُ ٱلْمُجَاوِرَة لِلسُّعُودِيَّة هي : _____

_____

The present-future tense أَلْمُضَارِعُ ٱلْمَرْفُوع

The present-future tense, أَلْمُضَارِعُ ٱلْمَرْفُوع, indicates the present habitual (*He writes*), the present progressive (*He is writing*) and the future tense (*He will write*). Its particular meaning depends on the context as well as on words that indicate the time of the action within the sentence.

Present habitual:

١. أَكْتُبُ رِسَالَة لِصَدِيقِي كُلَّ أُسْبُوع. . *I **write** a letter to my friend every week.*

Present progressive:

٢. أَكْتُبُ رِسَالَة لِصَدِيقِي. . *I **am writing** a letter to my friend.*

Future:

٣. أَكْتُبُ ٱلرِّسَالَة بَعْدَ سَاعَة. . *I **will** write the letter in an hour.*

٤. سَوْفَ أَكْتُبُ ٱلرِّسَالَة = سَأَكْتُبُ ٱلرِّسَالَة. . *I **will** write the letter.*

> The particle سَوْفَ or its abbreviation سَ indicates that the verb is in the future tense.

In أَلْمُضَارِعُ ٱلْمَرْفُوع the subject (doer) is indicated by a prefix or both a prefix and a suffix. For example, in the verb نَكْتُبُ (*we write / we are writing / we will write*) the prefix نَ is indicative of the subject pronoun نَحْنُ (we). In the verb يَكْتُبُونَ (*they write / they are writing / they will write*) the prefix يَ and the suffix ـُ ونَ are indicative of the subject pronoun هُمْ (they). Here is the full conjugation of أَلْمُضَارِعُ ٱلْمَرْفُوع in the singular and plural.

تَصْرِيفُ ٱلْمُضَارِعِ ٱلْمَرْفُوعِ

We study	(نَحْنُ) نَدْرُسُ	I study	(أَنَا) أَدْرُسُ
You (m. pl.) study	(أَنْتُمْ) تَدْرُسُونَ	You (m. s.) study	(أَنْتَ) تَدْرُسُ
You (f. pl.) study	(أَنْتُنَّ) تَدْرُسْنَ	You (f. s.) study	(أَنْتِ) تَدْرُسِينَ
They (m. pl.) study	(هُمْ) يَدْرُسُونَ	He studies	(هُوَ) يَدْرُسُ
They (f. pl.) study	(هُنَّ) يَدْرُسْنَ	She studies	(هِيَ) تَدْرُسُ

Prefixes in different verbs in the present-future tense can take ضَمَّة or فَتْحَة.

يَدْرُسُ ؛ يُعَلِّمُ ؛ يَتَكَلَّمُ ؛ يُشَاهِدُ

نَفْيُ ٱلْمُضَارِعِ ٱلْمَرْفُوعِ

Negation of the present-future tense

To negate a verb in the present-future tense put لا before the verb.

I don't study French.	لا أَتَعَلَّمُ ٱللُّغَةَ ٱلْفَرَنْسِيَّةَ .
They don't live in New York.	لا يَسْكُنُونَ فِي نيو يورك .

تَمْرِين ١٢. أُنْظُرُوا إِلَى تَصْرِيفِ ٱلْمُضَارِعِ ٱلْمَرْفُوع وَقُولُوا ثَلاث جُمَل صَحِيحَة

تَتَعَلَّقُ بِهِ. مَثَلاً: لِكُلِّ فِعْل فِي ٱلْمُضَارِعِ ٱلْمَرْفُوعِ بَادِئة.

Exercise 12. Look at the conjugation of the present-future tense and say three correct

statements regarding it. Example: *Every verb in the present-future*

tense has a prefix.

تَمْرِين ١٣. حَدِّدُوا ٱلْفِعْلَ ٱلْمُضَارِعَ وَضَمِيرَهُ ثُمَّ تَرْجِمُوا ٱلْجُمَل إِلَى ٱلإِنْجِليزِيَّة.

Exercise 13. Identify the present-future tense and its pronoun, then translate

the sentences into English.

١. نَجْلِسُ مَعًا كُلّ يَوْم وَنَدْرُسُ ٱلْعَرَبِيَّة وَنَلْعَبُ عَلَى ٱلْكُمبِيُوتِر.

٢. مَعَ مَنْ سَتُسَافِرُونَ إِلَى ٱلْمَغْرِب يَوْمَ ٱلسَّبْت؟

٣. كَمْ لُغَة تَعْرِفُ وَالِدَتُكِ؟

٤. مَتَى يَسْتَأْجِرُونَ ٱلشَّقَّة؟

٥. لِمَاذَا لا تُحِبِّينَ هٰذَا ٱلْمَطْعَم؟

٦. هَلْ تَعْرِفِينَ إِلَى أَيْنَ ذَهَبْنَ وَمَتَى سَيَرْجِعْنَ؟

٧. سَيَرْجِعُونَ مِنَ ٱلشُّغْل فِي ٱلسَّاعَة ٱلسَّادِسَة.

٨. هَلْ سَتَذْهَبُ غَدًا إِلَى ٱلْجَامِعَة فِي ٱلسَّاعَة ٱلْعَاشِرَة؟

٩. سَيُسَافِرْنَ فِي شَهْر دِيسَمْبِر (كَانُون ٱلأَوَّل) وَيَرْجِعْنَ فِي شَهْر فِبْرايِر (شُباط).

اَلْمُثَنَّى فِي ٱلْمُضَارِعِ ٱلْمَرْفُوع

The dual in the present-future tense

The dual is created by adding ان – to:

You (*m.* and *f. dual*)	أَنْتُمَا تَكْتُبَانِ	←	ان – + تَكْتُبُ	أَنْتَ
They (*m. dual*)	هُمَا يَكْتُبَانِ	←	ان – + يَكْتُبُ	هُوَ
They (*f. dual*)	هُمَا تَكْتُبَانِ	←	ان – + تَكْتُبُ	هِيَ

تَمْرِين ١٤. قُولُوا شَفَهِيًّا حَسَبَ ٱلْمِثَال.

Exercise 14. Say out loud according to the example.

١. هُوَ: **لا يَـدْرُسُ** ٱلْأَدَبَ ٱلْعَرَبِيّ فِي ٱلْجَامِعَة.

هِيَ: لا **تَـدْرُسُ** ٱلْأَدَبَ ٱلْعَرَبِيّ فِي ٱلْجَامِعَة.

أَنْتُمَا ، أَنْتِ ، هُنَّ ، هُمَا (f.) ، نَحْنُ ، أَنْتُمْ ، هُمْ ، أَنْتُنَّ

٢. هُوَ: **سَيُـحْـضِـرُ** ٱلْمَأْكُولَات وَٱلْمَشْرُوبَات لِلْحَفْلَة.

هِيَ: **سَـتُـحْـضِـرُ** ٱلْمَأْكُولَات وَٱلْمَشْرُوبَات لِلْحَفْلَة.

نَحْنُ ، أَنْتُنَّ ، هُمَا (m.) ، هُنَّ ، أَنْتِ ، أَنْتُمْ ، أَنْتُمَا ، هُمْ

All verbs in the present-future tense are conjugated in the same way.
They have the same prefixes and suffixes.

تَصْرِيفُ ٱلْمُضَارِعِ ٱلْمَرْفُوع

Conjugation of the present-future tense

أَنَا أ ━━━━━   نَحْنُ نـ ━━━━━

أَنْتَ تـ ━━━━━   أَنْتُمْ تـ ━━━━ ونَ   أَنْتُمَا تـ ━━━━ انِ

أَنْتِ تـ ━━━━ ينَ   أَنْتُنَّ تـ ━━━━ نَ

هُوَ يـ ━━━━━   هُمْ يـ ━━━━ ونَ   هُمَا يـ ━━━━ انِ

هِيَ تـ ━━━━━   هُنَّ يـ ━━━━ نَ   هُمَا تـ ━━━━ انِ

تَمْرِين ١٥. صَرِّفُوا ٱلْأَفْعَال شَفَهِيًّا ثُمَّ ٱكْتُبُوا ٱلتَّصْرِيف فِي دَفَاتِرِكُمْ.

Exercise 15. Conjugate the verbs out loud, then write the conjugation in your notebooks.

هُوَ: يَشْرَبُ ، يُسَافِرُ ، يَتَكَلَّمُ

تَمْرِين ١٦. صَرِّفُوا حَسَبَ ٱلضَّمَائِر.

Exercise 16. Conjugate according to the pronouns.

هُوَ يَتَخَرَّجُ: أَنَا ، هِيَ ، نَحْنُ ، أَنْتُمَا ، هُنَّ

هُوَ يَلْعَبُ: أَنْتَ ، أَنْتِ ، أَنْتُمْ ، هُمْ ، هُمَا (m.)

تَمْرِين ١٧ . إِخْتَارُوا ٱلْفِعْلَ ٱلْمُنَاسِب .   Exercise 17. Choose the appropriate verb.

١. ـــــــــــــــــــــ مَاجِد شُورْبَةَ ٱلطَّمَاطِم .   (تُحِبُّ ، يُحِبُّ)

٢. هُمَا لا ـــــــــــــــــــــ ٱلْفَرَنْسِيَّة .   (يَدْرُسْنَ ، يَدْرُسَانِ)

٣. كَمْ لُغَة ـــــــــــــــــــــ يَا مَرْيَم؟   (تَعْرِفِينَ ، تَعْرِفْنَ)

٤. سَـــــــــــــــــــــ عَنِ ٱلْكَاتِب نَجِيب مَحْفُوظ .   (تَكَلَّمْنَا ، نَتَكَلَّمُ)

٥. مَاجِد وَرَان ـــــــــــــــــــــ مِنَ ٱلْجَامِعَة هٰذِهِ ٱلسَّنَة . (يَتَخَرَّجَانِ ، تَتَخَرَّجَانِ)

٦. مَاذَا ـــــــــــــــــــــ يَا شَبَاب؟   (يَعْمَلُونَ ، تَعْمَلُونَ)

تَمْرِين ١٨ . إِمْلَؤُوا ٱلْفَرَاغَ بِٱلْفِعْلِ ٱلْمُنَاسِب بِٱلْمُضَارِعِ ٱلْمَرْفُوع .

Exercise 18. Fill in the blank with the appropriate verb in أَلْمُضَارِع ٱلْمَرْفُوع.

١. مَتَى ـــــــــــــــــــــ عَلَى ٱلْكُمْبِيُوتِر؟   (يَلْعَبُ – نَحْنُ)

٢. سَـــــــــــــــــــــ شَقَّة فِي هٰذِهِ ٱلْمَدِينَة .   (يَسْتَأْجِرُ – هُمْ)

٣. إِبْرَاهِيم وَأَحْمَد ـــــــــــــــــــــ فِي لَنْدَن .   (يَسْكُنُ – هُمَا)

٤. سَـــــــــــــــــــــ عِنْدَكَ فِي ٱلسَّاعَة ٱلْخَامِسَة .   (يَكُونُ – نَحْنُ)

٥. هَلْ ـــــــــــــــــــــ ٱلْعُنْوَان؟   (يَعْرِفُ – أَنْتُمَا)

٦. سَوْفَ لا ـــــــــــــــــــــ ٱلأَهْرَام فِي ٱلصَّيْف .   (يَزُورُ – هُمْ)

تَمْرِين ١٩. وَصَلَتْ رِسَالَة صَوْتِيَّة إِلَى ران. إِسْتَمِعُوا إِلَيْهَا ثُمَّ ٱقْرَؤُوهَا.

Exercise 19. A voice mail arrived for Rahn. Listen to it, then read it.

عَزِيزِي ران،

غَدًا سَيَكُونُ دَرْسُ ٱلْعَرَبِيَّة فِي ٱلسَّاعَة ٱلسَّادِسَة مَسَاءً فِي بِنَايَة ٱلْمَكْتَبَة، غُرْفَة رَقْم ٢٢٧. سَنَتَكَلَّمُ عَنِ ٱلْكَاتِبِ ٱلْمِصْرِيّ نَجِيب مَحْفُوظ. إِلَى ٱللِّقَاء غَدًا.

هَانِي.

تَمْرِين ٢٠. أَجِيبُوا.

Exercise 20. Answer.

١. مَنْ بَعَثَ هٰذِهِ ٱلرِّسَالَة؟

_____

٢. مَنْ هُوَ هَانِي فِي رَأْيِكُمْ؟

_____

٣. مَاذَا تَعَلَّمْتُمْ عَنْ ران مِنْ هٰذِهِ ٱلرِّسَالَة؟

_____

_____

٤. لِمَاذَا بَعَثَ هَانِي هٰذِهِ ٱلرِّسَالَة؟

هَانِي يُخْبِرُ (notifies) ران أَنَّ دَرْسَ ٱلْعَرَبِيَّة _____

_____

_____

تَمْرِين ٢١ . يَكْتُبُ ران رِسَالَة نَصِّيَّة (text message) إِلَى هَاني . سَاعِدُوهُ .

Exercise 21. Rahn is writing a text message to Hani. Help him.

_____

_____

تَمْرِين ٢٢ . جِدُوا مَعْلُومَات عَنِ ٱلْكَاتِب نَجِيب مَحْفُوظ فِي ٱلْإِنْتِرْنِت .

أَيْنَ عَاشَ وَبِأَيّ جَائِزَة فَازَ؟ أُذْكُرُوا أَسْمَاء ثَلَاثَة كُتُب كَتَبَهَا .

Exercise 22. Find information about the writer نَجِيب مَحْفُوظ on the Internet. Where did he live and what award did he receive? Give the titles of three of his books.

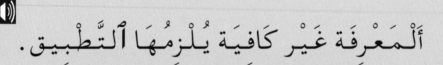

أَلْمَعْرِفَة غَيْر كَافِيَة يُلْزِمُهَا ٱلتَّطْبِيق .

Knowledge is not enough; it requires application.

والله علي ابن ابي طالب الغالب رضي الله تعالى عنه وكرم الله وجهه

Object Pronouns   ضَمَائِرُ ٱلنَّصْب

A pronoun that is attached to a verb indicates the object of the verb.

I do not know **the professor**.   لا أَعْرِفُ ٱلأُسْتَاذ .

⇓

I do not know **him**.   لا أَعْرِفُ + ه ⟸ لا أَعْرِفُهُ

		us	نَا	me	ـنِي
you (*dual, m. & f.*)	كُمَا	you (*m. pl.*)	كُمْ	you (*m. s.*)	كَ
		you (*f. pl.*)	كُنَّ	you (*f. s.*)	كِ
them (*dual, m.*)	هُمَا	them (*m. pl.*)	هُمْ	him	ه
them (*dual, f.*)	هُمَا	them (*f. pl.*)	هُنَّ	her	هَا

- The object pronouns are identical to the possessive pronouns except "me."
- Attaching pronouns to verbs is simple. Write the verb, then identify the appropriate object pronoun, and attach it to the verb.

We like the professor (f.) a lot.   نُحِبُّ ٱلأُسْتَاذَة كَثِيرًا .

⇓

*We like **her** a lot.* نُحِبُّهَا كَثِيرًا ⟸ نُحِبُّ + هَا

Exceptions:

1. For **you** (*pl. m.* أَنْتُمْ) in the past tense, add a silent و before the object

   pronoun to facilitate pronunciation.

   You (*pl. m.*) understood **her**.   فَهِمْتُمُوهَا ⟵ فَهِمْتُمْ + و + هَا

2. When you attach an object pronoun to a verb that ends with ‫ا‬و—, drop the ‫ا‬.

   They (*pl. m.*) welcomed **her**.   إِسْتَقْبَلُوهَا ⟵ إِسْتَقْبَلُوا + هَا

3. If the verb requires a preposition, attach the object pronoun to the preposition.

   We called **her**.   تَعَرَّفْنَا عَلَيْهَا.   ;   We met **her**.   إِتَّصَلْنَا بِهَا.

تَمْرِين ٢٣. حَوِّلُوا ٱلاسْم إِلَى ٱلضَّمِيرِ ٱلْمُنَاسِب شَفَهِيًّا حَسْبَ ٱلْمِثَال.

Exercise 23. Change the noun into the appropriate pronoun out loud according
      to the example.

مَا فَهِمْتُ ٱلسُّؤَال. ⟵ مَا فَهِمْتُهُ.

٢. لَا أُحِبُّ هٰذِهِ ٱلْفِكْرَة.	١. مَتَى بَعَثُوا ٱلرِّسَالَة؟
٤. كَتَبْتُ ٱلْكَلِمَات.	٣. قَرَأْنَا هٰذَا ٱلْكِتَاب.
٦. إِتَّصَلَتْ بِمَرْيَم.	٥. يُحِبُّ أُخْتَهُ كَثِيرًا.
٨. هَلْ تَعْرِفِينَ ٱلْعُنْوَان؟	٧. لِمَاذَا لَا تَفْتَحْنَ ٱلْبَاب؟
١٠. مَتَى تَعَرَّفْتُمَا عَلَى ٱلْأُسْتَاذَة؟	٩. رَأَيْنَا (we saw) وَالِدَهُ.

تَعَلَّمُوا هٰذِهِ ٱلْمُفْرَدَات

good, okay	حَسَنًا	It is late	أَلسَّاعَةُ مُتَأَخِّرَة
especially	خَاصَّةً	lecture	مُحَاضَرَة (ج) مُحَاضَرَات
ticket	تَذْكِرَة (ج) تَذَاكِر	bus	حَافِلَة (ج) حَافِلَات
		Good night	تُصْبِحُ عَلَى خَيْر

تَمْرِين ٢٤. إِمْلَؤُوا ٱلْفَرَاغِ بِٱلْكَلِمَةِ ٱلْمُنَاسِبَة.

Exercise 24. Fill in the blank with the appropriate word.

١. يَا ران، ٱلسَّاعَة _____ .   (مُتَأَخِّرَة ، مَكْتَبَة ، حَافِلَة)

٢. غَدًا عِنْدِي _____ فِي ٱلصَّبَاح. (خَاصَّةً ، تَذْكِرَة ، مُحَاضَرَات)

٣. أُسَافِرُ هٰذِهِ ٱلْمَرَّة بِـ _____ . (ٱلتَّذْكِرَة ، ٱلْمُحَاضَرَة ، ٱلْحَافِلَة)

٤. هَلِ ٱشْتَرَيْتَ _____ لِلْقِطَار؟   (حَافِلَة ، تَذْكِرَة ، فِكْرَة)

٥. تُصْبِحُ عَلَى _____ .   (خَيْر ، حَسَنًا ، خَاصَّةً)

Listen, then read.

إِسْتَمِعُوا ثُمَّ ٱقْرَؤُوا.

تُصْبِحُ عَلَى خَيْر

أَلْمَكَان: شَقَّة ران، مانهاتِن.

أَلْوَقْت: أَلسَّاعَة ٱلْعَاشِرَة وَٱلنِّصْف.

ماجد: يَا ران، أَلسَّاعَة مُتَأَخِّرَة وَغَدًا عِنْدِي مُحَاضَرَات فِي ٱلصَّبَاح.

ران: حَسَنًا، هَلِ ٱشْتَرَيْتَ تَذْكِرَة لِلْقِطَار؟

ماجد: لا. أُسَافِرُ هٰذِهِ ٱلْمَرَّة بِٱلْحَافِلَة.

ران: مُمْتَاز، سَأَرَاكَ قَرِيبًا، إِنْ شَاءَ ٱللّٰه، بَلِّغْ سَلامِي إِلَى ٱلْوَالِد وَٱلْوَالِدَة وَخَاصَّةً إِلَى ٱلْأُخْتِ ٱلصَّغِيرَة سَارَة.

ماجد: أَللّٰه يُسَلِّمُكَ، وَأَنْتَ أَيْضًا بَلِّغْ سَلامِي إِلَى ٱلْأُسْرَة، تُصْبِحُ عَلَى خَيْر.

ران: وَأَنْتَ مِنْ أَهْلِ ٱلْخَيْر.

حَافِلَة

قِطَار

Good night تُصْبِحُ عَلَى خَيْرٍ

Literally: May you get up in the morning and be in good condition.

لِلْمُذَكَّرِ (*m.*): تُصْبِحُ عَلَى خَيْرٍ.

لِلْمُؤَنَّثِ (*f.*): ⟵ تُصْبِحِينَ عَلَى خَيْرٍ.

لِلْجَمَاعَةِ (*pl.*): تُصْبِحُونَ عَلَى خَيْرٍ.

أَلْجَوَاب: ⟵ وَأَنْتَ / وَأَنْتِ / وَأَنْتُمْ مِنْ أَهْلِ ٱلْخَيْرِ.

The response: Good night.

Literally: May you (too) belong to the family of good.

Give my regards to بَلِّغْ سَلَامِي إِلَى

بَلِّغْ سَلَامِي إِلَى ٱلْوَالِدِ وَٱلْوَالِدَةِ.

Give my regards to (your) father and mother.

أَلْجَوَاب: أَللهُ يُسَلِّمُكَ. (لِلْمُذَكَّرِ *m.*)

أَللهُ يُسَلِّمُكِ. (لِلْمُؤَنَّثِ *f.*)

أَلْوَقْتُ كَٱلسَّيْفِ إِنْ قَتَلْتَهُ قَتَلَكَ.

Time is like a sword. If you kill it, it kills you.

تَمْرِين ٢٥ . أَلسَّاعَةَ ٱلآنَ ٱلْعَاشِرَة وَٱلنِّصْف بِٱللَّيْل . يَتَّصِلُ مَاجِد بِوَالِدَتِهِ

وَيُخْبِرُهَا أَنَّهُ يَخْرُجُ ٱلآنَ مِنْ شَقَّة ران وَسَيَأْخُذُ ٱلْحَافِلَة إِلَى

نِيو جِيرسي . وَالِدَتُهُ تَسْأَلُهُ فِي أَيّ سَاعَة سَتَصِلُ ٱلْحَافِلَة إِلَى

نِيو جِيرسي، وَمَاجِد يَقُولُ لَهَا إِنَّ ٱلْحَافِلَة سَتَصِلُ فِي ٱلسَّاعَة

ٱلثَّانِيَةَ عَشْرَةَ بِٱللَّيْل . تَكَلَّمُوا مَعَ زُمَلائِكُمْ ثُمَّ ٱكْتُبُوا ٱلْمُحَادَثَة .

Exercise 25. The time now is 10:30 p.m. Majid calls his mother and informs her

that he is now leaving Rahn's apartment and that he will take the

bus to New Jersey. His mother asks what time the bus will arrive

in New Jersey. Majid tells her that the bus will arrive at midnight.

Speak with your classmates, then write the conversation.

The Demonstrative Pronouns   إِسْمُ ٱلإِشَارَة

In the sentence أُسَافِرُ هُذِه ٱلْمَرَّة بِٱلْحَافِلَة (*I am traveling, this time, by bus*) the word هُذِه (*this*) is a demonstrative pronoun. Here are the demonstrative pronouns in the singular:

that / that is (m. s.)	ذُلِكَ	this / this is (m. s.)	هُـذَا
that / that is (f. s.)	تِـلْكَ	this / this is (f. s.)	هُـذِه

There are demonstrative pronouns also in dual and plural.

1. The demonstrative pronoun precedes the noun [as in English] and agrees with it in gender and number: هُـذَا الْـوَلَد (*this boy*), هُـذِه ٱلْبِـنْـت (*this girl*).
2. The demonstrative pronoun can function as an adjective or as a subject.

As an adjective

It must be followed by a noun **with the definite article** and its translation into English is: **this** or **that**: هُـذَا ٱلأُسْتَاذ (*this professor*), ذُلِكَ ٱلطَّالِب (*that student*). A construction of this type is called a *demonstrative phrase* and constitutes **one grammatical unit** in a given sentence.

As a subject

It must be followed by a noun **without the definite article** and its translation in English is: **this is** or **that is**: هُـذَا أُسْتَاذ (*this is a professor*), ذُلِكَ طَالِب (*that is a student*). A construction of this type constitutes a nominal sentence (جُـمْـلَة ٱسْمِـيَّة), where the demonstrative pronoun is the subject and the noun is the predicate.

Note.

If the demonstrative is the subject and it is followed by a noun **with the definite article** (أَلْ), you *must* separate them with a personal pronoun which agrees in gender and number with the subject.

⇓

This is **the** professor (*m.*) هٰذَا هُوَ ٱلْأُسْتَاذ.

⇓

This is **the** professor (*f.*) هٰذِه هِيَ ٱلْأُسْتَاذَة.

Remember.

This (demonstrative as adjective) هٰذَا ٱلـ ...

This is (demonstrative as subject) هٰذَا ...

Note. The demonstrative does not take the definite article.

تمرين ٢٦ . حَدِّدُوا دَوْرَ ٱسْمِ ٱلْإِشَارَة.

Exercise 26. Identify the role of the demonstrative (subject or adjective).

١. هٰذِه بِنْتِي أَمَل.

٢. هٰذَا طَبِيب أَسْنَان.

٣. هٰذَا ٱلْمَطْبَخ كَبِير.

٤. هٰذِه فِكْرَة مُمْتَازَة.

٥. هٰذِه غُرْفَة صَغِيرَة.

٦. هٰذِه أُخْت مَاجِد.

٧. مَنْ هٰذِه؟ هٰذِه زَوْجَة إِبْرَاهِيم.

٨. هٰذِه ٱلسَّجَّادَة جَمِيلَة.

Exercise 27. Change into a sentence. تمرين ٢٧ . حَوِّلُوا إِلَى جُمْلَة .

هٰذِهِ ٱلْجَامِعَة This is a university. ⟸ This university هٰذِهِ جَامِعَة .

_____ ٢. هٰذَا ٱلأُسْتَاذ   ١. هٰذَا ٱلطَّالِب _____

_____ ٤. هٰذِهِ ٱلسَّيَّارة   ٣. هٰذِهِ ٱلْفِكْرَة _____

_____ ٦. هٰذَا ٱلْكَاتِب   ٥. هٰذِهِ ٱلْجَرِيدَة _____

تمرين ٢٨ . إِقْرَؤُوا وَتَرْجِمُوا إِلَى ٱلإِنْجلِيزِيَّة .

Exercise 28. Read and translate into English.

٢. هٰذَا طَالِب جَدِيد .   ١. هٰذَا ٱلطَّالِب جَدِيد .

٤. هٰذِهِ فِكْرَة مُمْتَازَة .   ٣. هٰذِهِ ٱلْفِكْرَة مُمْتَازَة .

٦. هٰذِهِ أُسْتَاذَة عِرَاقِيَّة .   ٥. هٰذِهِ ٱلأُسْتَاذَة عِرَاقِيَّة .

٨. هٰذِهِ ٱلسَّجَّادَة جَمِيلَة .   ٧. مَنْ هٰذَا؟ هٰذَا إِبْرَاهِيم .

١٠. هٰذِهِ صُورَةُ ٱلأَهْرَام .   ٩. مَا هٰذَا؟ هٰذَا كِتَابُ ٱلْعَرَبِيَّة .

١٢. هٰذَا ٱلْمَنْظَر رَائِع .   ١١. هٰذِهِ ٱلشَّقَّة صَغِيرَة .

Prepositions   حُرُوفُ ٱلْجَرّ

about   عَنْ   ,   from   مِنْ

The prepositions عَنْ and مِنْ end with ن. In the first person,

singular and plural, the ن of the preposition مِنْ, and the ن of the

pronouns نِي and نَا turns into one ن with شَدَّة.

For example: عَنَّا ، مِنِّي.

Dual	Pl.	S.
	مِنَّا	مِنِّي
مِنْكُمَا	مِنْكُمْ	مِنْكَ
	مِنْكُنَّ	مِنْكِ
مِنْهُمَا	مِنْهُمْ	مِنْهُ
مِنْهُمَا	مِنْهُنَّ	مِنْهَا

تَمْرِين ٢٩ . أَضِيفُوا ٱلضَّمَائِر لِحَرْفِ ٱلْجَرّ "عَنْ" شَفَهِيًّا وَكِتَابِيًّا.

Exercise 29. Add pronouns to the preposition عَنْ out loud and in writing.

تَمْرِين ٣٠. إِمْلَؤُوا ٱلْفَرَاغ بِحَرْف ٱلْجَرِّ ٱلْمُنَاسِب.

Exercise 30. Fill in the blank with the appropriate preposition.

في	عَلَى	إِلَى	مَعَ	لِ	عِنْدَ	بِ	بَعْدَ	قَبْلَ	مِنْ
					at, with		after (time)	before (time)	

١. هَل _____ كَ صَفّ عَرَبِيّ _____ ٱلسَّاعَة ٱلسَّابِعَة؟

٢. _____ ٱلإِفْطَار شَاهَدْنَا ٱلتِّلْفَاز وَلَعِبْنَا _____ ٱلْكُمْبِيُوتِر.

٣. _____ فِكْرَة يَا رَان، لِمَاذَا تَدْرُس ٱلْعَرَبِيَّة؟

٤. سَيَذْهَبُونَ غَدَاً _____ ٱلْجَامِعَة _____ ٱلسَّاعَة ٱلْعَاشِرَة.

٥. قَدِمَ هَانِي _____ لُبْنَان _____ أَمْرِيكَا _____ أَرْبَع سَنَوَات.

٦. _____ فَضْلِكَ، أَيْنَ ٱلطَّرِيق _____ مَرْكَز ٱلشُّرْطَة؟

٧. سَأُسَافِر _____ ٱلصَّيْف _____ ٱلتَّخَرُّج _____ مِصْر.

٨. شُكْرَاً لَكَ _____ ٱلإِفْطَار ٱلْجَمِيل. لا شُكْر _____ وَاجِب.

٩. إِسْتَأْجَرَ شَقَّة _____ ٱلْقُرْب _____ مَرْكَز ٱلشُّرْطَة.

١٠. إِتَّصَلَ رَان _____ مَاجِد _____ أَنْ رَجَعَ _____ ٱلطَّبِيب.

١١. رَجَعَتْ _____ ٱلْبَيْت _____ مُنْتَصَف ٱللَّيْل.

١٢. كُنْتُ _____ ٱلأُرْدُنّ _____ عَمِّي _____ شَهْر.

Noun-noun phrase   أَلْإِضَافَة

The phrase شَقَّة رَان (Rahn's apartment) is a noun-noun phrase - إِضَافَة.
You already know that أَلْإِضَافَة consists of two nouns (or more) that
come after one another.

كِتَابُ ٱلطَّالِب   *The student's book (The book of the student)*

⇓   ⇓

أَلْمُضَاف   أَلْمُضَاف إِلَيْه

أَلْإِضَافَة can express:

1. **Possession**. As in English constructions that use the preposition "of" or the possessive "'s":

     Rami's car (The car of Rami)   سَيَّارَة رَامِي

     The professor's house (The house of the professor)   بَيْتُ ٱلْأُسْتَاذ

Note: When أَلْإِضَافَة expresses possession, أَلْمُضَاف إِلَيْه (the second noun)
could be replaced by a possessive pronoun that is attached to the first noun:

     His book   كِتَابُ ٱلطَّالِب ⟸ (كِتَابُ + ه) ⟸ كِتَابُه

     Her daughters   بَنَات دِينَا ⟸ (بَنَاتُ + هَا) ⟸ بَنَاتُهَا

2. **Modifying**. In Arabic and English, one noun can modify another. In English the first noun modifies the second (university professor, school bus, cheesecake), while in Arabic, the second noun modifies the first.

     Train station   مَحَطَّةُ ٱلْقِطَار

     The religion professor   أُسْتَاذُ ٱلدِّين

Note:

* The first noun of أَلإِضَافَة can not take any kind of definition. Only the second noun can be definite by being a proper noun, taking the definite article or a possessive pronoun. When the second noun is definite the whole إِضَافَة is definite, and when the second noun is not definite the whole إِضَافَة is not definite.

* أَلإِضَافَة constitutes **one grammatical unit** in a given sentence. It can fulfill different roles such as a subject, predicate, object, and time modifier.

تَمْرِين ٣١. إِضَافَة أَمْ ٱسْم وَصِفَة؟

Exercise 31. Noun-noun phrase or noun-adjective phrase?

٢. دَوْلَة عَرَبِيَّة		١. مَرْكَزُ ٱلشُّرْطَة	
٤. بِنَايَةُ ٱلْمَكْتَبَة		٣. أَلسَّاعَةُ ٱلرَّابِعَة	
٦. أَلْكَاتِبُ ٱلْمِصْرِيّ		٥. عُنْوَانُ ٱلشَّقَّة	
٨. عَصِيرُ ٱلْبُرْتُقَال		٧. أَللُّغَةُ ٱلْعَرَبِيَّة	
١٠. يَوْمُ ٱلسَّبْت		٩. أَلْوِلايَاتُ ٱلْمُتَّحِدَة	
١٢. مَدْرَسَة ثَانَوِيَّة		١١. بَيْت مَاجِد	
١٤. صُورَةُ ٱلأَهْرَام		١٣. أَلأَكْلُ ٱلْعَرَبِيّ	
١٦. شُورَبَة دَجَاج		١٥. أَلأَدَبُ ٱلْعَرَبِيّ	
١٨. أَلْحَضَارَةُ ٱلْعَرَبِيَّة		١٧. طَبِيب أَسْنَان	

🔊   تَعَلَّمُوا هٰذِهِ ٱلْمُفْرَدَات

end	نِهَايَة	answer	جَوَاب (ج) أَجْوِبَة
at, with, near	عِنْدَ	to bring	أَحْضَرَ (م) يُحْضِرُ
relatives, family	أَهْل	to buy	إِشْتَرَى (م) يَشْتَرِي
something	شَيْء (ج) أَشْيَاء	of course, certainly	طَبْعًا، بِٱلطَّبْع
perfect, all right	تَمَام	occasion, opportunity	مُنَاسَبَة
dancing	رَقْص	one time	مَرَّة (ج) مَرَّات
surprise	مُفَاجَأَة	to convey, give	بَلَّغَ (م) يُبَلِّغ
pain	وَجَع	moment	لَحْظَة (ج) لَحَظَات
head	رَأْس (ج) رُؤُوس	to invite	دَعَا (م) يَدْعُو
in that case, so	إِذًا، إِذَنْ	newspaper	جَرِيدَة (ج) جَرَائِد
only	فَقَطْ	a news item	خَبَر (ج) أَخْبَار
like (preposition)	كَ...	Don't (you *m. s.*) worry!	لا تَقْلَقْ!
phone	هَاتِف	and so on	إِلَى آخِرِه

تَمْرِين ٣٢. جِدُوا ٱلشَّاذّ.   Exercise 32. Which word does not fit (in each group)?

٢. جَوَاب ، أَجْوِبَة ، لَحْظَة   ١. مُحَاضَرَة ، مَرَّة ، حَضَارَة

٤. مُفَاجَأَة ، مُحَاضَرَات ، جَرِيدَة   ٣. أَهْل ، بَلَّغَ ، وَجَع

تَمْرِين ٣٣. أُكْتُبُوا كَلِمَات تَحْتَوِي عَلَى كُلّ مِنَ ٱلْجُذُورِ ٱلتَّالِيَةِ.

Exercise 33. Write words that contain each of the following roots.

١. قلق _____   ٢. نهي _____

٣. مرر _____   ٤. حضر _____

٥. جوب _____   ٦. نسب _____

تَمْرِين ٣٤. إمْلَؤُوا ٱلْفَرَاغَ بِٱلْكَلِمَةِ ٱلْمُنَاسِبَةِ.

Exercise 34. Fill in the blank with the appropriate word.

١. عِنْدِي _____ رَأْس.   (فَقَطْ ، وَجَع ، خَبَر)

٢. تُصْبِحِينَ _____ خَيْرٍ يَا إِيمَان.   (إِلَى ، فِي ، عَلَى)

٣. أَنَا بِخَيْر، كُلّ شَيْء _____ .   (هَاتِف ، فِكْرَة ، تَمَام)

٤. عِنْدِي _____ لَكِ.   (حَضَارَة ، مُحَاضَرَة ، مُفَاجَأَة)

٥. أَقْرَأُ _____ كُلّ يَوْم.   (ٱلْهَاتِف ، ٱلْجَرِيدَة ، ٱلْمُفَاجَأَة)

٦. _____ جَرِيدَة عَرَبِيَّة.   (إشْتَرَيْتُ ، بَلَّغْتُ ، أَكَلْتُ)

Exercise 35. Listen, then read.   تَمْرِين ٣٥ . إِسْتَمِعُوا ثُمَّ ٱقْرَؤُوا .

عِنْدِي مُفَاجَأَة لَكَ

أَلْمَكَان:	شَقَّة ران، مانهاتِن .
أَلْوَقْت:	يَوْمُ ٱلْخَمِيس . أَلسَّاعَة ٱلسَّادِسَة وَٱلنِّصْف مَسَاءً .

ران :   أَلُو ، مَاجِد؟

أبو مَاجِد : لا، أَنَا وَالِدُهُ .

ران :   أَهْلاً، مِنْ فَضْلِكَ، هَلْ مَاجِد فِي ٱلْبَيْت؟

أبو مَاجِد : مَنْ يَتَكَلَّمُ، ران؟

ران :   نَعَمْ، أَنَا ران، أَهْلاً .

أبو مَاجِد : أَهْلاً أَهْلاً يَا ران، نَعَمْ هُوَ فِي ٱلْبَيْت، لَحْظَة... يَا مَاجِد!

يَا مَاجِد ! ران عَلَى ٱلْهَاتِف...

ماجِد :   أَهْلاً يَا ران، مَا أَخْبَارُكَ؟

ران :   أَلْحَمْدُ لله، كُلّ شَيْء تَمَام، عِنْدِي مُفَاجَأَة لَكَ .

ماجِد :   مَا هِيَ ٱلْمُفَاجَأَة؟

ران :   أَدْعُوكَ (I invite you) لِحَفْلَة عَرَبِيَّة فِي نِهَايَةِ ٱلسَّنَة فِيهَا

مَأْكُولات عَرَبِيَّة وَمُوسِيقَى وَرَقْص .

ماجِد :   شُكْراً يَا ران وَمَا ٱلْمُنَاسَبَة؟

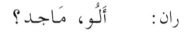

ران :   هٰذِهِ حَفْلَة صَغيرَة لِلْأَصْدِقَاء بِمُنَاسَبَة ٱلتَّخَرُّج .

ماجِد :   عَظِيم! وَأَيْنَ سَتَكُونُ ٱلْحَفْلَة؟

ران :   فِي شَقَّتِي طَبْعًا .

ماجِد :   وَمَتَى سَتَكُونُ؟

ران :   فِي ٱلشَّهْرِ ٱلْقَادِم، يَوْمَ ٱلسَّبْت،

ثَلاثَة وَعِشْرِينَ يُونْيُو (حُزَيْرَان) فِي ٱلسَّاعَة ٱلسَّابِعَة مَسَاءً .

June						
Su	Mo	Tu	We	Th	Fr	Sa
					1	2
3	4	5	6	7	8	9
10	11	12	13	14	15	16
17	18	19	20	21	22	23
24	25	26	27	28	29	30

ماجِد :   وَهَلْ تُرِيدُ مُسَاعَدَة (help)؟

ران :   لا تَقْلَق، سَأُحْضِرُ كُلّ شَيْء، سَأُحْضِرُ ٱلدَّجَاج وَٱللَّحْم وَٱلأَرُزّ

وَٱلْكَبَاب وَٱلْحُمُّص وَٱلْخُبْزَ ٱلْعَرَبِيّ وَٱلسَّلَطَة إِلَى آخِرِه .

ماجِد :   إِذًا، أَنَا سَأُحْضِرُ عَصِيرَ ٱلْبُرْتُقَال وَعَصِيرَ ٱللَّيْمُون وَٱلشَّاي

وَٱلْقَهْوَة وَٱلْحَلِيب (milk) وَٱلْكَاكَاو وَٱلسُّكَّر وَأَيْضًا ٱلْبَقْلاوَة .

ران :   شُكْرًا جَزِيلاً لَكَ يَا صَدِيقِي ٱلْعَزِيز. أَنْتَ كَأَخ لِي .

ماجِد :   لا شُكْرَ عَلَى وَاجِب .

ران :   عِنْدِي طَلَب (request) صَغِير، أُرِيدُ مُسَاعَدَتَكَ فِي كِتَابَة

ٱلدَّعْوَة لِلْحَفْلَة بِٱللُّغَة ٱلْعَرَبِيَّة .

ماجِد :   غَالٍ (read: g͟haalen) وَٱلطَّلَب رَخِيص .

غَالٍ وَٱلطَّلَب رَخِيص

Literally: precious and the request is cheap.

This expression is a polite way to positively answer a request. It means,

"No problem!" "Sure!" (*You are precious to me and your request is nothing*).

Exercise 36. True or false.   تَمْرِين ٣٦. صَوَاب أَمْ خَطَأ.

خَطَأ	صَوَاب	
○	○	١. دَعَا ران أَصْدِقَاءَهُ لِلْحَفْلَة.
○	○	٢. سَتَكُونُ ٱلْحَفْلَة فِي بَيْت مَاجِد.
○	○	٣. سَيُحْضِرُ ران ٱلْمَأْكُولات وَٱلْمَشْرُوبَات لِلْحَفْلَة.
○	○	٤. سَتَكُونُ ٱلْحَفْلَة فِي شَهْر يُونْيُو (حُزَيْرَان).
○	○	٥. طَلَبَ مَاجِد مِنْ ران مُسَاعَدَة بِكِتَابَة ٱلدَّعْوَة لِلْحَفْلَة.
○	○	٦. تَكَلَّمَ رَان مَعَ مَاجِد يَوْمَ ٱلْخَمِيس فِي ٱلْمَسَاء.
○	○	٧. سَيُحْضِرُ مَاجِد ٱلشَّاي وَٱلْقَهْوَة وَٱلْحَلِيب وَٱلسُّكَّر.
○	○	٨. سَتَكُونُ ٱلْحَفْلَة فِي نِهَايَة ٱلسَّنَة بِمُنَاسَبَة ٱلتَّخَرُّج.
○	○	٩. سَيُحْضِرُ ران ٱلدَّجَاج وَٱللَّحْم وَٱلْأَرُزّ وَٱلْخُبْزَ ٱلْعَرَبِيّ.

Exercise 37. Answer the questions. تَمْرِين ٣٧. أَجِيبُوا عَنِ ٱلأَسْئِلَة.

١. مَا هِيَ مُفَاجَأَة ران لِمَاجِد؟

_____

٢. مَا هِيَ مُنَاسَبَةُ ٱلْحَفْلَة؟

_____

٣. مَتَى سَتَكُونُ ٱلْحَفْلَة؟

_____

٤. مَاذَا طَلَبَ ران مِنْ مَاجِد؟

_____

٥. إِنْسَخُوا (copy) أَسْمَاءَ ٱلْمَأْكُولات وَٱلْمَشْرُوبَاتِ ٱلْمَذْكُورَة (mentioned)
في ٱلْمُحَادَثَة.

_____

_____

like, as كَ

كَ is a preposition and is added only to a noun.

كَ does not accept pronouns.

You are like a brother to me.	أَنْتَ كَأَخٍ لِي.
He speaks Arabic like the professor.	يَتَكَلَّمُ ٱلْعَرَبِيَّة كَٱلأُسْتَاذ.

The verbal noun (gerund)   أَلْمَصْدَر

أُرِيدُ مُسَاعَدَتَكَ فِي كِتَابَةِ ٱلدَّعْوَةِ بِٱللُّغَةِ ٱلْعَرَبِيَّةِ.

I want your help in writing the invitation in Arabic.

The words سَاعَدَ and مُسَاعَدَة and كِتَابَة are verbal nouns derived from the verbs
(to help) and كَتَبَ(to write). The verbal noun in Arabic is called أَلْمَصْدَر. It
corresponds to both the English infinitive (to help, to write) or the gerund
(helping, writing). Verbs in Form 1 have multiple patterns for أَلْمَصْدَر and they
are provided by the dictionary. Each one of the other Forms, with very few
exceptions, have a fixed pattern for أَلْمَصْدَر and these patterns should be
memorized. Here are some examples of أَلْمَصْدَر in different Forms:

(watching)	مُشَاهَدَة	شَاهَدَ	(writing)	كِتَابَة	كَتَبَ
(help)	مُسَاعَدَة	سَاعَدَ	(reading)	قِرَاءَة	قَرَأَ
(bringing)	إِحْضَار	أَحْضَرَ	(drinking)	شُرْب	شَرِبَ
(speaking)	تَكَلُّم	تَكَلَّمَ	(returning)	رُجُوع	رَجَعَ
(graduating)	تَخَرُّج	تَخَرَّجَ	(going)	ذَهَاب	ذَهَبَ
(learning)	تَعَلُّم	تَعَلَّمَ	(understanding)	فَهْم	فَهِمَ

تَمْرِين ٣٨. يَتَّصِلُ رَان بِأَمَل وَيَدْعُوهَا إِلَى ٱلْحَفْلَة. أَكْمِلُوا ٱلْمُحَادَثَة.

Exercise 38. Rahn calls Amal and invites her to the party. Complete the conversation.

أَلسَّابِعَة ، حَفْلَة ، ٱلتَّخَرُّج ، شَقَّتِي سَعِيدَة (happy) ، تَكُونُ ، ٱلْمَشْرُبَات

ران : أَدْعُوكِ (I invite you) يَا أَمَل لِحَفْلَة في _____ .

أَمَل : حَفْلَة في شَقَّتِكَ؟ أَيّ _____ ؟ مَا هِيَ ٱلْمُنَاسَبَة؟

ران : حَفْلَة نِهَايَة ٱلسَّنَة وَ _____ .

أَمَل : هٰذَا عَظِيم! شُكْرًا لَكَ، مَتَى سَ _____ ٱلْحَفْلَة؟

ران : يَوْمَ ٱلسَّبْتِ ٱلْقَادِم، ٢٣ يُونْيُو (حُزَيْرَان) في ٱلسَّاعَة _____

مَسَاءً.

أَمَل : وَهَلْ تُرِيدُ مُسَاعَدَة؟

ران : شُكْرًا لَكِ، أَنَا وَمَاجِد سَنُحْضِرُ كُلّ شَيْء، ٱلْمَأْكُولاتِ ٱلْعَرَبِيَّة

وَ _____ .

أَمَل : مُمْتَاز! أَنَا _____ جِدًّا لِهَٰذِهِ ٱلدَّعْوَة. إِلَى ٱللِّقَاء في ٱلْحَفْلَة.

ران : إِلَى ٱللِّقَاء.

تَمْرِين ٣٩. يَتَّصِلُ ران بِمَرْوان وَيَدْعُوهُ إِلَى ٱلْحَفْلَة. تَكَلَّمُوا مَعَ زُمَلائِكُمْ ثُمَّ ٱكْتُبُوا ٱلْمُحَادَثَة.

Exercise 39. Rahn calls Marwan and invites him to the party. Speak with your classmates, then write the conversation.

تَمْرِين ٤٠. وَصَلَتْ رِسَالَة نَصِّيَّة. إِقْرَؤُوهَا وَأَجِيبُوا عَنِ ٱلْأَسْئِلَة.

Exercise 40. A text message arrived. Read it and answer the questions.

أَنَا ٱلْآن فِي ٱلْقِطَار وَسَأَصِلُ (I will arrive) إِلَى مانهاتن فِي ٱلسَّاعَة ٱلسَّادِسَة وَٱلنِّصْف. إِنْتَظِرِينِي ([f.] wait for me) فِي مَحَطَّة ٱلْقِطَار وَسَنَذْهَبُ مَعًا (together) إِلَى ٱلْحَفْلَة. إِشْتَرَيْتُ لَهُ هَدِيَّة جَمِيلَة جِدًّا. مَاجِد.

١. مَنْ بَعَثَ ٱلرِّسَالَة ٱلنَّصِّيَّة؟ _____

٢. إِلَى مَنْ بَعَثَهَا؟ _____

٣. مَا هُوَ ٱلتَّأْرِيخ؟ _____

٤. لِمَنِ ٱلْهَدِيَّة؟ _____

تَمْرِين ٤١. وَصَلَتْ رِسَالَة نَصِّيَّة إِلَى مَاجِد. إِقْرَؤُوهَا وَأَجِيبُوا عَنِ ٱلْأَسْئِلَة.

Exercise 41. A text message arrived for Majid. Read it, then answer the questions.

سَأَنْتَظِرُكَ فِي مَحَطَّةِ ٱلْقِطَار. أَنَا أَيْضًا ٱشْتَرَيْتُ لَهُ هَدِيَّة جَمِيلَة، سَمَّاعَة (stethoscope). سَأَرَاكَ فِي ٱلسَّاعَة ٱلسَّادِسَة وَٱلنِّصْف. أَمَل.

١. مِمَّنْ (مِنْ مَنْ) هٰذِهِ ٱلرِّسَالَة؟
_____

٢. مَا هِيَ هَدِيَّة أَمَل لِرَان؟
_____

أَلْفِعْلُ ٱلسَّالِم وَٱلْفِعْلُ ٱلْمُعْتَل
The sound verb and the weak verb

In each Form (وَزْن) there are sound and weak verbs. Whether a verb is sound or weak is determined by its root (the three radicals).

The sound verb   أَلْفِعْلُ ٱلسَّالِم

A sound verb is a verb in which the three radicals of the root appear and are sounded (*you see them and hear them*) in all forms of the verb conjugation:

إِسْتَقْبَلَ (قبل) ، تَقَدَّمَ (قدم) ، يُعَلِّمُ (علم)

The weak verb   أَلْفِعْلُ ٱلْمُعْتَلّ

A weak verb is a verb in which one or more of the three radicals is omitted or altered in certain conjugations:

كَانَ (كون) ، مَدَّ (مدد) ، إِشْتَرَى (شري) ، دَعَا (دعو)

نَجِيب مَحْفُوظ

كَاتِب مِصْرِيّ مَشْهُور

فَازَ بِجَائِزَة نُوبِيل لِلآدَاب عَام ١٩٨٨ .

أَلذَّكِيّ يُعْرَفُ مِنْ إِجَابَاتِهِ وَٱلْحَكِيم يُعْرَفُ مِنْ أَسْئِلَتِهِ .

A clever person is known by his answers
and a wise person is known by his questions.

تَمْرِين ٤٢ . جِدُوا مَعْلُومَات عَنْ مِصْر في ٱلإِنترنت بِمَا فِيهَا ٱلْعَاصِمَة وَعَدَدُ

ٱلسُّكَّان وَٱلْعُمْلَة ونِظَامُ ٱلْحُكْم وَٱلدِّين وَٱلدُّوَلُ ٱلْمُجَاوِرَة وَمُدُن

مَرْكَزِيَّة وَٱللُّغَة ٱلرَّسْمِيَّة .

Exercise 42. Find information about Egypt on the Internet including the capital,
the population, the currency, the regime, the religion, neighboring
countries, important cities, and the official language.

UNIT 9

🔊

تَعَلَّمُوا هٰذِهِ ٱلْمُفْرَدَات

way, road	طَرِيق (ج) طُرُق	week	أُسْبُوع (ج) أَسَابِيع
since, ago (prep.)	مُنْذُ	to specialize	تَخَصَّصَ بِـ (م) يَتَخَصَّصُ بِـ
swimming	سِبَاحَة	child, baby	طِفْل (ج) أَطْفَال
self, the same	نَفْس	work	عَمَل (ج) أَعْمَال
fiancé	خَطِيب	hospital	مُسْتَشْفى (ج) مُسْتَشْفَيَات
preferred	مُفَضَّل	hobby	هِوَايَة (ج) هِوَايَات
in addition to	بِٱلْإِضَافَة إلى	embassy	سِفَارَة (ج) سِفَارَات
music	أَلْمُوسِيقَى	to study, learn	تَعَلَّمَ (م) يَتَعَلَّمُ
abroad	أَلْخَارِج	letter (correspondence)	رِسَالَة (ج) رَسَائِل
about (prep.)	عَنْ	sport	أَلرِّيَاضَة، رِيَاضَة
origin, descent	أَصْل	to obtain	حَصَلَ عَلَى (م) يَحْصُلُ عَلَى
		job, work, occupation	مِهْنَة (ج) مِهَن

تَمْرِين ١. أُكْتُبُوا كَلِمَات تَحْتَوي عَلَى كُلّ مِنَ ٱلْجُذُورِ ٱلتَّالِيَة.

Exercise 1. Write words that contain each of the following roots.

٢. سفر _____   ١. فضل _____

٤. سبح _____   ٣. خطب _____

٦. رسل _____   ٥. خصص _____

تَمْرِين ٢. إِمْلَؤُوا ٱلْفَرَاغ بِٱلْكَلِمَة ٱلْمُنَاسِبَة.

Exercise 2. Fill in the blank with the appropriate word.

١. هِوَايَتِي هِي _____ . (ٱلرِّسَالَة ، ٱلْأُسْبُوع ، ٱلْمُوسِيقَى)

٢. يَعْمَلُ خَطِيبِي في _____ . (ٱلْهِوَايَة ، ٱلسِّفَارَة ، ٱلْأُسْبُوع)

٣. ران هو طَبِيب _____ . (أَطْفَال ، هِوَايَة ، طَرِيق)

٤. نَذْهَبُ بَعْدَ _____ إِلَى ٱلْجَامِعَة. (ٱلْمِهْنَة ، ٱلرِّسَالَة ، ٱلْعَمَل)

٥. تَخَرَّجْتُ مِنَ ٱلْجَامِعَة _____ سَنَتَيْنِ. (نَفْس ، مُنْذُ ، عَن)

٦. خَطِيبَتِي أَمْرِيكِيَّة مِن _____ لُبْنَانِيّ. (أَصْل ، دَوْلَة ، طِفْل)

٧. يَذْهَبُونَ إِلَى ٱلْمَطْعَم كُلّ _____ . (رِيَاضَة ، أُسْبُوع ، سِفَارَة)

٨. هو _____ بِٱلْأَدَب ٱلْعَرَبِيّ. (تَتَعَلَّم ، مُفَضَّل ، يَتَخَصَّص)

Listen, then read.

إِسْتَمِعُوا ثُمَّ ٱقْرَؤُوا.

<h2 style="text-align:center">ران يَتَكَلَّمُ عَنْ نَفْسِهِ</h2>

بَحَثَ مَاجِد في ٱلْإِنْتِرْنِت عَنْ مَعْلُومَات عَنْ رَئِيس أَمْرِيكِيّ عَاشَ في ٱلْقَرْنِ ٱلثَّامِن عَشَر، وَعَنْ طَرِيقِ ٱلصُّدْفَة، عَثَرَ عَلَى مَوْقِع صَدِيقِهِ ران.

إِسْتَمِعُوا إِلَى مَا كَتَبَهُ ران عَنْ نَفْسِهِ ثُمَّ ٱقْرَؤُوا ٱلنَّصَّ.

Majid looked on the Internet for information about an American president who lived in the 18th century, and by chance he found Rahn's website.
Listen to what Rahn wrote about himself, then read the text.

إِسْمِي ران هَامِلْتُون. أَنَا أَمْرِيكِيّ وَأَسْكُنُ في "إِيطَالِيَا ٱلصَّغِيرة" في مَانْهَاتِن. تَخَرَّجْتُ مُنْذُ سَنَتَيْنِ من كُلِّيَّة ٱلطِّبّ في جَامِعَة نيو يورك وَٱلآن أَتَخَصَّصُ بِطِبّ ٱلْأَطْفَال في مُسْتَشْفَى "ماوُنْت سَايْناي" في مانهاتن. أُحِبُّ ٱلْأَطْفَال وَأُحِبُّ مِهْنَتِي كَثِيراً. هِوَايَاتِي ٱلْمُفَضَّلَة هي تَعَلُّمُ ٱللُّغَات وَٱلْمُوسِيقَى وَٱلرِّيَاضَة وَٱلسَّفَر إِلَى ٱلْخَارِج وَخَاصَّةً إِلَى ٱلدُّوَلِ ٱلْعَرَبِيَّة. كَمَا أُحِبُّ ٱلْأَكْلَ ٱللُّبْنَانِيّ كَثِيراً وَأَذْهَبُ إِلَى مَطْعَم لُبْنَانِيّ كُلَّ أُسْبُوع. لِي أَصْدِقَاء عَرَب كَثِيرُونَ في أَمْرِيكَا وَأَيْضاً في مِصْر

وَٱلأُرْدُنّ وَلُبْنَان وَٱلْمَغْرِب . خَطِيبَتِي أَمْرِيكِيَّة مَسِيحِيَّة مِنْ أَصْل لُبْنَانِيّ

ٱسْمُهَا رِيم وَتَعْمَلُ فِي ٱلسِّفَارَة ٱللُّبْنَانِيَّة فِي وَاشِنْطِن دِي سِي .

هِيَ أَيْضًا تُحِبُّ ٱلْمُوسِيقَى بِٱلإِضَافَة إِلَى ٱلسِّبَاحَة وَكِتَابَة ٱلرَّسَائِل

ٱلإِلِكْتِرُونِيَّة . لَهَا عَائِلَة كَبِيرَة فِي لُبْنَان . أَذْهَبُ كُلّ يَوْم خَمِيس بَعْدَ

ٱلْعَمَل إِلَى جَامِعَة نِيو يُورك وَأَتَعَلَّمُ ٱللُّغَة ٱلْعَرَبِيَّة مَع ٱلأُسْتَاذ هَانِي .

هُوَ أُسْتَاذ مُمْتَاز، مُتَخَصِّص بِٱللُّغَة ٱلْعَرَبِيَّة وَٱلأَدَب ٱلْعَرَبِيّ .

likewise, as, just as   كَمَا

كَمَا is followed by a verb.

Likewise, I like Lebanese food a lot.   كَمَا أُحِبُّ ٱلأَكْلَ ٱللُّبْنَانِيّ كَثِيرًا.

Exercise 3. Answer out loud.   تَمْرِين ٣ . أَجِيبُوا شَفَهِيًّا .

١. لِمَاذَا يُحِبُّ ٱلدُّكْتُور ران ٱلسَّفَر إِلَى ٱلدُّوَل ٱلْعَرَبِيَّة؟

٢. أَيْنَ تَعَرَّفَ ران عَلَى خَطِيبَتِه رِيم؟ خَمِّنُوا (guess).

٣. يُحِبُّ ران ٱلأَكْلَ ٱللُّبْنَانِيّ، وَأَنْتُمْ؟ مَا ٱلأَكْلُ ٱلْمُفَضَّل بِٱلنِّسْبَة لَكُمْ؟
(with regard to you [m. pl.])

تَمْرِين ٤ . قُولُوا ثَلاثَة أَشْيَاء تَعْرِفُونَهَا عَنْ ران . تَكَلَّمُوا مَعَ زُمَلائِكُمْ .

Exercise 4. Say three things that you know about Rahn. Talk with your classmates.

تَمْرِين ٥ . حَدِّدُوا ٱلأَشْيَاءَ ٱلصَّحِيحَة بِٱلنِّسْبَة لِران .

Exercise 5. Identify the correct statements about Rahn.

٢ . يَدْرُسُ ٱللُّغَة ٱلْعَرَبِيَّة في جَامِعَة نيو يورك .	١ . هُوَ خَطِيب رِيم .
٤ . يَعْمَلُ في جَامِعَة نيو يورك .	٣ . هو طَبِيب أَطْفال .
٦ . مِنْ هِوَايَاتِه ٱلْمُفَضَّلَة ٱلْمُوسِيقَى وَٱلرِّيَاضَة .	٥ . هو زَوْج رِيم .
٨ . يَسْكُنُ بِٱلْقُرْب مِنَ ٱلسِّفَارَة ٱللُّبْنَانِيَّة .	٧ . لا يُحِبُّ ٱلأَكْلَ ٱللُّبْنَانِيّ .
١٠ . تَخَرَّجَ من جَامِعَة كُولُومْبِيا مُنْذُ سَنَتَيْن .	٩ . هو عَرَبِيّ مَسِيحِيّ .
١٢ . تَعْمَلُ خَطِيبَتُهُ في ٱلسِّفَارَة ٱللُّبْنَانِيَّة .	١١ . يُحِبُّ ٱللُّغَة ٱلْعَرَبِيَّة .

تَمْرِين ٦ . أُكْتُبُوا نَفْس ٱلنَّصّ (صَفْحَة ٣٣٦–٣٣٥) . إِبْدَؤُوا : "إِسْمُهُ رَان هَامِلْتُون ."

Exercise 6. Write the same text (pp. 335-336) starting with "His name is رَان هَامِلْتُون ."

تَمْرِين ٧. أُكْتُبُوا أَسْئِلَة لِلْأَجْوِبَة .   Exercise 7. Write questions for the answers.

١. أَلسُّؤَال : _____ ؟

أَلْجَوَاب : لا . رِيم عَرَبِيَّة مَسِيحِيَّة .

٢. أَلسُّؤَال : _____ ؟

أَلْجَوَاب : يَعْمَلُ ٱلدُّكْتُور ران في مُسْتَشْفى في مَدِينَة نيو يورك .

٣. أَلسُّؤَال : _____ ؟

أَلْجَوَاب : أَتَعَلَّمُ ٱللُّغَة ٱلْعَرَبِيَّة مَعَ ٱلْأُسْتَاذ هَاني .

٤. أَلسُّؤَال : _____ ؟

أَلْجَوَاب : يَسْكُنُ ران بِٱلْقُرْب مِنْ جَامِعَة نيو يورك .

٥. أَلسُّؤَال : _____ ؟

أَلْجَوَاب : أَدْرُسُ ٱللُّغَة ٱلْعَرَبِيَّة في ٱلْجَامِعَة كُلّ يَوْم خَمِيس .

إِذَا كَانَ بَيْتُكَ مِنْ زُجَاج فَلا تَرْمِ ٱلنَّاس بِٱلْحِجَارَة .

If your house is made of glass don't throw stones at others.

(Meaning: don't be a hypocrite.)

تَمْرِين ٨. إِمْلَؤُوا ٱلْفَرَاغ بِٱلْكَلِمَة ٱلْمُنَاسِبَة.

Exercise 8. Fill in the blank with the appropriate word.

هِوَايَاتِي ، بِٱلْإِضَافَة ، بِٱلْقُرْب ، مَسِيحِيَّة ، كَثِيرًا ،
كُلّ ، مُتَخَصِّص ، ٱلطِّبّ ، مُسْتَشْفَى ، ٱلسِّفَارَة

١. أَسْكُنُ ——————— مِنْ جَامِعَة نِيو يُورك.

٢. رَان طَبِيب أَطْفَال وَيَعْمَلُ فِي ——————— "مَاوُنْت سَايْنَاي".

٣. تَعْمَلُ رِيم فِي ——————— ٱللُّبْنَانِيَّة.

٤. يُحِبُّ رَان مِهْنَتَهُ ———————.

٥. ——————— هِيَ ٱلْمُوسِيقَى وَٱلرِّيَاضَة وَٱلسَّفَر إِلَى ٱلْخَارِج.

٦. ——————— يَوْم خَمِيس أَتَعَلَّمُ ٱللُّغَة ٱلْعَرَبِيَّة فِي ٱلْجَامِعَة.

٧. أَلْأُسْتَاذ هَانِي ——————— بِٱللُّغَة ٱلْعَرَبِيَّة وَٱلْأَدَب ٱلْعَرَبِيّ.

٨. ——————— إِلَى ٱلْمُوسِيقَى تُحِبُّ رِيم أَيْضًا كِتَابَة ٱلرَّسَائِل.

٩. خَطِيبَة رَان أَمْرِيكِيَّة ——————— مِنْ أَصْل لُبْنَانِيّ.

١٠. دَرَسَ رَان فِي كُلِّيَّة ——————— فِي جَامِعَة نِيو يُورك.

تَمْرِين ٩ . تَتَكَلَّمُ رِيم، خَطِيبَة ران، مَعَ صَدِيقَتِهَا رَشِيدَة وتُخْبِرُهَا لِأَوَّل مَرَّة عَنْ خَطِيبِهَا ران، أَيْنَ يَسْكُنُ ومَاذَا يَعْمَلُ وبِمَاذَا يَتَخَصَّصُ ٱلآنَ وَمَتَى تَخَرَّجَ مِنَ ٱلْجَامِعَة وما هِي هِوَايَاتُهُ. رَشِيدَة تَتَعَلَّمُ ٱللُّغَة ٱلْعَرَبِيَّة في جَامِعَة نيو يُورك وتَعْرِفُ ٱلْأُسْتَاذ هَانِي . تَكَلَّمُوا مع زُمَلائِكُمْ ثُمَّ ٱكْتُبُوا ٱلْمُحَادَثَة في دَفَاتِرِكُمْ .

Exercise 9. Rim, Rahn's fiancée, talks with her friend Rashida and informs
her, for the first time, about her fiancée Rahn, where he lives,
what he does, what he specializes in now, when he graduated
from university and, what his hobbies are. Rashida studies Arabic
at New York University and she knows Professor Hani. Talk with
your classmates, then write the conversation in your notebooks.

تَمْرِين ١٠ . تَكَلَّمُوا مَعَ زُمَلائِكُمْ عَنْ أَنْفُسِكُمْ ثُمَّ ٱكْتُبُوا ٱلنَّصّ في دَفَاتِرِكُمْ .
"إسْمِي ... . أَنَا ... "

Exercise 10. Talk with your classmates about yourselves, then write the text
in your notebooks. "My name is ... I am..."

تَمْرِين ١١. أَكَلْتُمْ في مَطْعَم لُبْنَانِيّ في مانهاتن. أُكْتُبُوا عَنْ هٰذِه

ٱلتَّجْرِبَة (experience). مَتَى ذَهَبْتُمْ؟ مع مَنْ ذَهَبْتُمْ؟ مَاذَا أَكَلْتُمْ

وماذا شَرِبْتُمْ؟ كَيْفَ ٱلْأَسْعَار بِهٰذا ٱلْمَطْعَم وما رَأْيُكُمْ في

ٱلطَّعَام؟ إِسْتَعْمِلُوا ٱلْكَلِمات ٱلتَّالِيَة:

Exercise 11. You ate at a Lebanese restaurant in Manhattan. Write about this experience. When did you go? With whom did you go? What did you eat and drink? How are the prices in this restaurant and what is your opinion of the food? Use the following words:

we ate	أَكَلْنَا	we went	ذَهَبْنَا
delicious	لَذِيذ	we drank	شَرِبْنَا
week	أُسْبُوع	before, since, ago	قَبْلَ، مُنْذُ
pita bread	أَلْخُبْزُ ٱلْعَرَبِيّ	friend	صَدِيق (ج) أَصْدِقَاء
very good	جَيِّد جِدًّا	family	عَائِلَة
coffee	أَلْقَهْوَة	street	شَارِع
tea	أَلشَّاي	kebab (roasted beef)	أَلْكَبَاب
food	أَلطَّعَام، أَلْأَكْل	Hummus (chick peas)	أَلْحُمُّص
tasty	طَيِّب، لَذِيذ	Fattoush (vegetable salad)	أَلْفَتُّوش
after (+ verb)	بَعْدَ أَنْ	Tabbouleh (vegetable salad)	أَلتَّبُّولَة
price	سِعْر (ج) أَسْعَار	experience	تَجْرِبَة
sweets	أَلْحَلَوِيَّات	reasonable	مَعْقُول

أَلْجُمْلَة ٱلاِسْمِيَّة وَٱلْجُمْلَة ٱلْفِعْلِيَّة

Nominal and verbal sentences

There are two main sentence patterns in Arabic: nominal sentence

أَلْجُمْلَة ٱلاِسْمِيَّة and verbal sentence أَلْجُمْلَة ٱلْفِعْلِيَّة. In Arabic,

as in English, every sentence must have a subject and a predicate.

The nominal sentence   أَلْجُمْلَة ٱلاِسْمِيَّة

جُمْلَة ٱسْمِيَّة هِيَ جُمْلَة تَبْدَأُ بِٱسْم .

A nominal sentence is a sentence that starts with a noun.

(In grammar إِسْم means: *noun*)

أَلْبَيْت كَبِير .

⇩   ⇩

(predicate) أَلْخَبَر   أَلْمُبْتَدَأ (subject)

(The new thing about the subject)   (The word that starts the sentence)

The predicate (أَلْخَبَر) must agree in gender and number with the subject أَلْمُبْتَدَأ.

My fiancée (f. s.) is an Arab.   خَطِيبَتِي عَرَبِيَّة .

Maryam, Nawal, and Muna are Egyptians.   مَرْيَم وَنَوَال وَمُنَى مِصْرِيَّات .

The **subject** (أَلْمُبْتَدَأ) can be a common noun (إِسْم) such as أَلأُسْتَاذ, a proper

noun (إِسْم عَلَم) such as أَلْعِرَاق or نَبِيل, a personal pronoun (ضَمِير) such as

هو, or a demonstrative pronoun (إِسْمُ ٱلإِشَارَة) such as هٰذا.

The **predicate** (أَلْخَبَر) can be a common noun (إِسْم), a proper noun

(إِسْم عَلَم), an adjective (صِفَة) such as كَبِير, a prepositional phrase

(جَار وَمَجْرُور) such as فِي ٱلْبَيْت, or a verb (فِعْل) such as ذَهَبَ.

جَار وَمَجْرُور   Prepositional phrase

Prepositional phrase is a preposition (جَار) followed by a noun or a pronoun

(مَجْرُور). Examples: أَمَامَهُ , بِٱلْبَنْك , مُنْذُ سَنَتَيْنِ , أَمَامَ ٱلْمَحَطَّة.

تَمْرِين ١٢. إِنْسَخُوا ثَلاث جُمَل ٱسْمِيَّة مِنَ ٱلنَّصّ (صَفْحَة ٣٣٥-٣٣٦).

Exercise 12. Copy three nominal sentences from the text (pp. 335-336).

_____ .١

_____ .٢

_____ .٣

تَمْرِين ١٣. حَدِّدُوا ٱلْمُبْتَدَأ في كُلّ جُمْلَة ثُمَّ ٱكْتُبُوهُ في ٱلْعَامُودِ ٱلْمُلائِم.

Exercise 13. Identify the subject in each sentence, then write it in the

appropriate column.

٢. مِنْ أَيْنَ هٰذِهِ ٱلْمُوسِيقَى؟		١. أَلْكِتَاب جَدِيد.
٤. هِوايَتُهَا مُشَاهَدَةُ ٱلأَفْلام.		٣. هٰذِه بِنْتِي.
٦. وَالِدُهُ مِن لُبْنَان.		٥. رِيم خَطِيبَة ران.
٨. لَيْلَى مُوَظَّفَة في ٱلْجامِعَة.		٧. هُمْ مِنْ سُورِيَا.
١٠. هٰذا بَيْت أُسْرَة هاني.		٩. هِيَ خَطِيبَة ران.

إِسْمُ ٱلإِشَارَة	ضَمِير	إِسْم عَلَم	إِسْم
Demonstrative	Pronoun	Proper noun	Noun

			أَلْكِتَاب

تَمْرين ١٤. حَدِّدُوا ٱلْخَبَر في كُلّ جُمْلَة ثُمَّ ٱكْتُبُوهُ في ٱلْعَامُودِ ٱلْمُلائِم.

Exercise 14. Identify the predicate in each sentence, then write it in the

        appropriate column.

١. هَاني أُسْتَاذ.

٢. بَيْتُهَا بِلَنْدَن.

٣. ألدَّرْس سَهْل (easy).

٤. لَيْلَى لُبْنانِيَّة.

٥. هٰذِهِ مَرْيَم.

٦. هِيَ مُوَظَّفَة بِٱلْبَنْك.

٧. مُحَمَّد مِنَ ٱلْعِرَاق.

٨. ألْمَتْحَف أَمَامَ ٱلْمَحَطَّة.

٩. نَادِيَة تَدْرُسُ في ٱلْجامِعة.

١٠. ران طَبيب أَطْفَال.

فِعْل	جَار ومَجْرُور	صِفَة	إسْم عَلَم	إسْم
Verb	Prepositional phrase	Adjective	Proper noun	Noun

				أُسْتَاذ

Note:

If the predicate (أَلْخَبَرَ) is a noun, it is possible to insert between the

subject (أَلْمُبْتَدَأَ) and the predicate (أَلْخَبَرَ) a personal pronoun

(هُوَ ، هِيَ ، هُمْ ، هُنَّ ، هُمَا), although it is not necessary. The

personal pronoun must agree in gender and number with the subject:

١. هاني أُسْتَاذ. = هاني هُوَ أُسْتَاذ.   هاني *is a professor.*

٢. هٰذِهِ مَرْيَم. = هٰذِهِ هِيَ مَرْيَم.   This is *مَرْيَم.*

If the subject (أَلْمُبْتَدَأَ) is a demonstrative such as هٰذا or هٰذه, and the

predicate (أَلْخَبَرَ) is a noun **with the definite article (أَلْ)**, **you must**

separate them with a personal pronoun:

   This is *the student.*   ٣. هٰذا هُوَ ٱلطَّالِب.

   This is *the car.*   ٤. هٰذِهِ هِيَ ٱلسَّيَّارة.

        If not separated, the meaning is changed: *this student, this car.*

If the predicate (أَلْخَبَرَ) is an adjective, it is indefinite:

   The student is new.   ٥. أَلطَّالِب جَدِيد.

   The university is big.   ٦. أَلْجَامِعَة كَبِيرَة.

تَمْرِين ١٥. حَدِّدُوا ٱلْمُبْتَدَأَ وَٱلْخَبَر.

Exercise 15. Identify the subject and the predicate.

١. أَلْكِتَاب جَدِيد.   ٢. زَوْجَتُهُ مُوَظَّفَة في بَنْك.

٣. هٰذا هُوَ ٱلْقُرْآنُ ٱلْكَرِيم.   ٤. أَخُوهُ وَأُخْتُهُ في نيو يورك.

٥. في ٱلصَّفّ طَالِب.*   ٦. أُسرتُهُ في ٱلأُرْدُنّ.

٧. هَانِي مَسِيحِيّ مِنْ لُبْنَان.   ٨. هٰذا أَبُو سَامِي.

٩. أَمَامَ ٱلْمَحَطَّة مَتْحَف.   ١٠. مَنْ هُمْ؟ **

---

*   If the subject (أَلْمُبْتَدَأَ) is indefinite, and the predicate (أَلْخَبَر) is a prepositional phrase, the predicate precedes the subject. It is called "the fronted predicate" (أَلْخَبَرُ ٱلْمُقَدَّم): *In the classroom (there is) a student.* في ٱلصَّفّ طَالِب.

**   The question word مَنْ in the sentence مَنْ هُمْ؟ has the same grammatical function as the answer. A possible answer could be, هُمْ طُلاب *They are students.* In this sentence هُمْ is the subject (أَلْمُبْتَدَأَ) and طُلاب is the predicate (أَلْخَبَر) therefore, the grammatical function of مَنْ in the sentence, مَنْ هُمْ؟ is equal to the grammatical function of the word طُلاب - the predicate.

The verbal sentence   أَلْجُمْلَة ٱلْفِعْلِيَّة

جُمْلَة فِعْلِيَّة هِيَ جُمْلَة تَبْدَأُ بِفِعْل.

A verbal sentence is a sentence that starts with a verb.

The student ate.

أَكَلَ ٱلطَّالِب.

⇓   ⇓

أَلْفِعْل   أَلْفَاعِل

(subject - the doer)   (predicate - the action)

The student ate an apple.

أَكَلَ ٱلطَّالِب تُفَّاحَة.

⇓

(direct object) أَلْمَفْعُول بِه

(The receiver of the action is the direct object)

I wrote the letter.

كَتَبْتُ ٱلرِّسَالَة.

⇓   ⇓

أَلْفِعْل + أَلْفَاعِل   أَلْمَفْعُول بِه

A conjugated verb includes both predicate فِعْل and subject فَاعِل.

Note:

In the verbal sentence (ٱلْجُمْلَة ٱلْفِعْلِيَّة) the verb could be preceded by:

1. Question words:

Who opened the window? ١. **مَنْ** فَتَحَ ٱلشُّبَّاك؟

Did you read the story, students? ٢. أَقَرَأْتُمُ ٱلْحِكايَة يا طُلاب؟

2. Negation words:

Muna didn't write the letter. ٣. **مَا** كَتَبَتْ مُنَى ٱلرِّسَالَة.

Sami does not study French. ٤. **لا** يَدْرُسُ سامي ٱلْفَرَنْسِيَّة.

تَمْرِين ١٦. حَدِّدُوا ٱلْفِعْل وَٱلْفَاعِل وَٱلْمَفْعُول بِهِ في ٱلْجُمَل ٱلتَّالِيَة.

Exercise 16. Identify the predicate, subject and object in the following sentences.

٢. تَعَلَّمُوا ٱلْمُوسِيقَى في أَمْرِيكَا. ١. يُعَلِّمُ هَانِي ٱللُّغَة ٱلْعَرَبِيَّة.

٤. أَتَعَلَّمُ ٱللُّغَة ٱلْإِسْبَانِيَّة. ٣. شَرِبَ رامِي ٱلْقَهْوَة.

٦. يُحِبُّ ران مِهْنَتَهُ. ٥. أَكَلْنَا ٱلْكَبَاب وَٱلْحُمُّص.

٨. هَلْ زُرْتِ ٱلْأَهْرَام؟ ٧. مَتَى كَتَبَتْ رِيم هٰذِهِ ٱلرِّسَالَة؟

١٠. نُحِبُّ ٱلرِّيَاضَة وَٱلْمُوسِيقَى. ٩. نَقْرَأُ ٱلْقُرْآنَ ٱلْكَرِيم كُلَّ يَوْم.

تَعَلَّمُوا هٰذِهِ ٱلْمُفْرَدَات

not, not to be	لَيْسَ	solution	حَلّ (ج) حُلُول
I am not	لَسْتُ	to come	قَدِمَ (م) يَقْدَمُ
convinced	مُتَأَكِّد	madness	جُنُون
it is possible	يُمْكِنُ	to move	إِنْتَقَلَ (م) يَنْتَقِلُ
going	أَلذَّهَاب	problem	مُشْكِلَة (ج) مَشَاكِل
always	دَائِمًا	relationship	عَلاقَة (ج) عَلاقَات
distance	بُعْد	employee	مُوَظَّف (ج) مُوَظَّفُونَ
married	مُتَزَوِّج	to think, assume	ظَنَّ (م) يَظُنُّ

Exercise 17. Change into the singular.   تَمْرِين ١٧. حَوِّلُوا إِلَى ٱلْمُفْرَد.

١. هُمْ أَطْفَال.   ٢. عَلاقَات جَيِّدَة   ٣. أَصْدِقَاء عَرَب

٤. مِهَن جَدِيدَة   ٥. هٰذِهِ سِفَارَات عَرَبِيَّة.   ٦. كِتَابَةُ ٱلرَّسَائِل

٧. مَشَاكِل كَبِيرَة   ٨. أَرْبَعَة أَسَابِيع   ٩. مُسْتَشْفَيَات أَمْرِيكِيَّة

١٠. مُوَظَّفُونَ جُدُد   ١١. هِوَايَاتِي ٱلْمُفَضَّلَة   ١٢. حُلُول جَدِيدَة

إِسْتَمِعُوا إِلَى ٱلْمُحَادَثَة ثُمَّ ٱقْرَؤُوهَا. Listen to the conversation, then read.

هَاني سَعيد خُوري

ماجِد: يا ران، أَنْتَ دَائِمًا تَتَكَلَّمُ عَنْ هَاني، مَنْ هُوَ هَاني؟

ران: هَاني سَعيد خُوري هُوَ أُسْتَاذي في جَامِعَة نيو يورك وَيُعَلِّمُ

فِيهَا ٱللُّغَة ٱلْعَرَبِيَّة وَٱلْأَدَبَ ٱلْعَرَبِيّ.

ماجِد: هَلْ هُوَ عَرَبِيّ مُسْلِمٌ؟

ران: لا. هُوَ عَرَبِيّ مَسيحِيّ.

ماجِد: كَمْ سَنَةَ لَهُ في أَمْريكَا؟

ران: قَدِمَ إِلَى أَمْريكَا من لُبْنَان مُنْذُ سَبْع سَنَوَات.

ماجِد: وَأَيْنَ يَسْكُنُ؟

ران: يَسْكُنُ في مَدِينَة أَلْبَني في شَقَّة كَبيرَة وَجَميلَة.

ماجِد: يَسْكُنُ في مَدِينَة أَلْبَني وَيَعْمَلُ في مَدِينَة نيو يُورك؟

هَلْ يُسَافِرُ كُلَّ يَوْم من أَلْبَني إِلَى نيو يورك؟ هٰذا جُنُون!

ران: لا. إِسْتَأْجَرَ شَقَّة صَغيرَة بِٱلْقُرْب مِنَ ٱلْجَامِعَة وَيُسَافِرُ إِلَى أَلْبَني

يَوْمَ ٱلثُّلاثَاء وَيَوْمَ ٱلْجُمْعَة.

ماجِد: أَلْبُعْد بَيْنَ أَلْبَني ونيو يورك كَبير وهٰذِهِ مُشْكِلَة.

ران: وَٱللهِ مُشْكِلَة كَبيرَة. ولٰكِنْ ما هو ٱلْحَلّ؟

ماجِد: هَلْ هُوَ مُتَزَوِّج؟

ران: طَبْعًا. لَهُ زَوْجَة ٱسْمُهَا لَيْلَى وثَلاثة أَوْلاد هُمْ رامي وبُشْرَى وأَميرَة.

ماجِد: مَاذَا تَعْمَلُ زَوْجَتُهُ؟

ران: أَظُنُّ أَنَّهَا مُوَظَّفَة في جامِعَة ٱلْبَني ولٰكِنْ لَسْتُ مُتَأَكِّدًا.

ماجِد: وَٱللهِ أُريدُ ٱلتَّعَرُّف عَلَيْه.

ران: هٰذِهِ فِكْرَة. هَلْ يُمْكِنُكَ ٱلذَّهاب مَعي يَوْمَ ٱلْخَميسِ ٱلْقادِم إلى دَرْسِ ٱلْعَرَبِيَّة في ٱلْجامِعَة؟

ماجِد: عَظيم، سَأَذْهَبُ مَعَكَ.

"By God"   وَٱللهِ

The word وَٱللهِ is an oath comprised of وَ (an oath marker) and أَللهِ. In daily use it has become part of informal speech indicating one's commitment to the truthfulness, seriousness and sincerity of one's utterance. It is also used as a polite and intimate register for requests: *please, I beg you, I urge you*, etc. It is widely used by all social classes and in a variety of social interactions.

تَمْرين ١٨. أَجيبُوا شَفَهِيًّا ثُمَّ ٱكْتُبُوا ٱلْأَجْوِبَة في دَفَاتِركُمْ.

Exercise 18. Answer out loud, then write the answers in your notebook.

١. مَنْ هُوَ ٱلْأُسْتَاذ هَاني؟

٢. أَيْنَ يَسْكُنُ وَأَيْنَ يَعْمَلُ؟

٣. ما ٱسْمُ زَوْجَة هاني وَأَيْنَ تَعْمَلُ؟

٤. كَمْ وَلَدًا وكَمْ بِنْتًا لِهَاني؟

٥. ما هِيَ ٱلْعَلاقَة بَيْنَ ران وَهَاني؟

٦. ما هِيَ مُشْكِلَة هاني؟

٧. لِمَاذا تَرَكَ هاني لُبْنَان وَٱنْتَقَلَ هو وَأُسْرَتُهُ إلَى أَمْريكَا؟

تَمْرين ١٩. حَدِّدُوا ٱلْأَشْيَاءَ ٱلصَّحيحَة بِٱلنِّسْبَة لِهَاني.

Exercise 19. Identify the correct statements about Hani.

٢. هو طَالِب في جَامِعَة نيو يورك .   ١. هُوَ أُسْتَاذ .

٤. يُحِبُّ ٱلْمُوسيقَى .   ٣. هُوَ ٱبْن سَعيد .

٦. لَهُ وَلَد وَبِنْتَانِ .   ٥. هو زَوْج لَيْلَى .

٨. لَهُ شَقَّة كَبيرَة في أَلْبَني .   ٧. يُعَلِّمُ ٱلْأَدَبَ ٱلْعَرَبِيَّ .

١٠. هو من لُبْنَان .   ٩. هو عَرَبِيّ مُسْلِم .

١٢. إِسْتَأْجَرَ شَقَّة في مَدينَة نيو يورك .   ١١. تَعْمَلُ زَوْجَتُهُ في أَلْبَني .

تَمْرِين ٢٠ . تَرْجِمُوا شَفَهِيًّا ثُمَّ ٱكْتُبُوا ٱلتَّرْجَمَة في دَفَاتِرِكُمْ.

Exercise 20. Translate out loud, then write the translation in your notebooks.

1. He is a Christian Arab.

2. Hani and Layla have a big apartment.

3. This is a big problem.

4. Hani has three children.

5. She is an employee at the university.

6. She came to London with the family.

7. Hani and his wife have a big problem.

8. In my opinion, she is Muslim.

تَمْرِين ٢١ . إِسْأَلُوا زُمَلاءَكُمْ ثَلاثَة أَسْئِلَة عَنْ هَاني .

Exercise 21. Ask your classmates three questions about Hani.

تَمْرِين ٢٢ . يُرِيدُ هَاني كِتَابَة نَصّ عَنْ نَفْسِه "لِلْفِيسْبُوك" كَمَا فَعَلَ ران .

سَاعِدُوهُ. إِبْدَؤُوا بِ : إِسْمِي هَاني سَعِيد خُوري .

Exercise 22. Hani wants to write a text about himself for Facebook as Rahn did.

   Help him. Begin with "My name is Hani Sa'id <u>Khuri</u>..."

تَمْرِين ٢٣ . تُرِيدُ لَيْلَى أَيْضاً كِتَابَة نَصّ عَنْ نَفْسِها "لِلْفِيسْبُوك." سَاعِدُوهَا.

إِبْدَؤُوهُ بِ: "إِسْمِي لَيْلَى يُونِس خُوري."

Exercise 23. Layla wants also to write a text about herself for Facebook.

   Help her. Begin with "My name is Layla Yunis <u>Khuri</u>."

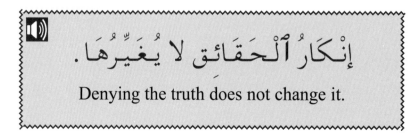

إِنْكَارُ ٱلْحَقَائِق لا يُغَيِّرُهَا.
Denying the truth does not change it.

Ending vowels أَلإِعْرَاب

The last letter of definite and indefinite nouns and adjectives takes a vowel to indicate the grammatical role of the word in the sentence. Ending vowels are used in classical Arabic, Qur'anic recitations, religious texts and formal speeches. Beyond their grammatical role they add beauty and rhythm to texts recited. In the standard language, ending vowels are usually omitted in speaking and reading aloud. However, they are needed in two cases:

• When a word has a possessive pronoun:

هَـذا بَيْتُهُ .   *This is his house.*

• Before *'alif waṣla* (هَمْزَةُ ٱلْوَصْل) to facilitate pronunciation:

أَدْرُسُ ٱلأَدَبَ ٱلْعَرَبِيَّ .   *I study Arabic literature.*

Definite nouns and adjectives

The student wrote the letter to the professor.

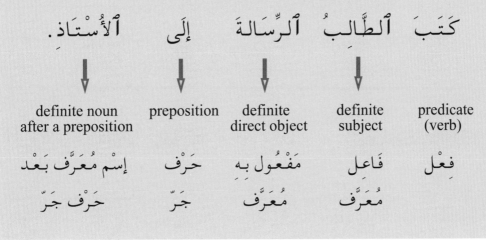

كَتَبَ   ٱلطَّالِبُ   ٱلرِّسَالَةَ   إِلَى   ٱلأُسْتَاذِ .

definite noun after a preposition	preposition	definite direct object	definite subject	predicate (verb)
إِسْم مُعَرَّف بَعْد حَرْف جَرّ	حَرْف جَرّ	مَفْعُول بِه مُعَرَّف	فَاعِل مُعَرَّف	فِعْل

Hani is the professor.

هَانِي هُوَ ٱلْأُسْتَاذُ.

⬇   ⬇

Definite predicate   definite subject

خَبَر مُعَرَّف   مُبْتَدَأ مُعَرَّف

Ending vowels - Definite nouns and adjectives

- A definite subject or predicate takes ضَمَّة.

- A definite direct object takes فَتْحَة.

- A definite noun after a preposition takes كَسْرَة.

تَمْرِين ٢٤ . أَضِيفُوا ٱلْحَرَكَاتِ فِي أَوَاخِرِ ٱلْكَلِمَاتِ ٱلْبَارِزَةِ وَٱشْرَحُوا ٱلسَّبَب .

Exercise 24. Add vowels to the end of the bold words and explain the reason.

١ . ألْأُسْتَاذ مِنْ بَيْرُوت .   ٢ . ذَهَبَ رَامِي إلى ٱلطَّبِيب .

٣ . هٰذِهِ هِيَ ٱلْمُوَظَّفَة .   ٤ . أَدْرُسُ ٱلْعَرَبِيَّة .

٥ . ذَهَبْنَا مَعَ هٰذِهِ ٱلْأُسْتَاذَة .   ٦ . أَذْهَبُ إلى ٱلْجَامِعَة بَعْدَ ٱلظُّهْر .

٧ . كَتَبْنَا ٱلْمُحَادَثَة .   ٨ . مَنْ فَتَحَ ٱلشُّبَّاك (window)؟

٩ . ألطَّبِيب فِي ٱلْمَكْتَب .   ١٠ . تَكَلَّمَ ٱلْأُسْتَاذ مَعَ ٱلطَّالِب .

تَمْرِين ٢٥. تَرْجِمُوا وشَكِّلُوا ٱلْكَلِمَاتِ ٱلْبَارِزَة.

Exercise 25. Translate and add ending vowels to the bold words.

1. Rim works at the **embassy** in Washington.

2. I saw the **professor** at the **museum**.

3. The **library** is in this **building**.

4. We graduated from this **university**.

5. He will return **home** (to the home) in the **evening**.

Note:

1. Don't analyze the grammatical role of words in Arabic sentences by using the English translation. In many cases the grammatical roles are different. For example: in the Arabic sentence: لِنَبِيل بَيْت بِـلُبْنَان (*Nabil has a house in Lebanon*) the word بَيْت is the subject of the Arabic sentence, while in the English translation the word *house* is the object. Remember, in Arabic, everything that someone has or does not have is the subject.

2. The demonstrative adjective (هٰذا هٰذه ‒ إِسْمُ ٱلإِشَارَة) is part of the noun and does not affect the ending vowels. For example, in the sentence:

    أَسْكُنُ في هٰذا ٱلْبَيْتِ (*I live in this house*), the word ٱلْبَيْتِ takes كَسْرَة because it is definite and influenced by the preposition في.

3. When you add ending vowels, ignore proper nouns.

تَمْرِين ٢٦. إِمْلَؤُوا ٱلْفَرَاغَ بِٱلْكَلِمَة ٱلْمُنَاسِبَة.

Exercise 26. Fill in the blank with the appropriate word.

١. لِمَاذَا لا تُحِبِّينَ هٰذِهِ ــــــــــ؟ (ٱلْمَدِينَةُ ٱلْمَدِينَةَ ٱلْمَدِينَةِ)

٢. يَدْرُسُ ران ــــــــــ ٱلْعَرَبِيَّة. (ٱللُّغَةُ ٱللُّغَةَ ٱللُّغَةِ)

٣. بَيْتُهُ بِٱلْقُرْب مِنَ ــــــــــ. (ٱلْجَامِعَةُ ٱلْجَامِعَةَ ٱلْجَامِعَةِ)

٤. ــــــــــ من لُبْنَان. (أَلأُسْتَاذُ أَلأُسْتَاذَ أَلأُسْتَاذِ)

٥. يُحِبُّ ران ــــــــــ ٱللُّبْنَانِيّ كَثِيرًا. (ٱلأَكْلُ ٱلأَكْلَ ٱلأَكْلِ)

Indefinite nouns and adjectives

Marking indefinite nouns, subjects, predicates, and objects is simple.

They take the same vowel as their definite counterparts, but this vowel is

doubled. For example: a definite subject takes ضَمَّة, while an indefinite

subject takes double ضَمَّة. The same changes occur in nouns and

adjectives with فَتْحَة and كَسْرَة.

- Double ضَمَّة is called: تَنْوِينُ ٱلضَّمّ
- Double فَتْحَة is called: تَنْوِينُ ٱلْفَتْح
- Double كَسْرَة is called: تَنْوِينُ ٱلْكَسْر

How to pronounce double vowels

Double vowels are pronounced as regular vowels with the addition of the **sound nuun**. (You have learned this previously in words like شُكْراً , أَهْلاً , عَفْواً)

This phenomenon is called تَنْوِين (Nunation). For example: وَلَدٌ (*waladun*), رِسَالةٌ (*risalatan*), مَكْتَبٍ (*maktaben*).

To facilitate pronunciation تَنْوِينُ ٱلْكَسْر is pronounced like the "en" in the word "**ten.**" فِي سَيَّارَةٍ كَبِيرَةٍ (read: *fi sayyaraten kabiraten*) – *in a big car*.

A student wrote a letter to a professor.

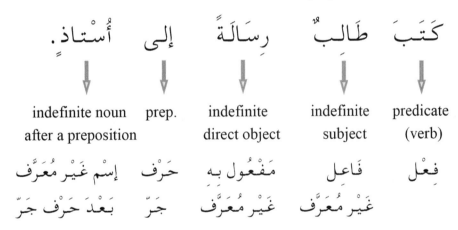

She is a student.

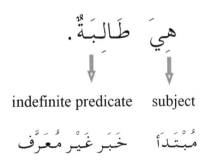

Ending vowels - Indefinite nouns and adjectives

- An indefinite subject or a predicate takes تَنْوِينُ ٱلضَّمّ.

- An indefinite direct object takes تَنْوِينُ ٱلْفَتْح.

- An indefinite noun after a preposition takes تَنْوِينُ ٱلْكَسْر.

تَمْرِين ٢٧. أَضِيفُوا ٱلْحَرَكَاتِ فِي أَوَاخِرِ ٱلْكَلِمَاتِ ٱلْبَارِزَةِ وَٱشْرَحُوا ٱلسَّبَب.

Exercise 27. Add vowels to the end of the bold words and explain the reason.

٢. هٰذِهِ **ٱلشَّقَّة كَبِيرَة**.		١. **أَلأُسْتَاذ مِصْرِيّ**.	
٤. رِيم **مُوَظَّفَة** فِي ٱلسِّفَارَة.		٣. **أَلأُسْتَاذَة لُبْنَانِيَّة**.	
٦. نَادِيَة **طَالِبَة** فِي ٱلْجَامِعَة.		٥. رَجَعَتْ قَبْلَ **سَاعَة**.	
٨. زُرْتُ (I visited) بَارِيس قَبْلَ **شَهْر**.		٧. تَعَرَّفْنَا عَلَى **طَبِيب مِصْرِيّ**.	
١٠. لِهَانِي **زَوْجَة** ٱسْمُهَا لَيْلَى.		٩. هٰذِهِ **حِكَايَة جَمِيلَة**.	

تَمْرِين ٢٨. تَرْجِمُوا وَشَكِّلُوا ٱلْكَلِمَاتِ ٱلْبَارِزَة.

Exercise 28. Translate and add ending vowels to the bold words.

1. He graduated from the **university** a **year** ago.

2. The **student** sent (أَرْسَلَ) a **letter** to the **professor**.

3. She is a **professor** at the **university**.

4. I read a **story** (حِكَايَة) in **Arabic** in front of (أَمَام) the **students**.

ألْعَائِلَة وٱلأَقَارِب

father	وَالِد	father	أَب (ج) آبَاء
mother	وَالِدَة	mother	أُمّ (ج) أُمَّهَات
brother	أخ (ج) إخْوَة	husband	زَوْج (ج) أَزْوَاج
sister	أُخْت (ج) أَخَوَات	wife	زَوْجَة (ج) زَوْجَات
brother of	أخُو	uncle (paternal)	عَمّ (ج) أَعْمَام
father of	أبُو	uncle (maternal)	خَال (ج) أَخْوَال
son	إبْن	grandfather	جَدّ (ج) أَجْدَاد
daughter	بِنْت	grandmother	جَدَّة (ج) جَدَّات
cousin (m.)	إبْن عَمّ/خَال	grandson	حَفِيد (ج) أَحْفَاد
cousin (f.)	بِنْت عَمّ/خَال	granddaughter	حَفِيدَة (ج) حَفِيدَات
relative	قَرِيب (ج) أَقَارِب	my parental grandfather	جَدِّي لأَبِي
heart	قَلْب (ج) قُلُوب	to die	مَاتَ (م) يَمُوتُ
as for	أمَّا ... فَ...	to have mercy	رَحِمَ (ج) يَرْحَمُ

أَلْعَائِلَة وَٱلْأَقَارِب

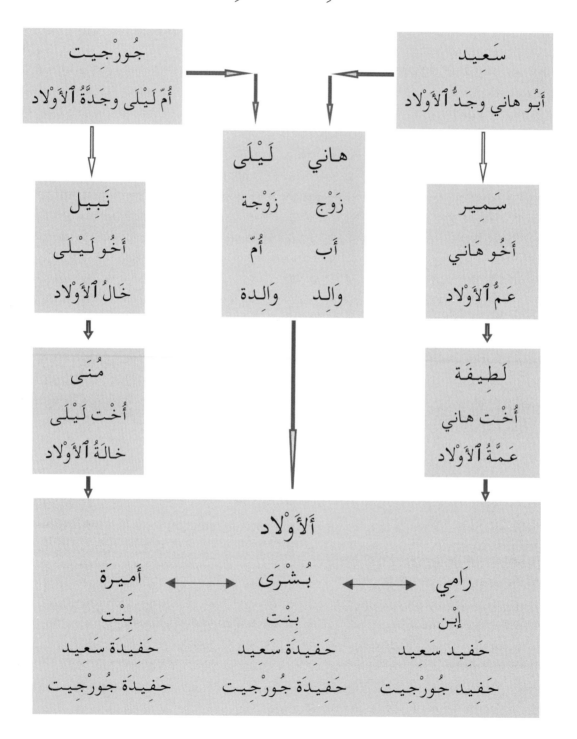

جُورْجِيت	سَعِيد
أُمّ لَيْلَى وجَدَّةُ ٱلْأَوْلاد	أَبُو هاني وجَدُّ ٱلْأَوْلاد

هاني	لَيْلَى
زَوْج	زَوْجة
أَب	أُمّ
وَالِد	وَالِدة

نَبيل	سَمِير
أَخُو لَيْلَى	أَخُو هَاني
خَالُ ٱلْأَوْلاد	عَمُّ ٱلْأَوْلاد

مُنَى	لَطِيفَة
أُخْت لَيْلَى	أُخْت هاني
خَالَةُ ٱلْأَوْلاد	عَمَّةُ ٱلْأَوْلاد

أَلْأَوْلاد

أَمِيرَة	بُشْرَى	رَامِي
بِنْت	بِنْت	إِبْن
حَفِيدَة سَعِيد	حَفِيدَة سَعِيد	حَفِيد سَعِيد
حَفِيدَة جُورْجِيت	حَفِيدَة جُورْجِيت	حَفِيد جُورْجِيت

Exercise 29. True or false.   تَمْرِين ٢٩. صَوَاب أَمْ خَطَأ.

١. لَطِيفَة عَمَّة رَامِي وَأَمِيرَة.   ٢. سَمِير خَال رَامِي وَبُشْرَى.

٣. جُورْجِيت جَدَّة سَمِير وَمُنَى.   ٤. لِهَانِي وَلَيْلَى ثَلَاثَة أَوْلَاد.

٥. لَطِيفَة زَوْجَة نَبِيل.   ٦. نَبِيل وَلَيْلَى وَمُنَى إِخْوَة.

٧. مُنَى عَمَّة رَامِي.   ٨. لِبُشْرَى عَمّ ٱسْمُهُ نَبِيل.

٩. مُنَى أُخْتُ ٱلأُمّ.   ١٠. بُشْرَى حَفِيدَة سَعِيد.

١١. سَعِيد زَوْج جُورْجِيت.   ١٢. لِسَمِير أَخ وَأُخْت.

Exercise 30. Fill in the blank.   تَمْرِين ٣٠. إِمْلَؤُوا ٱلْفَرَاغ.

١. هَانِي _____ لَيْلَى.   ٢. أَمِيرَة _____ لَيْلَى.

٣. جُورْجِيت _____ رَامِي.   ٤. لِهَانِي _____ أَوْلَاد.

٥. _____ أُمُّ ٱلأَوْلَاد.   ٦. رَامِي ٱبْنُ _____ .

٧. _____ أَخُو سَمِير.   ٨. لَيْلَى _____ هَانِي.

٩. لَطِيفَة _____ هَانِي.   ١٠. هَانِي _____ رَامِي.

١١. سَعِيد _____ بُشْرَى.   ١٢. أَمِيرَة _____ سَعِيد.

Listen, then read.

رَامِي يَتَكَلَّمُ عَنْ نَفْسِهِ

أَنَا رَامِي وَهٰذِهِ عَائِلَتِي. إِسْمُ وَالِدِي هَانِي وَٱسْمُ وَالِدَتِي لَيْلَى. لِي أُخْتَانِ صَغِيرَتَانِ بُشْرَى وَأَمِيرَة. جَدِّي سَعِيد، يَرْحَمُهُ ٱلله، مَاتَ قَبْلَ أَرْبَعِ سَنَوَات، وَجَدَّتِي رَوَان، يَرْحَمُهَا ٱلله، مَاتَتْ قَبْلَ سَبْعِ سَنَوَات.

عَمِّي وَعَمَّتِي هُمَا سَمِير وَلَطِيفَة وَخَالِي وَخَالَتِي هُمَا نَبِيل وَمُنَى. خَالِي نَبِيل تَخَرَّجَ مِنَ ٱلْجَامِعَة مُنْذُ سَبْعِ سَنَوَات وَٱلآن يَعْمَلُ طَيَّارًا فِي خُطُوطِ ٱلطَّيَرَانِ ٱلْأَمْرِيكِيَّة "دِلتَا،" أَمَّا خَالَتِي مُنَى فَتَخَرَّجَتْ مِنَ ٱلْجَامِعَة مُنْذُ أَرْبَعِ سَنَوَات وَٱلآن تَعْمَلُ طَبِيبَة فِي مُسْتَشْفَى "مَاوُنْت سَيْنَاي" فِي مَانهاتِن. هِيَ مُتَخَصِّصَة بِٱلْقَلْب.

إِلْيَاس، ٱبْنُ خَالَتِي لَطِيفَة، يَدْرُسُ ٱلْعُلُومَ ٱلسِّيَاسِيَّة فِي جَامِعَة نيو يُورك وَسَيَتَخَرَّجُ بَعْدَ ثَلَاثِ سَنَوَات. أُحِبُّ عَائِلَتِي كَثِيرًا.

Exercise 31. Answer.   تَمْرِين ٣١. أَجِيبُوا.

١. مَاذَا يَعْمَلُ نَبِيل؟   ٢. مَاذَا تَعْمَلُ مُنَى؟   ٣. مَنْ هِيَ لَطِيفَة؟

٤. مَنْ هُوَ إِلْيَاس؟   ٥. مَاذَا يَدْرُسُ إِلْيَاس؟   ٦. مَتَى سَيَتَخَرَّجُ إِلْيَاس؟

يَرْحَمُهُ ٱللّٰه. ، رَحِمَهُ ٱللّٰه.

May God have mercy upon him.

"May God have mercy upon him" رَحِمَهُ ٱللّٰه or يَرْحَمُهُ ٱللّٰه is said when

talking about someone who has died. For a female you say, يَرْحَمُهَا ٱللّٰه or

رَحِمَهَا ٱللّٰه. From the same three radicals رحم, the words أَلْمَرْحُوم (the late,

deceased (*m. s.*) and أَلْمَرْحُومَة (*f. s.*) are formed.

أَمَّا ... فَـ ...   As for...

... فَـ ... أَمَّا can be used to indicate something different from what has been

said before: عَمِّي نَبِيل طَيَّار، أَمَّا زَوْج خَالَتِي مُنَى فَهُوَ مُهَنْدِس.

My (paternal) uncle is a pilot, as for the husband of my (maternal) aunt, he is

an engineer.

When a sentence starts with أَمَّا the subject of the sentence follows it. The rest

of the sentence is preceded by فَـ. This فَـ has no English equivalent and is

therefore not translated into English.

تَمْرِين ٣٢. إِسْتَمِعُوا وَٱمْلَؤُوا ٱلْفَرَاغ. Exercise 32. Listen and fill in the blank.

هٰذِهِ _____ رَامِي. إِسْم _____ هَانِي وَٱسْمُ _____

لَيْلَى. لَهُ _____ بُشْرَى وَأَمِيرَة. جَدُّهُ سَعِيد، _____

ٱلله، مَاتَ قَبْلَ أَرْبَع _____ وَجَدَّتُهُ رَوَان، يَرْحَمُهَا ٱلله، _____

مُنْذُ سَبْع سَنَوَات. عَمُّهُ وَعَمَّتُهُ _____ سَمِير وَلَطِيفَة، وَخَالُهُ وَخَالَتُهُ

هُمَا _____ وَمُنَى. نَبِيل _____ مِنَ ٱلْجَامِعَة مُنْذُ سَبْع

سَنَوَات وَٱلآن _____ طَيَّاراً فِي _____ ٱلطَّيَران "دْلْتَا"، أَمَّا

خَالَتُهُ مُنَى _____ مِنَ ٱلْجَامِعَة مُنْذُ أَرْبَع سَنَوَات وَٱلآن تَعْمَل

_____ فِي مُسْتَشْفَى "مَاوُنْت سَايْنَاي" فِي مانهاتِن.

إِلْيَاس، ٱبْنُ خَالَتِهِ لَطِيفَة، _____ ٱلْعُلُومَ ٱلسِّيَاسِيَّة فِي

وَسَيَتَخَرَّجُ بَعْدَ _____ سَنَوَات. يُحِبُّ رَامِي عَائِلَتَهُ _____ .

🔊

تَعَلَّمُوا هٰذِهِ ٱلْمُفْرَدَاتِ

heart	قَلْب (ج) قُلُوب	pilot	طَيَّار (ج) طَيَّارُونَ
always	دَائِمًا	line	خَطّ (ج) خُطُوط
busy	مَشْغُول	airlines	خُطُوطُ ٱلطَّيَرَان
the second	أَلثَّانِي	specialized	مُتَخَصِّص

Listen, then read.

إِسْتَمِعُوا ثُمَّ ٱقْرَؤُوا.

🔊

نَبِيل يَتَحَدَّثُ عَنْ نَفْسِهِ

إِسْمِي نَبِيل. أَنَا طَيَّار وَأَعْمَلُ فِي خُطُوطِ ٱلطَّيَرَانِ ٱلْأَمرِيكِيَّة "دِلْتَا." لِي أُخْتَانِ، وَاحِدَة ٱسْمُهَا لَيْلَى وَٱلثَّانِيَة ٱسْمُهَا مُنَى. تَعْمَلُ لَيْلَى سِكْرتِيرَة فِي قِسْمِ ٱلْعُلُومِ ٱلسِّيَاسِيَّةِ فِي جَامِعَة ٱلْبَنِي.

زَوْجُ أُخْتِي ٱسْمُهُ هَانِي وَيَعْمَلُ أُسْتَاذًا فِي جَامِعَة نيو يورك. لِأُخْتِي لَيْلَى وَلَد وَبِنْتَان. أُخْتِي ٱلثَّانِيَة، مُنَى، تَسْكُنُ فِي مانهاتِن حَيْثُ تَعْمَلُ طَبِيبَة فِي مُسْتَشْفَى "ماونت سايناي." هِيَ طَبِيبَة مُمْتَازَة مُتَخَصِّصَة فِي ٱلْقَلْب وَدَائِمًا مَشْغُولَة وَتَعْبَانَة.

Exercise 33. Answer out loud.   تَمْرِين ٣٣ . أَجِيبُوا شَفَهِيًّا .

٢ . مَا عَلاقَة (connection) نَبِيل بِهَانِي؟   ١ . مَاذَا يَعْمَلُ نَبِيل؟

٤ . مَا ٱلْعَلاقَة بَيْنَ نَبِيل ومُنَى ولَيْلَى؟   ٣ . أَيْنَ تَعْمَلُ لَيْلَى؟

تَمْرِين ٣٤ . جِدُوا ٱلتَّرْجَمَة في ٱلنَّصّ (صَفْحَة ٣٦٧) وَٱنْسَخُوهَا .

Exercise 34. Find the translation in the text (p. 367) and copy it.

1. Delta Airlines _____

2. I have two sisters. _____

3. My brother in-law (the husband of my sister) _____

4. The Department of Political Science _____

5. Lyla has a son and two daughters . _____

6. She is always busy and tired. _____

مَصَائِب قَوْم عِنْدَ قَوْم فَوَائِد .

Misfortunes of some people are benefits of others.

تَعَلَّمُوا هٰذِهِ ٱلْمُفْرَدَات

half	نِصْف	lawyer	مُحَامٍ (مُؤَنَّث: مُحَامِيَة)
to rest	إِرْتَاحَ (م) يَرْتَاحُ	to wake up	صَحَا (م) يَصْحُو
to continue	وَاصَلَ (م) يُوَاصِلُ	sixth	أَلسَّادِس، سَادِس
period of time	مُدَّة	to eat breakfast	فَطَرَ (م) يَفْطُرُ

Listen, then read.

إِسْتَمِعُوا ثُمَّ ٱقْرَؤُوا.

أَمَل

لِنَبِيل بِنْت ٱسْمُهَا أَمَل. هِيَ مُحَامِيَة وتَعْمَلُ في شَرِكَة ٱقْتِصَادِيَّة (commercial) كَبِيرَة. تَصْحُو مِنَ ٱلنَّوْم ٱلسَّاعَة ٱلسَّادِسَة صَبَاحًا.

وبَعْدَ أَنْ تَفْطُرَ وتَقْرَأَ ٱلْجَرِيدَة ٱلصَّبَاحِيَّة، تَذْهَبُ إلى عَمَلِهَا. تَعُودُ أَمَل إلى ٱلْبَيْت ٱلسَّاعَة ٱلثَّامِنَة وٱلنِّصْف مَسَاءً وبَعْدَ أَنْ تَشْرَبَ ٱلْقَهْوَة وتَرْتَاحَ قَلِيلاً تُوَاصِلُ عَمَلَهَا لِمُدَّة سَاعَة أَوْ سَاعَتَيْنِ. هِيَ دَائِمًا مَشْغُولَة بِٱلْعَمَل، ولٰكِنْ تُحِبُّ مِهْنَتَهَا كَثِيرًا.

صَبَاحًا = في ٱلصَّبَاح ، مَسَاءً = في ٱلْمَسَاء
In the evening　　　　　　　　in the morning

بَعْدَ ، بَعْدَ أَنْ   After

1. The preposition بَعْدَ can be followed by a noun or a verb in أَلْمَاضِي
or أَلْمُضَارِع.

2. The noun comes directly after the preposition: بَعْدَ أُسْبُوع *after a week*,
بَعْدَ سَاعَة *after an hour*.

3. The verb comes after أَنْ which is added to the preposition:

بَعْدَ أَنْ شَرِبَ ٱلْقَهْوَة   *After he drank coffee*

بَعْدَ أَنْ يَشْرَبَ ٱلْقَهْوَة   *After he drinks/will drink coffee*

4. A verb in أَلْمُضَارِع that follows أَنْ has some changes in its conjugation,
for example: أَنْ يَشْرَبَ instead of يَشْرَبُ, and is called
أَلْمُضَارِع ٱلْمَنْصُوب.

تَمْرِين ٣٥. أَجِيبُوا شَفَهِيًّا ثُمَّ ٱكْتُبُوا ٱلْأَجْوِبَة فِي دَفَاتِرِكُمْ.

Exercise 35. Answer out loud, then write the answers in your notebooks.

١. مَنْ هِيَ أَمَل؟   ٢. مَتَى تَصْحُو مِنَ ٱلنَّوْم؟

٣. مَاذَا تَعْمَلُ؟   ٤. أَيْنَ تَعْمَلُ؟

٥. مَاذَا تَعْمَلُ بَعْدَ أَنْ تَفْطُرَ؟   ٦. مَتَى تَعُودُ إِلَى ٱلْبَيْت؟

تَمْرِين ٣٦. أَمَل تَتَحَدَّثُ عَنْ نَفْسِهَا. تَكَلَّمُوا مَعَ زُمَلائِكُمْ ثُمَّ ٱكْتُبُوا ٱلنَّصّ.

Exercise 36. Amal talks about herself. Talk with your classmates, then write the text.

تَمْرِين ٣٧. أُكْتُبُوا أَسْئِلَة لِلْأَجْوِبَة.   Exercise 37. Write questions for the answers.

١. أَلسُّؤَال: _____ ؟

أَلْجَوَاب: يَعْمَلُ نَبِيل في شَرِكة ٱلطَّيَرَان ٱلأَمْرِيكِيَّة "دِلْتَا."

٢. أَلسُّؤَال: _____ ؟

أَلْجَوَاب: زَوْجَتِي هِيَ لَيْلَى.

٣. أَلسُّؤَال: _____ ؟

أَلْجَوَاب: لِهَانِي وَلَيْلَى وَلَد وبِنْتَان.

٤. أَلسُّؤَال: _____ ؟

أَلْجَوَاب: تَسْكُنُ أُخْتِي مُنَى في مانهاتن.

٥. أَلسُّؤَال: _____ ؟

أَلْجَوَاب: بِنْت نَبِيل مُحَامِيَة.

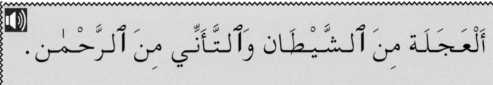

أَلْعَجَلَة مِنَ ٱلشَّيْطَان وَٱلتَّأَنِّي مِنَ ٱلرَّحْمَن.

Haste is from Satan and patience is from God.

تَمْرِين ٣٨. لائِمُوا بَيْنَ ٱلْعَرَبِيَّة وَٱلإِنجِليزِيَّة.

Exercise 38. Match the Arabic with the English.

a. My sister's husband (my brother in-law)   ١. لِنَبِيل أَخ وَأُخْت.

b. We read the morning newspaper.   ٢. قِسْمُ ٱلْعُلُومِ ٱلسِّيَاسِيَّة

c. He works as a pilot.   ٣. زَوْج أُخْتِي

d. Commercial (economic) company   ٤. يَعْمَلُ طَيَّارًا.

e. After she drinks coffee   ٥. لِأُخْتِي وَلَد وَبِنْتَان.

f. At 6:30   ٦. مُتَخَصِّص فِي ٱلْهَنْدَسَة

g. The political Science Department   ٧. مَشْغُولَة وَتَعْبَانَة

h. Nabil has a brother and a sister.   ٨. تَعْمَلُ مُحَامِيَة.

i. Busy and tired (*f. s.*)   ٩. شَرِكَة ٱقْتِصَادِيَّة

j. She works as a lawyer.   ١٠. فِي ٱلسَّاعَة ٱلسَّادِسَة وَٱلنِّصْف

k. Specializes in engineering   ١١. نَقْرَأُ ٱلْجَرِيدَة ٱلصَّبَاحِيَّة.

l. My sister has a son and two daughters.   ١٢. بَعْدَ أَنْ تَشْرَبَ ٱلْقَهْوَة

Exercise 39. Who am I? تَمْرِين ٣٩. مَنْ أَنَا؟

هاني ، لَيْلَى ، ران ، رِيم ، نَبِيل ، مُنَى ، أَمَل ، رامي

١. أَنَا طَيَّار وَأَعْـمَـلُ في شَرِكَةِ ٱلطَّيَـرانِ ٱلْأَمْرِيكِيَّة "دِلْتَا." _____

٢. أَنَا مُوَظَّفَة في جَامِعَة ٱلْبَـني. _____

٣. أَنَا مُحَامِيَة في شَرِكَة ٱقْتِصَادِيَّة كَبِيرَة. _____

٤. أَنَا طَبِيبَة في مُسْتَشْفَى "ماونت سايناي." _____

٥. صَدِيقِي أُسْتَاذ في جَامِعَة نيو يورك وَيُعَلِّمُ ٱللُّغَة ٱلْعَرَبِيَّة. _____

٦. _____ _____

٧. _____ _____

٨. _____ _____

تَمْرِين ٤٠. مُنَى تَتَحَدَّثُ عَنْ نَفْسِهَا. تَكَلَّمُوا مَعَ زُمَلائِكُمْ.

Exercise 40. Muna talks about herself. Talk with your classmates.

تَمْرِين ٤١. صِفُوا عَائِلَتَكُمْ لِزُمَلائِكُمْ.

Exercise 41. Describe your family to your classmates (use a picture).

تَمْرين ٤٢. إِمْلَؤُوا ٱلْفَرَاغَ بِٱلْكَلِمَةِ ٱلْمُلائِمَة.

Exercise 42. Fill in the blank with the appropriate word.

١. بَعْدَ أَنْ تَفْطُرَ وتَقْرَأَ ٱلْجَريدَةَ، تَذْهَبُ إِلَى ــــــــــــــ .

١. عَمَلِهِ   ٢. عَمَلِهَا   ٣. عَمَلِهِمْ   ٤. عَمَلِهِنَّ

٢. لِهَاني ثَلاثَةُ أَوْلاد. ــــــــــــــ طُلّاب في ٱلْمَدْرَسَة.

١. نَحْنُ   ٢. أَنْتُمْ   ٣. هُمْ   ٤. هُنَّ

٣. لِرامي أُخْتَان. واحِدَة كَبيرَة ــــــــــــــ صَغيرَة.

١. وَٱلثَّانِيَة   ٢. وَٱلثَّالِثَة   ٣. وَٱلرَّابِعَة   ٤. وَٱلْخَامِسَة

٤. تَعْمَلُ لَيْلَى سِكْرِتيرَة و ــــــــــــــ هَاني أُسْتَاذاً.

١. أَعْمَلُ   ٢. تَعْمَلُ   ٣. يَعْمَلُ   ٤. تَعْمَلينَ

٥. نَبيل خَال بُشْرَى أَمَّا سَمير فَهُوَ ــــــــــــــ .

١. أَبُوهَا   ٢. أَخُوهَا   ٣. عَمُّهَا   ٤. زَوْجُهَا

٦. سَعيد هُوَ أَبُو هَاني أَمَّا نَبيل فَهُوَ ــــــــــــــ لَيْلَى.

١. أَبُو   ٢. أَخُو   ٣. زَوْج   ٤. إِبْن

The hundreds   أَلْمِئَات

سِتُّمِائَة	٦٠٠	مِائَة ، مِئَة	١٠٠
سَبْعُمِائَة	٧٠٠	مِائَتَانِ ، مِائَتَيْنِ	٢٠٠
ثَمَانِيمِائَة	٨٠٠	ثَلاثُمِائَة	٣٠٠
تِسْعُمِائَة	٩٠٠	أَرْبَعُمِائَة	٤٠٠
		خَمْسُمِائَة	٥٠٠

أَلْف   ١٠٠٠

- The number 100 has two spellings—old and new. In the old spelling there is a silent ١ after the letter م even though the vowel of the م is كَسْرَة.

- The number 200 has two endings: ـَانِ — and ـَيْنِ — . Using one or the other depends on the grammatical role of the word in the sentence. The meaning is the same.

- The last letter of the number in the hundreds (between 300 to 900) can take ضَمَّة or فَتْحَة or كَسْرَة based on the grammatical situation. For example: ثَلاثُمِائَة or ثَلاثَمِائَة or ثَلاثِمِائَة.

Three-digit numbers

Three-digit numbers consist of ones, tens, and hundreds. In order to say a number such as 122, 154, or 173, you must first say the hundreds, then وَ + the ones, and then وَ + the tens. Here is an example: the number 173 is said in Arabic: مِائَة وَثَلاثة وَسَبْعُونَ (Literally: one hundred and three and seventy).

تَمْرِين ٤٣ . قُولُوا ٱلأَعْدَادَ شَفَهِيًّا ثُمَّ ٱكْتُبُوهَا.

Exercise 43. Say the numbers out loud, then write them.

١. ١٢٥   مِائَة وخَمْسَة وَعِشْرُونَ

٢. ٣٥١   _____

٣. ٢٧٦   _____

٤. ٨٩٣   _____

٥. ١٩٥٧   أَلْف وتِسْعُمِائة وسَبْعَة وَخَمْسُونَ

٦. ١٩٨٨   _____

٧. ١٩٩٥   _____

٨. ٢٠٠٥   أَلْفَان وَخَمْسَة

٩. ٢٠٠٩   _____

تَعَلَّمُوا هٰذِهِ ٱلْمُفْرَدَات

west	غَرْب	source	مَصْدَر (ج) مَصَادِر
to move	تَحَرَّكَ (م) يَتَحَرَّكُ	light	نُور
middle, center	وَسَط	heat	حَرَارَة
to continue	إِسْتَمَرَّ (م) يَسْتَمِرُّ	life	حَيَاة
until	حَتَّى	Earth	أَلْكُرَة ٱلْأَرْضِيَّة
		east	شَرْق

حُلُّوا ٱللُّغْز. مَا ٱلْخَطَأُ في هٰذا ٱلنَّصِّ؟   Solve the riddle. What is wrong in this text?

أَلشَّمْس هِيَ مَصْدَرُ ٱلنُّور وَٱلْحَرَارَة وَٱلْحَيَاة على ٱلْكُرَة ٱلْأَرْضِيَّة. كُلَّ صَبَاح تُشْرِقُ ٱلشَّمْس مِنَ ٱلشَّرْق وَتَتَحَرَّكُ إلى وَسَطِ ٱلسَّمَاء في ٱلظُّهْر، وَتَسْتَمِرُّ في تَحَرُّكِهَا حَتَّى تَغْرِبُ في ٱلْغَرْب.

نِزَار قَبَّانِي

شَاعِر سُورِيٌّ مُعَاصِر

إِنَّهُمْ يُرِيدُونَ أَنْ يَفْتَحُوا ٱلْعَالَم
وَهُمْ عَاجِزُونَ عَنْ فَتْحِ كِتَاب.

They want to conquer the world but they

are unable to open a book.

تَمْرِين ٤٤ . جِدُوا مَعْلُومَات عَنْ نِزَار قَبَّانِي فِي ٱلإِنْترنْت.

Exercise 44. Find information about Nizar Qabbani on the Internet.

تَمْرِين ٤٥ . جِدُوا مَعْلُومَات عَنْ سُورِيَا فِي ٱلإِنْترنت بِمَا فِيهَا ٱلْعَاصِمَة وَعَدَدُ
ٱلسُّكَّان وَٱلْعُمْلَة ونِظَامُ ٱلْحُكْم وَٱلدِّين وَٱلدُّوَلُ ٱلْمُجَاوِرَة وَمُدُن
مَرْكَزِيَّة وَٱللُّغَة ٱلرَّسْمِيَّة.

Exercise 45. Find information about Syria on the Internet including the capital,
population, currency, regime, religion, neighboring
countries, important cities, and official language.

ألمسجد الأقصى

ألمسجد الأقصى

COMMON PHRASES   مُصْطَلَحَات شَائِعَة

Script	Print	Letter
أ	أ	'alif
ب بـ	ب بـ	baa
تـ تـ	تـ ت	taa
ثـ ثـ	ثـ ث	thaa
جـ جـ جـ	جـ جـ ج	jiim
حـ حـ حـ	حـ حـ ح	ḥaa
خـ خـ خـ	خـ خـ خ	khaa
د	د	daal
ذ	ذ	dhaal
ر	ر	raa
ز	ز	zaai
سـ سـ س	سـ س	siin
شـ شـ ش	شـ ش	shiin

Script	Print	Letter
صص	ص ـص	ṣaad
ضض	ض ـض	ḍaad
ط	ط	ṭaa
ظ	ظ	DHaa
ع ع ع ع	ع ـع ـعـ عـ	ʿayn
غ غ غ غ	غ ـغ ـغـ غـ	ghayn
ف ف ف	ف ـف ـفـ فـ	faa
ق ق ق	ق ـق ـقـ قـ	qaaf
ك كا كل ك	ك كا كلـ كـ	kaaf
ل ل	ل ـل	laam
م م م م	م ـم ـمـ مـ	miim
ن ن	ن ـن	nuun
ه ه ه ه	ه ـه ـهـ هـ	haa
و	و	waaw
ي ي	يـ ي	yaa

Review questions   أَسْئِلَة لِلْمُراجَعَة

أ . صَوَاب أَمْ خَطَأ (true or false)

1. Silent letters at the end of words do not lengthen.

2. A word in Arabic can start with سُكون or شَدَّة.

3. In the month of رَمَضـان Muslims fast from sunset to sunrise.

4. In the word إيـرَان you should lengthen only the *fatḥa* before the *'alif*.

5. سُـورَةُ أَلْفَاتِـحـة is the first chapter in the Qur'an.

6. The word لِمـاذا is a preposition.

7. The letter ق does not have a similar sound in English.

8. The word مَسِيـحِيّ is an adjective derived from the word مَسِيح.

9. A connected ك at the end of a word shifts downward.

10. In the phrase جـامِـعـة كـاليـفـورنيا the ة in جـامِـعـة is silent.

11. When the vowel at the end of a word is doubled, the sound "*nuun*" is added to the vowel.

12. The capital of Egypt is Damascus.

13. Iran is an Islamic country that does not speak Arabic.

14. The meening of إلـى أَللّـقـاء is: See you.

15. The phrase ما شَـاء اللة is said after finishing dinner.

16. The word لبـنـان is definite.

17. أَلإِضافة can express only possession.

18. In the phrase صَدِيقِي ٱلْعَزِيز the second word is an adjective.

19. The title خَلِيفة is given to the Islamic rulers after the death of Prophet Muhammad.

20. أَللهُ أَكْبَر translates as: God is merciful.

21. The pronoun كَ can function as a possessive or an object pronoun.

22. نَجِيب مَحْفوظ was the first president of Egypt.

23. أَلْجُمْلة ٱلْفِعْلِيَّة is the subject of أَلْمُبْتَدَأ.

23. The translation of هذا كَلْب is: this dog.

24. يَرْحَمُهُ ٱلله is said when talking about someone who has died.

25. The word بَعْد is a preposition.

26. The proverb يَوْم عَسَل ويَوْم بَصَل means: one of those days.

27. خُبْز عَرَبيّ means: pita bread.

28. شُوربة دَجَاج means: meat soup.

29. The holiday at the end of the month of Ramadan is عِيدُ ٱلْمِيلاد.

30. The *kunia* أَبُو نَبِيل indicates that the person is being called by his father's name.

31. Modern Standard Arabic (MSA) is the mother tongue of the Arabs.

32. نِزار قَبَّانِي is a Syrian poet.

33. The greeting تُصْبِح على خَيْر is said in the morning.

34. The words تَكَلَّمَ ، كَلِمَة ، كَلام share the same root.

35. Non-human plural is treated as feminine singular.

ب . أَحِيطُوا ٱلْجَوَابَ ٱلصَّحِيح (Circle the correct answer)

1. Which of the following is إِضَافَة ؟

A. بِنْت عَمَّتي   B. جَامِعَة سُورِيَّة   C. ٱلصَّفُّ ٱلأَوَّل

2. The correct translation of: "Why didn't you (*m. s.*) go to the university?" is:

A. مَتَى ذَهَبْتَ إلى ٱلجَامِعَة؟   B. لِمَاذَا مَا ذَهَبْتَ إلى ٱلجَامِعَة؟

C. لِمَاذَا ذَهَبْتَ إلى ٱلجَامِعَة؟   D. إلى أَيْنَ ذَهَبْتَ؟ إلى ٱلجَامِعَة؟

3. تَخَرَّجَ خَالِد مِنَ ٱلْجَامِعَة مُنْذُ سَنَتَيْن. – A possible question could be:

A. أَيْنَ تَخَرَّجَ خَالِد؟   B. لِمَاذَا تَخَرَّجَ خَالِد؟   C. مَتَى تَخَرَّجَ خَالِد؟

4. Which word is not a preposition?

A. أَلآن   B. أَمَام   C. بِ   D. عِنْدَ

5. The translation of: "Their (*f. pl.*) school" is:

A. مَدْرَسَتُهُمْ   B. مَدْرَسَتُهُنَّ   C. مَدْرَسَتُكُمْ   D. مَدْرَسَتُكُنَّ

6. The subject in a nominal sentence is called:

A. فَاعِل   B. خَبَر   C. مُبْتَدَأ   D. فِعْل

7. لا شُكْرَ عَلى واجِب is answer to :

A. مَبْرُوك   B. شُكْرًا   C. عَفْوًا   D. أَهْلاً

8. The answer to مَعَ مَنْ تَحَدَّثْتِ بِالتِّلِفون؟ is:

A. تَحَدَّثْتِ مَعَ أُخْتِي.   B. تَحَدَّثْتُ مَعَ أُخْتِي.

C. تَحَدَّثْتْ مَعَ أُخْتِي.   D. أَتَحَدَّثْ مَعَ أُخْتِي.

9. Fill in the blank: هذهِ بُيُوت ـــــــــــــــــ

A. أَكْبَر   B. كِبَار   C. كَبِير   D. كَبِيرَة

10. The translation of كَمِ ٱلساعة؟ is:

    A. I have a watch.   B. What time is it?

    C. How many watches?   D. How many hours?

Audio Tracklist

UNIT 1:

U1. Conversation 1. P. 1.mp3
U1. Conversation 2. P. 13.mp3
U1. Conversation 3. P. 31.mp3
U1. Conversation 4. P. 32.mp3
U1. Exercise 19. P. 16.mp3
U1. Exercise 4. P. 5.mp3
U1. Exercise 6. P. 7.mp3
U1. Exercise 7. P. 7.mp3
U1. Exercise 10. P. 9.mp3
U1. Exercise 14. P. 11.mp3
U1. Exercise 20. P. 16.mp3
U1. Exercise 22. P. 18.mp3
U1. Exercise 23. P. 18.mp3
U1. Exercise 25. P. 19.mp3
U1. Exercise 29. P. 21.mp3
U1. Exercise 32. P. 23.mp3
U1. Exercise 33. P. 24.mp3
U1. Exercise 35. P. 26.mp3
U1. Exercise 36. P. 26.mp3
U1. Exercise 37. P. 27.mp3
U1. Exercise 38. P. 27.mp3
U1. Exercise 39. P. 27.mp3
U1. Exercise 40. P. 28.mp3
U1. Exercise 41. P. 28.mp3
U1. Exercise 44. P. 34.mp3
U1. Exercise 46. P. 35.mp3
U1. Exercise 50. P. 39.mp3
U1. Exercise 53. P. 41.mp3
U1. Proverb. P. 41.mp3
U1. The Arabic alphabet. P. 3.mp3
U1. Vocabulary. P. 30.mp3

Unit 2:

U2. Conversation 1. P. 42.mp3
U2. Conversation 2. P. 65.mp3
U2. Exercise 5. P. 45.mp3
U2. Exercise 7. P. 47.mp3
U2. Exercise 9. P. 48.mp3
U2. Exercise 11. P. 49.mp3
U2. Exercise 13. P. 51.mp3
U2. Exercise 21. P. 55.mp3
U2. Exercise 24. P. 60.mp3
U2. Exercise 25. P. 61.mp3
U2. Exercise 27. P. 63.mp3
U2. Exercise 31. P. 66.mp3
U2. Exercise 34. P. 67.mp3

U2. Exercise 35. P. 68.mp3
U2. Exercise 41. P. 75.mp3
U2. Exercise 46. P. 80.mp3
U2. Proverb. P. 82.mp3
U2. Vocabulary. P. 53.mp3

Unit 3:

U3. Conversation 1. P. 83.mp3
U3. Conversation 2. P. 107.mp3
U3. Conversation 3. P. 122.mp3
U3. Exercise 5. P. 86.mp3
U3. Exercise 12. P. 95.mp3
U3. Exercise 14. P. 97.mp3
U3. Exercise 16. P. 99.mp3
U3. Exercise 18. P. 101.mp3
U3. Exercise 20. P. 103.mp3
U3. Exercise 22. P. 104.mp3
U3. Exercise 24. P. 105.mp3
U3. Exercise 28. P. 109.mp3
U3. Exercise 30. P. 113.mp3
U3. Exercise 32. P. 116.mp3
U3. Exercise 35. P. 118.mp3
U3. Exercise 36. P. 118.mp3
U3. Proverb. P. 105.mp3
U3. Proverb. P. 117.mp3
U3. Proverb. P. 125.mp3
U3. The Op Chapter. P. 112.mp3
U3. Vocabulary. P. 90.mp3
U3. Vocabulary. P. 106.mp3
U3. Vocabulary. P. 119.mp3

Unit 4:

U4. Conversation 1. P. 126.mp3
U4. Conversation 2. P. 153.mp3
U4. Conversation 3. P. 161.mp3
U4. Exercise 4. P. 129.mp3
U4. Exercise 6. P. 133.mp3
U4. Exercise 8. P. 134.mp3
U4. Exercise 10. P. 135.mp3
U4. Exercise 13. P. 136.mp3
U4. Exercise 14. P. 137.mp3
U4. Exercise 15. P. 138.mp3
U4. Exercise 16. P. 139.mp3
U4. Exercise 18. P. 140.mp3
U4. Exercise 20. P. 141.mp3
U4. Exercise 22. P. 142.mp3
U4. Exercise 24. P. 143.mp3
U4. Exercise 26. P. 144.mp3

U4. Exercise 28. P. 145.mp3
U4. Exercise 30. P. 146.mp3
U4. Exercise 33. P. 149.mp3
U4. Exercise 34. P. 149.mp3
U4. Exercise 36. P. 150.mp3
U4. Exercise 41. P. 158.mp3
U4. Proverb. P. 140.mp3
U4. Proverb. P. 142.mp3
U4. Proverb. P. 149.mp3
U4. Proverb. P. 160.mp3
U4. Proverb. P. 164.mp3
U4. The Arabic letters. P. 148.mp3
U4. Vocabulary. P. 126.mp3
U4. Vocabulary. P. 137.mp3
U4. Vocabulary. P. 151.mp3
U4. Vocabulary. P. 159.mp3

Unit 5:

U5. Bayt plus pos…nouns. P. 180.mp3
U5. Conversation 1. P. 166.mp3
U5. Conversation 2. P. 175.mp3
U5. Conversation 3. P. 184.mp3
U5. Days of the Week. P. 178.mp3
U5. Exercise 12. P. 177.mp3
U5. Pronunciation… P. 186.mp3
U5. Proverb. P. 172.mp3
U5. Proverb. P. 190.mp3
U5 Proverb. P. 192.mp3
U5. Taha Husayn…ayings. P. 206.mp3
U5. Tens P. 203.mp3
U5. Text- Dina an…amily. P. 189.mp3
U5. Text-Sandra…riends. P. 196.mp3
U5. Vocabulary. P. 165.mp3
U5. Vocabulary. P. 173.mp3
U5. Vocabulary. P. 182.mp3
U5. Vocabulary. P. 194.mp3

Unit 6:

U6. Conversation 1. P. 209.mp3
U6. Conversation 2. P. 221.mp3
U6. Conversation 3. P. 230.mp3
U6. Exercise 8. P. 214.mp3
U6. Exercise 11. P. 217.mp3
U6. Exercise 28. P. 234.mp3
U6. Exercise 33. P. 237.mp3
U6. Exercise 35. P. 240.mp3
U6. Proverb. P. 216.mp3
U6. Proverb. P. 233.mp3
U6. Proverb. P. 237.mp3
U6. Riddle. P. 225.mp3
U6. Saying. P. 247.mp3
U6. The time. P. 218.mp3

U6. The ordinal numbers. P. 218.mp3
U6. Vocabulary. P. 207.mp3
U6. Vocabulary. P. 219.mp3
U6. Vocabulary. P. 228.mp3

Unit 7:

U7. 'ila + pronouns. P. 282.mp3
U7. bi + pronouns. P .281.mp3
U7. Conjug. past tense. P. 260.mp3
U7. Conversation 1. P. 249.mp3
U7. Conversation 2. P. 256.mp3
U7. Conversation 3. P. 268.mp3
U7. Conversation 4. P. 277.mp3
U7. Conversation 5. P. 286.mp3
U7. Exercise 33. P. 279.mp3
U7. fi + pronouns. P. 281.mp3
U7. li + pronouns. P. 252.mp3
U7. ma'a + pronouns. P. 252.mp3
U7. Proverb. P. 263.mp3
U7. Proverb. P. 264.mp3
U7. Proverb. P. 276.mp3
U7. Proverb. P. 284.mp3
U7. Proverb. P. 290.mp3
U7. Saying. P. 291.mp3
U7. Vocabulary. P. 248.mp3
U7. Vocabulary. P. 254.mp3
U7. Vocabulary. P. 267.mp3
U7. Vocabulary. P. 284.mp3

Unit 8:

U8. Conjugation. P…ense. P. 302.mp3
U8. Conversation 1. P. 293.mp3
U8. Conversation 2. P. 312.mp3
U8. Conversation 3. P. 324.mp3
U8. Exercise 2. P. 294.mp3
U8. Exercise 19. P. 307.mp3
U8. Exercise 25. P. 314.mp3
U8. Exercise 28. P. 317.mp3
U8. Exercise 31. P. 321.mp3
U8. Exercise 36. P. 326.mp3
U8. Exercise 40. P. 330.mp3
U8. Exercise 41. P. 331.mp3
U8. li'anna + pronouns. P. 296.mp3
U8. min + pronouns. P. 318.mp3
U8. Proverb. P. 294.mp3
U8. Proverb. P. 298.mp3
U8. Proverb. P. 308.mp3
U8. Proverb. P. 313.mp3
U8. Saying. P. 332.mp3
U8. Vocabulary. P. 292.mp3
U8. Vocabulary. P. 311.mp3
U8. Vocabulary. P. 322.mp3

Unit 9:

U9. Conversation 1. P. 351.mp3
U9. Exercise 9. P. 340.mp3
U9. Exercise 11. P. 341.mp3
U9. Exercise 17. P. 350.mp3
U9. Exercise 32. P. 366.mp3
U9. Nizar Qabban...aying. P. 378.mp3
U9. Proverb. P. 338.mp3
U9. Proverb. P. 354.mp3
U9. Proverb. P. 368.mp3
U9. Proverb. P. 371.mp3
U9. Riddle. P. 377.mp3

U9. Text about Amal. P. 369.mp3
U9. Text about Nabil. P. 367.mp3
U9. Text about Rahn. P. 335.mp3
U9. Text about Rami. P. 364.mp3
U9. The hundreds. P. 375.mp3
U9. Vocab. P. 333.mp3
U9. Vocab. P. 350.mp3
U9. Vocab. P. 361.mp3
U9. Vocab. P. 369.mp3
U9. Vocab. P. 367.mp3
U9. Vocab. P. 377.mp3